# HER MAJESTY'S
# VIETNAM
# SOLDIER

# HER MAJESTY'S
# VIETNAM
# SOLDIER

## GUY BRANSBY

Published 1992 by
The SPA Ltd,
Units 7/10, Hanley Workshops,
Hanley Road, Hanley Swan,
Worcs.

A MEMBER OF

British Library Cataloguing in Publication Data
A catalogue record for this book is available from the
British Library




ISBN  1 85421 167 6




Designed and Produced by Images Design and Print Ltd.
Printed and Bound in Great Britain by Billing and Sons Limited.

# CONTENTS

# DEDICATION

To Mother Dear, Dad and 'Odge (Roger).

# ACKNOWLEDGEMENTS

Major (retired) Morley Thomas BEd (South Wales Borders and Royal Army Educational Corps) for his patient efforts to improve the abysmal technical standard of my writing.

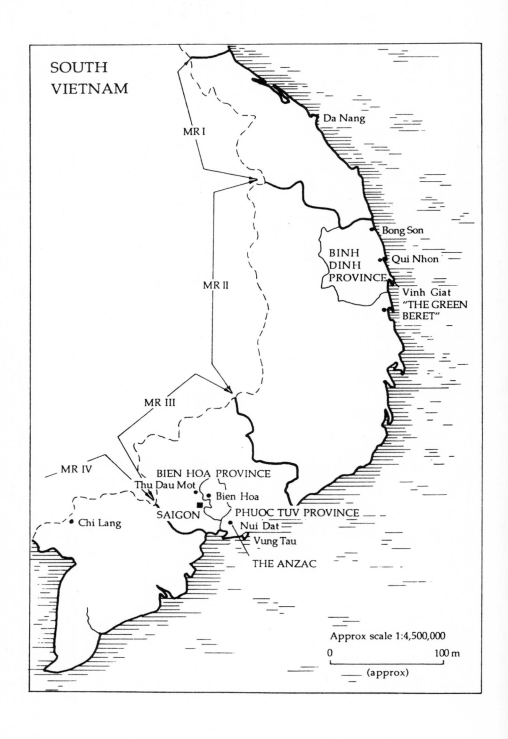

SOUTH
VIETNAM

MR I

Da Nang

Bong Son

BINH
DINH
PROVINCE

Qui Nhon

MR II

Vinh Giat
"THE GREEN
BERET"

MR III

MR IV

BIEN HOA PROVINCE
Thu Dau Mot

Bien Hoa

Chi Lang

SAIGON

PHUOC TUV PROVINCE

Nui Dat

Vung Tau

THE ANZAC

Approx scale 1:4,500,000

0                    100 m

——— (approx)

# THE SONG OF THE VUNG-TAU BAR-GIRL
(To the tune of "This Old Man, he played one . . ." etc)

*Uck-Da-Loi,*[1] Cheap Charlie[2]
He no buy me Saigon tea[3],
Saigon tea cost many, many pee[4]
*Uck-Da-Loi* he Cheap Charlie.

*Tant-Tay-Lan,*[5] Number One[6]
He leave me with baby son,
Baby son is many, many fun
*Tant-Tay-Lan* he Number One.

Anon (1964-72, Phuoc Tuy Province, South Vietnam)

## NOTES

1.  The peasant Vietnamese word for "Australian". Literally "Big red rat" after the mistaken identity of the orange Kangaroo signs on their vehicles.

2.  A spendthrift.

3.  A bar-girl's non-alcoholic token "drink".

4.  Short for *piastre*, the larger denomination in Vietnamese currency. The smaller denomination was *dong*.

5.  The peasant Vietnamese word for "New Zealander". Literally "New Westener". They had no idea where New Zealanders come from.

6.  The best. Conversely, the worse, was "Number Ten". The nadir was *"Number Wenty Welft"*.

# FOREWORD

This is a true story. However, I have, in some places, been deliberately a little imprecise over the names of persons, military units and other cosmetic detail. The events recounted are from fairly recent history and I believe that people deserve the option of their privacy.

Any scholar of the subject, or participant in it, will easily be able to accurately identify the details, if they wish to.

It is neither a scholarly history nor an account of personal heroism – as there was surely none. It is only a series of 'scenes' from a tiny part of a small and lesser known aspect of a war – and an era – that continues to intrigue. I was the very least soldier in Vietnam and it is only as a chronicler that I presume to write of those times.

I have tried to let the character that I was then escort you through and, on occasions, express his feelings about it all. I am sure that several different types of judgement will be passed on both him and his world. However, I do so hope that they are touched with a little generosity. There was much basically good intention about in those days.

GHB

# PROLOGUE

The North Vietnamese Colonel political officer, as he turned out to be, having emerged from the neck high grass on the far side of the small clearing and ducked carefully under a branch of prickly bamboo, now stood up and faced me. I was intrigued by the way that he looked exactly like a North Vietnamese or Viet Cong officer from the illustrations in the training manual: black peasant pyjamas, albeit with military pockets and epaulettes, to keep alive the idea of popular insurrection, rather than regular invasion; an immaculately maintained set of American webbing that tended to indicate a higher ranking officer, the lower ranks usually had Chinese webbing; and an incredibly large and powerful Soviet pistol that he was currently drawing from its holster with the intention of shooting me dead.

I felt that some sort of reaction was probably expected of me. I raised my M16 rifle and squeezed the trigger. Nothing happened. I had cleaned it that dawn, about half-an-hour earlier, but had forgotten to recock it. I cocked it. I removed the protective plastic dust cover from the end of the barrel that I had also forgotten about and squeezed the trigger again. Again nothing happened. The safety catch was still on.

Fortune could have been excused if she had abandoned me at this point. I had already had more chances than a soldier deserves. The pistol was now levelled and my rather square body must have been a reasonable target at about fifteen metres.

Salvation arrived in the form of a shatteringly violent explosion in my right ear. A dark hole appeared in the political colonel's breast bone, that showed from the open "v" of his unbuttoned shirt front and he was flung straight backwards across the clearing. The Company Support Section Sergeant had fired his SL rifle from behind me. It felt as if he had used my right shoulder as a weapon rest.

I had temporarily forgotten, during the few seconds of my meeting with the North Vietnamese officer, that I was not alone. A sturdy Australian infantry company surrounded me.

Our 7.62 machine gunner now reacted from somewhere to my left and filled the air with an eardrum-cracking cacophony. Of the column that followed the fallen officer, I saw the next man's neck nearly sliced through. The man behind him turned to escape but a round smashed through his spine and for a moment neat pink segments of vertebrae were exposed before his legs buckled and he was thrown onto his face. Still more men beyond him dropped into the long grass, and the chilling screams and sobs of a maimed man rang out.

The higher staccato of the Soviet and Chinese made weapons almost immediately burst out in answer to ours. The concussion caused by so many mini-explosions in such a small area shook one's senses and hurt the ears and sinuses.

The near reflex actions induced by military training took over to save our lives. The contact rule of jungle war was "run, down, crawl, observe, sights, fire". Suddenly we were all running towards, but not into, the enemy. We threw ourselves down into any areas that offered cover. We crawled a few paces to deceive on our exact locations. We observed the battlefield situation and those with an enemy in view, which was not me, got him in their sights and fired.

Once a contact (a small battle) has started, the golden rule of jungle silence can be abandoned. Above the racket of musketry, commanders shouted orders and men called warnings or encouragement to their friends.

I was a New Zealand artillery forward observer (FO) serving an Australian infantry company. Instinctively I drew my "shooting map" and technical bits from my jungle green leg pocket, located our position and prepared a target to send by radio to the guns as soon as my company commander wanted it. There was, however, another FO in the company. I was his understudy. This was the first operation of my tour and the last one of his. I was to replace him. He was by the company commander and so called up the gun fire. Within minutes the oscillating whistling sound of a 105 millimetre shell on the final part of its journey could be heard approaching over the tree tops. It crashed into the enemy position and produced a series of whoops and cheers from our side, as it never failed to do. The jungle would absorb much of its lethal effect on the enemy but it cheered us up and, presumably, had a correspondingly depressing effect on them. A round of battery fire followed and six rounds exploded almost simultaneously with a shuddering roar.

Back on the fire base at Nui Dat the little New Zealand howitzers would be springing back onto their haunches with the effort of spiting their lethal forty pound pointed cylinders, packed with high explosive, up to eleven kilometres. The shells would climb up into the beautiful blue and gold tropical sky high above our mostly twilight world beneath the jungle canopy. At the height of their trajectory, about five hundred feet, there would be an excellent overview of the ANZAC defended province of Phuoc Tuy.

If one could have hovered there for a while, it would have been possible to have seen the Long Hai mountain range and the town of Vung Tau by the coastal curve to the South. To the West could be seen the ominous Nui Din mountain range. The Eastern border was the beautiful bright, white sand and bright blue water of the South China Sea. To the North the jungle stretched away endlessly; on to the "demilitarized zone" of the bloodthirsty border between the Vietnams and on across North Vietnam and to the hills of China.

The North/South highway divided the province down the middle. The Song Rai river meandered down the Eastern half. The water tendrils and swamps of the Mekong Delta peeped into the South West corner. One would have been able to see a few little dusty hamlets too: Ba Ria and Dat Do just South of the centre and Xyen Moc slightly to the East.

Around these areas, one might have been able to make out the long suffering, traditionalist South Vietnamese endeavouring to live, move and have their normal being. In the shimmering waterlogged paddy fields, whole families would be working thigh deep. Others would be hoeing in red earth vegetable patches and tropical fruit groves. A few could even be glimpsed at the jungle's edge gathering latex so that the rubber industry might survive. Grubby shopping lanes and fly infested markets teemed and scooter-taxis, mopeds, rickshaws and ox-carts competed with military vehicles to kick up red dust.

Interesting people of all classes abounded. There were the shrivelled and dignified elderly, scores of pretty urchin children, sleek youths and ladies who, even if they lived in a house that was a piece of corrugated iron perched on four bamboo poles, had better deportment than a duchess.

One might also have been able to spot the odd off duty bronzed Australasian trooper, within the while villa and shanty settlements. He would be kitted out in a neatly fitting and pressed British style jungle green uniform. Long black lace-up boots, a tight and scrubbed canvas belt, a rifle held across his body, and on his head he would wear a rakish beret or a dashing Cavalier-like slouch hat.

One would be able to see plenty more signs of the military over the two thousand and four hundred square kilometres of Phuoc Tuy. There were the fire lanes running through the jungle – great bulldozed strips that were intended to provide speedy despatch routes for relief columns. Unfortunately, however, they could also canalise troops into ambush.

There were great bare patches containing the fortified ovals of the Fire Support Bases, where artillery and mortars worked to serve the patrolling infantry. There were the long standing bases like Nui Dat and the Horseshoe, and temporary ones, established for a particular operation, and often called after a wife or sweetheart. ("Coral" or "Alison")

Tactically spaced trucks and tracked armoured personnel carriers moved along the roads, containing alert and watchful men – rifles and machine guns covering the passing scene.

The floating observer would certainly have been far from alone in the skies above the province for, apart from the soaring and diving shells and mortar bombs, a multitude of aircraft would have shared his eyrie.

The Vietnam war has often been called the helicopter war, and in almost every direction the silhouette of some sort of these mechanical insects would be seen. There would be the little observer, plastic bubble and meccano-set, Souix and gigantic twin-rotor Chinooks with every conceivable object slung beneath them: tanks, bulldozers, giant water bladders, and containers the size of garages. The trusty medium sized Iroquois work horses commuted regularly around the military locations, and every so often the chopper gun-ships – Cobra or Iroquois would cruise by, shark-like and aloof. The air seemed never to be free of the thudding of rotors.

Higher still there would be fixed wing aircraft: twin Pilatus Porter observer planes, Phantom and Skyhawk jets. And, far, far up, no more than vapour trails, mammoth United States B52 bombers would draw their many parallel white lines across the sky.

On the open country and even through the jungle, the starburst scars where bomb and shell had bitten and torn at the land over the many years of war could be seen everywhere.

Most of the airborne view would, of course, have been jungle. From the sky it looked deceptively soft, green and cosy. However, the dark and damp world beneath the tree canopy was, even without war, a difficult place to live in.

The humidity exhausted men quickly. Movement was difficult because of thick and clawing vegetation, criss-cross streams in deep fissures and stinking swamps. The fauna was mostly hostile. A sudden encounter with an Asian elephant or a tiger might not be too likely, but regular association with a host of smaller biting creatures was. There was a large variety of poisonous snakes, scorpions and spiders. Every flying insect, including a breed of butterfly, nipped. Tiny blood-sucking, and crab-like, bamboo ticks dropped down onto passers by. In wet areas leeches got down the tops and even through the lace-holes of boots to suck and bloat on blood.

One was always grimy, sweaty and tired. One was always covered in small insect bites and sores. One's dirty green uniform chafed. One's feet were damp. Equipment rubbed. Scratches, cuts and wounds never seemed to congeal and heal. There were insect, animal and plant borne diseases. There was often stomach pains and nausea from a necessarily hurried and unhygienic lifestyle.

On top of all this had been superimposed a particularly vicious war. The neutral jungle provided cover for both sides alike. It provided cover for men, but also for booby traps of explosion, flying metal, or sprung spikes and jaws. It provided cover for ambush killings and unmanned mechanical ambush of an exploding row of grenades that tore a column to bits from a flank, or mines that fired a powerful directional jet of mini ball-bearings from the front that could saw a row a men in half. The jungle meant that opposing sides would come suddenly upon each other, at point blank range, and only the fastest on the draw would live.

The contact seemed to have moved away from me, and so I took the chance to make a more detailed study of the scene around me. I was lying alongside the dead political Colonel. He lay arched backwards over his pack, which was soaked with the blood of his exit wound. His face was turned towards me. He was not particularly young. He looked as if he was in his late forties and was of neat and almost dapper appearance. His grey hair was well trimmed and styled. Very curiously, he had quite pale blue eyes, although in all other aspects he seemed completely Asian. Perhaps he was partially French. The long barrelled pistol lay across his stomach. His right hand still held the butt and his fore finger was round the trigger.

After one last glance at his sightless stare, I looked beyond him. All the way across the clearing and into the long grass and bamboo clumps on the far side lay the sprawled bodies of black uniformed men. I looked over to my left and just past a small crop of young rubber trees in the centre of the clearing and a wave of overwhelming sadness swept over me, for there lay a dark green clad figure. At least one of our own had fallen.

The enemy decided to break contact and retreat back in the direction from which they had come. My artillery colleague now moved the howitzer fire to the path of their withdrawal to give them the added hazard of having to run through a constantly erupting wall of flying sharp shrapnel bits.

The firing stopped suddenly leaving the ears ringing. The calls to each other of the Company headquarters support section, as they swept the area, could now be distinctly heard – reassuringly mundane and domestic.

The fighting part of the "contact" was now over, but the follow up actions would continue for a couple of hours. The enemy bodies would have to be thoroughly searched for information. ANZAC force headquarters would want the North Vietnamese identity cards, weapons and dead portraits – our medic carried a camera for this macabre purpose – as soon as possible and so a helicopter would be despatched to winch down a line to us and gather all this up. Our dead would be taken away in plastic bags by

16

the same method, and the deceased enemy would achieve the purest state of communism possible by being buried near to where they fell in a communal all ranks grave.

The useful combat equipment of all dead men would be distributed amongst the living, in accordance with the earliest battlefield customs. It is not looting or a studied insult to the dead, but a simple necessity against the frugality of campaign. Both Western and Communist forces of all nationalities did cut off fingers to steal rings, took gold teeth, watches and money. However, such actions are contrary to international agreements and national military regulations and any British Commonwealth personnel caught at it were punished.

What had just passed was a company headquarters "contact". This is not so unusual in jungle terrain. The enemy column had passed between our point and flanking platoons and met the very head of our particular octopus. The company executives and their support section had, therefore, to fight the battle. Alas, the inconsiderate jungle deprived many of their more usual distant managerial roles. I had been to the fore at the start of it all, only because the Company Commander had waved the FO party ahead of his, for what was intended to be a brief period, while his party paused to try and get a reticent radio set to talk to them.

The result of those murderous few minutes was that they left five dead on the ground. Blood trials leading away suggested that they had carried still more off with them. There were also large puddles of arterial blood evidencing that a critically wounded man had been taken away. That afternoon, we heard a single shot a few kilometres distant as either he, or one of his companions, ended his misery. Another company found him a few days later.

We had one dead and no wounded. I had nearly collided with him that dawn as he was coming from, and I was going to, the field convenience area. He was a teenage Australian National Serviceman with a pleasant, shy, urbane aspect and a prematurely receding hairline. He looked as if he was going to be one of those very worthy, but rather dull, men who marries young and becomes a steady husband, father and uncle – highly popular with all generations of a large clannish family – but now he never would be. Now he would be a framed uniformed photograph on a side table. He would be referred to with respect and sadness. As the generations passed, however, he would be referred to less and less, until finally he would not be referred to at all and young people would wonder who he was. One day his photograph and his memory would go to the dump when someone was moving house or having a clear out.

"That's your Uncle Bob," people would say. Albeit he never got a chance to practice his role. I have an "Uncle Albert", my father's only brother. He was killed at eighteen at the Battle of the Somme. I expect that families of many nations have a very young, uniformed, optimistically smiling, framed, faded brown and doomed relative kept somewhere.

We had grinned sheepishly at the circumstances of our meeting. His body looked so small and sad as it was carried away by his friends. Even big men seem to look small and sad under such circumstances. The impression was always the same to me; then and later in Indo-China, in Kashmir, in West Belfast, at Ajax Bay and in the hills round Port Stanley. I never learned to acquire a matter-of-fact, professional attitude to it or grieve any the less – whether they were friends, allies or foes.

While still keeping my rifle at the ready, and not abandoning my position in the all-round defence posture of the company HQ against counter-attack, I stood up and surveyed the scene of my first close quarter military event.

The sensations of the soft, dewy, green and chirping jungle dawn that we had started out in seemed shattered forever. The little clearing, and its surrounds, were filled with smashed flesh and bone. The scarlet blood stood out in brilliant contrast to the greens of the jungle.

In my heart I had always known what the coal face of soldiering and war must be, but it did not at all reduce the traumatic effect of confrontation with it.

How peripherally military and distant now seemed the four preceding years in home based forces, where the warless and, therefore, goalless vacuum had to be filled by preparing for formal inspections by Generals, tense practice manoeuvres and elegant social functions.

Four evenings earlier I had been in the cocktail lounge of the Civic Hotel in Auckland, surrounded by people as fashionable and exquisite as any in the world. I had bought drinks for a gorgeous long-haired, long-legged mini-skirted girl. Tonight that bar, and all the others like it in the Western world, would again open, and wit and sexual interest would blossom. Our life of dirt and death could not have been more remote and different from that and other norms of our youthful generation.

An invasion, backed by the entire communist world, brought the allied armies to Vietnam – but what brought the individuals there? Some came on holy crusade, some came because they were soldiers by profession and because their army happened to be there and others came because they were conscripts and their personal preferences were not invited.

Indeed, why was I there? An English youth, whose government had backed away from its traditional allies in this war and who, apart from ownership of a glorious box of lead redcoats when small, had never shown any martial inclination or attributes.

The journey to this, and four other alarming campaigns, had started in an unexceptional way some four years earlier one mid-sixties springtime.

# PART ONE

## A PASSAGE THROUGH THE BRITISH ARMY

*In a word, let your deportment be haughty and insolent to your inferiors, humble and fawning to your superiors, solemn and distant to your equals.*

Advice to officers of the British Army. Anon. 1782

"I hope you don't mind me calling you back here?" said the Major in charge of my local recruiting depot. Without waiting to see if I did mind being called back there, he went on:

"A little matter has cropped up and I felt I should meet you and have a short chat."

He was youthful, but already distinguished looking, and wore a dark brown Harris Tweed three piece suit that pulsed Saville Row quality. The Sergeants I had seen on my first visit had been magnificent in blue dress uniforms with ceremonial belts and sashes. They had helped me fill in my enlistment application for the British Army. I had not expected to be called back and have the privilege of being spoken to by an Officer.

The Major crossed an exquisite brown tweed leg, revealed a hand-tooled suede "chuka" boot, and continued:

"You see the Colonel, my area commander, who I am sure you will know as soon as I mention his name. (he did and I did not – but tried to look as though I might) Likes to glance through the applicants from the various districts and, of course, your name was of special interest to him!"

He stared expectantly at me and I began to wonder uneasily if the Colonel was the owner of a dented car, a beer-stained suit or a distressed daughter.

"Naturally, as you went to the same school as he did (the penny dropped with great relief) and as you have the basic educational requirements, he is asking why you have not applied for a Commission and he wants me to see you about it. May I ask then why you wish to enlist in the ranks?" He looked enquiringly at me.

"Ah well, it's over a debt," I said. I could tell that I had pitched that wrongly, as his face immediately clouded over at the thought of the military inheriting the financially irresponsible.

"A debt of honour to the Nation." His face cleared slightly. I tried not to sound too pompous but I was obviously still not getting it right as I seemed to have totally bemused him. A completely different tack was necessary.

"You see, Sir, I should have been in the last batch of National Servicemen, before the Socialists abolished it. It was waived because I had a chance of a university place – but in the event I didn't – well not immediately – or rather went to a university in France for eighteen months, then got a place at university here but I don't think I am cut out for an academic career – they are a pretty wet lot – and anyway all the chaps in my class from school have done their National Service – they must be just about finished by now – and if they had to do it, I felt I should." I paused. He masked any excitement with a yawn and possibly took his eyes momentarily from the teenage typists in Surbiton High Street.

Something more was probably required, so I went on:

"And . . . er . . . actually I was asked to leave boarding school a few months early, (Expelled is the correct technical term. It was as a result of a combination of being seen drinking beer in a theatre bar, a village maiden with eyes in which a man might happily have drowned himself and a more than usually retarded public school headmaster of the times.) and I was never a prefect or anything; I have always been a bit thick and dozy and I thought a short period in the ranks would sort me out. Mind you, in some ways I'm not looking forward to that!" I finished and burst into guffaws of conspiratorial laughter – but stopped quickly before the Major's continuing deadpan.

"I see," he said vaguely.

"Anyway, the Colonel has told me to put it to you. Are you prepared to at least consider applying for a Commission? It doesn't necessarily mean that you will get one. You still have to pass RCB*." A savage glee came into his delivery of the last sentence.

"Oh yes," I said, wishing to sound an obliging and patriotic type.

"I'll definitely consider it."

"Good," he said.

"Sign here."

I hastily considered the pros and cons of service in the ranks versus commissioned service. The minimum period in the ranks was two years, whereas the minimum period for the officer was three years. However, the lifestyle might even out as it could be three soft years instead of two harsh ones. I was yet to discover that the fighting arm junior officer is about the most harassed person in the British Army. It was all very difficult. Then a completely erroneous thought struck me. How

---

* Regular Commissions Board.

unexpectedly well, for a more than usually common commoner, I had been doing of late with the debutante set. A mistaken invitation to one of the current season's cocktail parties had already opened up vistas of aristocratic romance and beauty. I had not totally deserted my secretaries, shop girls, and girls I met in bars, of course – but forbidden trysts, against beautiful backdrops, with fair temporary escapees from ancestral home and finishing school was a world of excitement and enchantment.

Just think, I thought, how even more smoothly I might glide through this strata if I had a magnificent set of regimentals for the right occasions? Especially one of those with the tight cavalry pants and spurs, a short tunic and chain mail epaulettes, gold cross-belts and glittering black fitted boots.

I seized the Major's offered gold Parker. Beautiful flaxen haired, clear eyed, fine bone structured, slender girls. Alabaster bodies. Delicate wrists and ankles. Shapely legs and pretty knees. Sweet cut-glass accents. Laughter like the tinkling of silver bells. Girls who walked hand-in-hand with you across their father's estates wearing tweeds and wellies – the sun tinting a peaches and cream complexion, the wind stirring the gold of her head. Girls who wore silver buckled, black patent leather shoes and silken mini-dresses in the evening. Girls who held cute little fingers before their cute little lips to bid you "sh" as they spirited you from the drawing room. Girls who crumpled and stained your dinner suit and intoxicated you with their scent and quality. Girls as traditionally lovely as an English willow tree on a Summer's day!

I signed with a flourish and that was, with a few short interludes, nearly the last time I was to see my country regularly for fifteen years. I was to depart while not far out of my teens and return a middle-aged man. United Kingdom based girls were to be forever safe from me. By the time I returned, all those upon whom I had once had such despicable, caddish and bounderish designs would be married and matronly with near grown-up children.

Other girls of many types there were to be; exotic, thrilling and foreign. However, the memory of European girls of my late fifties' and early sixties' sexual debut and youth has never fully faded.

The splendid parade and Mess uniforms also did not get as much wear as I might have wished, as the modern battlefield is not a good place to draw colourful attention to oneself.

I caught the very tail end of a military era when going to the same school as, knowing, or being the son of someone in high places, might help. Not that, even then, it bypassed all barriers – but it could at least get one noticed. Selection for commissioning today seems to be by meticulously fair open competition and academic qualities. Most young Officers have university degrees. Perhaps that is why so many seem unable to speak, dress, operate a knife and fork or live with any impressive style.

Once the interview ended, I had a few months more in which to make my dandified and irresponsible way across Belgravia, South Kensington and the home counties before the Regular Commissions Board received a candidate that both the Major and I considered to be far from promising.

I fell off the scaffolding contraption and landed with an unpleasant sound, in the wet mud at the Gurkha Officer's feet.

"Well tried," he said sparingly to the current hapless candidate on the initiative test phase of the RCB, who had so planned the movement of his fellow syndicate members, some string, two short planks, and a dustbin full of concrete, that they were now (with the recent exception of myself) festooned across the obstacle structure and not in a neat pile on the far side – as they were supposed to be.

"Right, number thirty-four," he said, managing to make out my candidate number through my pale brown glutinous mud coating. "Your turn next."

My heart sank. Everything was going disastrously. On the preceding arrival evening I had met a jolly group of local garrison troops as I was returning from the dining hall and had foolishly accepted their kind invitation to join them in the village pub. I had thus started this crucial day weary and hung-over.

However, hung-over or at my most astute, nothing could have improved my performance on the lead-in IQ test. I got some of the things into the holes by using force, but I could certainly not decide who was the odd man out in a row of shapes or arrange them in a "logical" order. Albeit I had tried – even though they were occupations that could not have recorded anything of value about the arranger.

At the impromptu short address session, all that had come instantly to my mind was an account of the migratory patterns of Scandinavian aupair girls around Southwest London. It had seemed to go down like a lead balloon with the Directing Staff. My suggested solutions to the written appreciation paper, on a ficticious political and military situation in the Middle East, would, I realized in retrospect, have been a Sarajevo-like catalyst to launch World War Three.

However, I had, of course, hurled my thick-set and fairly undamagable body all over the assault course with great gusto and a total lack of finesse but – unless the British Army had some intention of raising a corps of berserkers – I doubted that that was the most significant part of it all.

Now I stood poised on the brink of the most embarrassing and humiliating public display yet of my incompetence.

"Follow me, and I'll show you the problem and explain what we want," chirped the staff officer.

My problem certainly had a more spectacular setting then the others. A short canal had been dug off at right angles to an existing river. The canal was about five metres wide and its even banks rose about three metres above the murky water. Opposite each other on either bank two identical small jetties protruded a few feet.

The task, the Major explained, was to get all six syndicate members, which included myself, and the ubiquitous dustbin of concrete, which was not to be thrown or stood on as it was a wounded Field Marshal, from one side to the other. To assist me to bring this about, I had two planks, neither of which would reach more than a third of the way across the gap, and a few small pieces of rope.

I would have solved none of the tests so far set had I been invited to do so – and there seemed no reason, at this point, to suppose that I was to find inspiration now.

To make matters worse, the Board hierarchy chose this moment to descend from the mansion and see how it was all going. A row of shooting sticks erected to one side, supporting in order: a Major General, a Brigadier and a full Colonel. From within their scarlet general staff cap bands and gorget patches and above field grey moustaches, unblinking steely eyes now examined me.

"Right. I'll give you a few minutes to think about it," said the Staff Major. "Then off you go. By the way, a Royal Marines demonstration team did this one in three minutes. You get five."

The only thing that anyone who came near this place demonstrated, I decided, was a total abandonment of their senses.

"Go!" trilled the Major.

Necessity is certainly the master of invention. Total desperation helps even more.

The gap was too wide to jump. The planks neither separately nor tied together would reach . . . but wait! If a plank was extended by just over half its length and as many men as possible weighted down the part still on the bank, we had a gap that was jumpable by a highly agile man.

I quickly got my heavies on a plank and, miracle of miracles, one of my light athletes sprang across the gap and landed, just, on the other side. I sent a couple more across and passed the other plank, as ours had rocked dangerously with the last man. Now we could withdraw our plank considerabley, so that it, and its twin on the other side, needed only two men to anchor them. At this mid point we passed the concrete Field Marshal carefully across the smaller gap. I pulled my plank well back as it was to be weighted down by my weight alone. The farther side pushed theirs still further out and the very last man of my team stepped across.

I was now alone on the original bank. I tossed my plank and the unused bits of rope to the others and they extended their plank as far as possible and all piled onto the other end. They clung on to each other to stay on. The difficult bit was nigh.

I took off like a maniac from my "run-up" making sure I did not pause to think for a moment of the ghastly thing that I was about to do. I leaped from the solid jetty towards the narrow diving-board extending out over the drop. After a brief and awful weightless interlude, I crashed into my companions, who kindly absorbed my momentum and clutched me into the mutually supportive packet.

"OK," said the Major.

"The stop watch is off. You've made it just within the time."

A wave of giddy relief passed over me and my syndicate stepped off their end of the plank. In the milli-second that followed before the plank and I took a dive, I managed to grasp two of the others and unbalance them. They in turn snatched still more until the whole knot was teetering. Being the first that was about to go had its advantage. Before I overbalanced backwards, I jumped straight back and down and clutched at the wooden edge. As I swung there above the water, my entire team avalanched past me. I struggled back onto the wooden platform to the continuing rhythm of mighty splashes as the last in the chain lost the air-clawing battle and plummeted down to the water.

There seemed a distinct possibility that manslaughter was about to be added to my list of crimes for the day. The three shooting sticks had collapsed inwards to resemble a small teepee. Their occupants lay helplessly across each other. There was no question that they were only moments away from Intensive Care. It was a terrible thing to have done to men unaccustomed to strong emotion. Their chests heaved, their eyes streamed and the complexions matched their gorget patches as they struggled for breath.

The Gurkha Major's high pitched nasal honking seemed to go on forever and even masked quite a bit of the waterlogged bad language that emanated from the bowels of the earth nearby.

The final event of the Board was interview by the entire inquisition. It was after this that I knew that I had confirmed myself as an oafish buffoon who could not possibly be entrusted with a directing role in the ongoing noble saga of the British military.

I entered the imposing room and nodded and smiled courteously to the head of the Board. At the sight of me, the General quickly looked down at his papers and shielded his face to hide the twitchings at the corners of his mouth. There were winks, nudges and a few snorts and hisses and other symphon-like sounds of suppressed mirth from various parts of the semi-circular table. Still shaking slightly – but having otherwise brought himself under control, the General tried to silence the others with a glance.

"School . . . been a year at university – but don't like it . . . and want to join us," he said, going over my record, and seeming to be biting his tongue.

"Ever worked?" It came out as a near screech and he clapped his hand across his mouth.

"I mean student vacation jobs," he said after a pause. "A lot of chaps do that sort of thing these days – very educational from many points of view."

He looked enquiringly at the wall above me, as though he did not trust himself to look at me. I wondered if my sports and hobbies were not featuring as topics because, apart from rugby, they involved rowing, punting and swimming. I think one mention of water would have finished off the entire Board at a stroke.

"I am a dancehall bouncer at weekends," I said. Surprised, the entire Board looked directly at me for a moment.

There was silence. I had stunned them. I went on, "About a year ago I was offered the job by a chap who runs an agency and saw me public spiritedly remonstrate with a fellow, who was spoiling an evening for the majority, and give him the old arse . . . I mean . . . seat-of-the-trousers back-of-the-collar treatment out of the portals. It is very well paid and you meet lots of girls – but you wreck a few of the firms' dinner suits."

Why not go on, I thought, things cannot get any worse. Unfortunately they could.

"Flinging someone down the steps of a dance hall!" said the General and, obviously unable to resist it: "Well, I suppose it could be called man management." The last few words came out in a momentum gathering and exploding roar.

The table shrieked to a man. All inhibition overridden, they fell back convulsed. The General, his eyes bulging helplessly was giving out deep rhythmic monotone bellows. At one part of the table a Royal Artillery Lieutenant-Colonel was being thumped on the back by those on either side. Some of the senior officers seemed to be on the point of strokes and heart attacks. A cavalry Colonel looked as if he was about to pass quietly, but happily, away. All were red-faced with laughter and many were wiping their eyes.

No one was capable of dismissing me, so I tried vainly to make a respectful and dignified exit from the Board's presence.

In the hall, I passed the bewildered Staff Sergeant orderly and the gleeful smirks of the waiting competitors. I could still hear the echoing menagerie of hyena and kookaburra sounds by the time I reached my barrack room on the other side of the compound and started to sadly pack my kit.

No-one is more devoted to the collective spirit and principles of the British peoples than I, I thought. They would never have a more faithful potential servant. I should have loved to have served in a leadership role – where I might have fired others.

Never mind, I thought, by the time I was on the train home. I can still serve. I shall go and see old hairy-suit next week and tell him, or preferably one of his sergeants, that the ranks of one of the Southern regiments are about to be swollen by a devoted private soldier.

When I got home that Friday evening, my parents, who seemed to have remained remarkably optimistic about me – despite having owned me for about twenty years – asked me cheerfully how it all went.

I could not tell them the hurtful truth. But by a few vague "all rights" and "not too bads", I prepared them for yet another notch in my remarkably consistent failure record.

The following Monday morning, I found a wafer thin official envelope in my mail slot at university. Its inconsequential dimensions unquestionably meant a rejection slip and so I was not at all prepared for a simple one liner that said I was to be enrolled at Mons Officer Cadet School within a few months.

I was later to discover that of the eighty of us who attended that particular RCB only three were selected.

What could that highly professional and skilled body have seen that always seemed to escape my parents and headmasters? Perhaps they saw the single-mindedness of intent beneath the cloddishness or perhaps it was just that they felt that very occasionally it would do no harm to infuse a little humour into what was otherwise, no doubt, a very serious business.

Fenwick, Sargeaunt, Beezley and I were standing at the counter of the Public Bar of the Old Crown Inn in Kingston-on-Thames looking in four different directions. It was the type of thing we did fairly often. They were my friends. Our friendship was, however, little more than an occasional administrative grouping as we all seemed to be loners. Certainly none of us depended on any of the others for anything. We shared a background, a sense of humour and some interests. Our families knew each other. We called on each other occasionally, but usually just drifted together because we all happened to be in the same fashionable location. We could resume a lapsed conversation after an interlude of a few moments or several years. Our friendship, however, has lasted thirty years and is, in its distant way, as profound and as significant as any.

"I joined the Army last week," I said.

"Ah-ha!" shouted Fenners in a sort of "yoiks – Tally-Ho" style.

"Make sure you go in a Guards regiment – become a proper red-coat! Refound the Empire. They are all degenerating under their own home-grown despots. If most of that lot got a few swift kicks in the pants from a highly bulled British toe-cap, the lot of ordinary world citizens would be improved no end. Mind you, I did my National Service in the RAF. I was a signaller. It was good fun and the uniform caused me to be seduced a lot."

He nudged my arm to draw my attention to the upper reaches of a pair of shapely black stockings bending over a table within his arc.

I knew already that Fenners had been in the RAF and, as he got more attention from girls than most, it seemed likely that such things had befallen him reasonably frequently in the past.

"I thought about joining the Army," said Sarg with one of his usual rather graceful depreciative Gallic hand gestures. "But I want to carry on studying a bit longer." Having spoken, he drifted back to the insouciance that seemed to send girls frantic with sexual interest.

"I'm joining the HAC*," said Beezley. "They have these super uniforms with lots of braid and busbies and things and they have super functions at Amoury House in the City. I went to one last week with Patrick, whose in it; we got absolutely pissed and thrown out of the Royal Garden Hotel later. It was super. They do some hard field training some weekends – but with any luck, it won't be too frequently."

He beamingly returned the shy smile of a pretty red-haired and duffel-coated girl at the far end of the bar.

We could be found fairly often either collectively or individually, in places of younger public gathering. It was prompted by the reasonably constant instinct that nature sends to young humans to find mates and the fact that we liked to drink beer and laugh a lot. Our beat extended around the areas of South West London where we lived and roughly followed the line of the urban Thames Valley to include such places as Esher, East Molesey, Hampton Court, Kingston, Twickenham, Richmond, South Kensington and Belgravia. We would go anywhere that seemed interesting without fear or favour. Public bars, saloon bars, lounge bars, cocktail bars, palais, night-clubs (smart or sleazy), top London hotels and occasionally, and sometimes with an invitation, the odd private function. We were equally indiscriminating over the female friendships we struck up. No race, creed, colour, nationality, class or political view could debar. The sole requirement was to be pretty, or if it was late in the evening, mere geographical proximity might do.

---

* Honourable Artillery Company.

Drunkenness and lechery are unfortunately not always compatible and so our existences were ones of constant fine line planning to ensure that a. did not prejudice b. and vice versa. Needless to say, failures in one direction or another were far from infrequent.

We were at variance wherever we went. British youth in that late Fifties and early Sixties era seemed to be mainly divided into: the Teddy Boy types; working class "James Deans" whose girls were mostly not worth the fight it would probably take to filch them; dapperly dressed "Mods;" various categories of the intellectually pretentious, who seemed to try and look as if they had assisted in the storming of the Winter Palace and who generally tended to overact their imagined roles in life; and the County Set, with their rust jersey and spotty cravat wearing, thigh slapping chaps and fey young ladies.

Inadvertently and unplanned between us, we had a sort of decadent and dandified Old School failed gentleman look in dress. Our appearances and lifestyles probably achieved a concoction of the evil Sir Jasper, Max Berboem and Oscar Wilde. (Not that we shared any of the latter's more fundamental interests.) We all went in for tailored shirts with extra deep collars and cuffs, waisted and flaired jackets and stove-pipe trousers worn over chisel-toed boots. Hair was longish and swept back and other accoutrements could be bright waist-coats, cascading silk top-pocket handkerchiefs, tightly rolled brollies and old-school ties.

Fenwick, who had inherited central London properties, usually wore dark three-piece suits along with his dark roguish good looks.

Sargeaunt lived with his parents on a large and beautiful ocean going launch that berthed on either the Thames or the Seine depending on which location his scientist father's work took them to. He had spent some of his school days in France and had a few French additives with his basically British ensembles.

"Sarg" had the sad task of trying to resolve a tragic personal conflict. His aristocratic disdain and distant manner was irresistible to girls. However, there are some things what cannot be done while maintaining the portrait pose of an Eminent Victorian. He, therefore, worried a lot and did not score as often as he might have. We, all felt for him. He was also very heftily built and, when necessary, would help me deal with any local resistance encountered on patrol.

Beezley must have seemed the ultimate Bertie Wooster to most that encountered him in those days. He charged up to girls with a jolly horsey-set style of braying naive confidence and friendliness that never seemed to fail. One would have thought that this "upper-class twit" would reap only mimicry and contempt. But he never did. In fact, Beezley belonged to a very stylish emigré Czarist Russian family, and perhaps this background gave him indefinable subtleties that disarmed all. He affected the country dandy for the most part and, sometimes, after he had been riding, would spend the entire Saturday evening in his riding coat, stock, breeches and mahogany top boots. One got an intimation of when such an evening was imminent by the trilling of a hunting horn as his open sports car approached. This used to startle public bars in particular.

I envied them all, as I seemed to be the one of no particularly distinctive character. I envied Fenwick his cunning charm, Sargeaunt his nonchalant wit and Beezley his carefree exuberance.

I lived with my parents and younger brother in a river-bordering house near Hampton Court. In my London wartime childhood at my grandparents' house in Streatham, when I used to escape to play on bomb-sites with Cockney street arabs, they called me "Pikey" (Gypsy) because I have a dark look.

I believe we caused little harm during our era. Girls who were seduced were treated with courtesy and friendliness. They were bought drinks and meals. They were flattered and praised. They laughed a lot at our idiot humour and were seen safely, and unimpregnatedly, home. Males only got their heads punched if they were unprovokedly aggressive or offensive and publicans must have been reasonably rewarded financially for putting up with us. Indeed, we probably brought them extra business as people followed us in out of curiosity. We were generally friendly and good mannered, if occasionally slightly loud, to all and did not use bad language.

We all, for the most part, followed the poet Laurie Lee's pronouncement on love affairs; that is that they should be short as: "the memories are few but they are all roses." The ideal in compressed romance was probably an early evening meeting with a mid-evening, probably "al fresco", affectionate interlude enabling one to get back to the bar before closing time. One could also have "mystery tour" type awakenings in any part of Greater London and the Home Counties and learn such ancillary skills as fast drain-pipe descending and dressing on the run.

The Old Crown Inn in Kingston-upon-Thames, usually tended to be our early Saturday evening first base. It was probable that we had initiated its popularity as one of the first young and mixed community bars in the area. We used to go there when only just legally old enough to do so to chat over a beer and play the juke box. We liked the simple tuneful and happy rock and dream pop of the late fifties and early sixties, before later groups brought dreary intellectual pretension to it all.

Other young sets had gradually followed us into the Crown and the old codgers, bar flies, and more usual public bar natives had moved out. The plainness of the bar's aspect and the sincerity of its Victorian utility furniture seemed to have established it as a Bohemian locale. Bohemians, Beathicks or Hippies; the type goes on and on. To us they formed a sump for failures and inadequates. Ubiquitous, conformist and predictable, they try to camouflage themselves under a load of scruffy fashions, hair, contrived in-house vocabulary, unskilled "art", drugs, hand-outs, unwashed sex, and pretend revolution. They could not have existed outside the welfare-dispensing capitalist democracy they professed to hate.

Despite our lack of respect, however, we were not averse to trying to mingle with their younger and prettier female fringe members. Not that they had any pretty female members who were other than very young. A little humour, charm and drink-buying was usually adequate. Perhaps we made a change from the pubic-bearded, half-baked-philosophy-dispensing characters they were used to. We certainly had nothing profound to say. A simulated conversion, before irrefutable logic, to the prostration of the weak was an occasional idea. The newly absolved fascist might then be rewarded by brief entry, or entries, into Elysium.

In retrospect, I do so hope that none of those silly, lovely girls, were too crushed when, with the dawn, all she probably glimpsed of the new disciple was a twinkling pair of hand-made boots as he fled back to the establishment.

"Oops, look at the time," said Fenners. "Nearly half-past nine. The deadline for just standing about here drinking and chatting. We must get amongst the young comelies. Time to make a move. If we get separated get a taxi back to my place with whatever you've got. Stand by to order the Trumpeter to sound the Charge!"

We contemplated the current array of baggy painter's smocks, jeans and artless hair with a measure of disappointment. At that moment four very striking conventional girls walked in, obviously attracted by the sounds and sights of youth that emanated into the street from the open double doors that Summer night.

They had taken care over their presentation with neat and pretty figure-displaying clothes and enhancing hair and make-up. They were thrown into fits of giggles by the process of ordering a drink.

"We've just come down here," said one in a North country accent.

"We're on holiday. We're dying to get to know some of the people."

And as I look back down the years, I like to remember their suddenly up-turned faces sparkling like dew flecked wild roses as four fleeting Prince Charmings materialized at their sides.

"So you really have joined the Army," said Denise, sitting fully-clothed, from the waist up, a few evenings later in a small copse in Richmond Park.

"You went on about it, but I never thought you would."

With her beautiful elfin face, small and perfect body, incredible part-Burmese eyes, stockings, suspenders and exposed girlish detail, she was like a slightly naughty, but fabulous, contemporary wood nymph.

"I don't suppose you'll see me again, will you?"

For a moment I thought her large eyes filled with large tears. She had been my very first and my foremost love for quite a while. Together we had discovered the totally magical, private world of young bodies. In my memory, her physical star has never waned and never shall. Her bower was often only the quieter recesses of suburbia but Cleopatra, Sheba or Hollywood goddesses, with all their luxury, could not have been more exciting or magnificent.

"Oh darling! They'll cut your hair. You'll come to see me, won't you?" exclaimed a naked Susan, moving cat-like on a sofa in Epsom the following afternoon. She was a firm and athletic classical hunting-goddess statue with a lovely, gentle face. I doubted that it would be possible to contemplate such wonders again.

Jo and Babs, in similar circumstances over the next few days, on acres of soft and sumptuous fitted carpeting in country houses in Egham and Virginia Water respectively, laughed at the news of my imminent military departure with the careless laughter of the privileged, pretty and spoilt. Janine, my beautiful, dark and mysterious Parisienne girl, seemed sad in a beautiful, dark and mysterious way, but between her extremes of ferocious passion and icy cool, I, as an Englishman, was never altogether sure of what she thought or felt.

Under the "every dog has its day" rule, that was very much my blessed era.

Although some try it, a permanent unmarried affair just becomes a hybrid that satisfies no feelings of quality and we were all too young, in those particular times, for serious matters. I deemed it best to sever all such ties at the start of a new life, rather than wait for the difficult circumstances, that would unquestionably come, to spoil perfection.

I went on my way with a temporarily heavy heart. However, I have unending happiness from the odd poignant and exquisite image that will unexpectedly and randomly flash back down the years as graphic and as thrilling as it was in its original reality.

Loving, love and loveliness for their own sakes are not so unusual amongst those of incompletely developed sensitivities. To have held those girls' youth to you was to have held the very Springtime itself in your arms.

"I shouldn't worry," said Hébert, a decadent French aristocrat, occasional member of our Old Guard in the Palm Court Lounge in Richmond towards the end of the week. "You're certain to be cashiered within a few months for conduct prejudicial to the females in the garrison."

With a communal shriek, Fenwick, Sargeaunt and Beezley, drinks slopping, fell back into the potted foliage.

I greeted the two dashing young blades from Esher and their pretty, but wan, young ladies with genuine pleasure and bought them all a drink. The Old Crown had only just opened and was nearly empty, so a short spell of cheery light conversation would be quite agreeable. I met this group occasionally on my travels.

I was probably the only one that noticed the stirrings from the collection of black leather and grease down by the juke box.

The chaps, with great gusto and animation, recounted the latest action-packed events in the lives of their motor cars, while I hid my total disinterest in all machinery behind a cheery grin. The two anaemic girls waited on the fringe with unaltering glassy eyes and limp fractional smiles. I got the impression that their expressions would not have changed had anyone said anything interesting, funny, disgusting or committed an unsociable act. They both, however, had exquisite and delicate wrists and ankles, lovely natural fair hair and thin but rounded hips.

This was, of course, a respectable gathering so I quickly elevated my thoughts back to the saga of internal combustion engines and found I was a mask of concern over some tragedy, or other, that had recently befallen a carburettor.

The four hefty yobs had obviously decided that the time was right for their move. They had allocated their forces in such a way that two would chat up the girls while the other two took care of the escorts. Probably I did not count, as I was just another arbitrary gutless toff who would be impotent before the physicality of the working class.

"What're two classy birds like you doing with these ponces?" said the spokesman, and largest, by way of introduction, thrusting his rough face into our circle.

The chaps had no idea what to do, except to try to politely smile it off and hope that they would go away.

"Aye say old chep!" said the chief job in a ghastly parody of an educated accent.

"Oo do you think your looking at?" He suddenly seized both lapels of one of the Esher blades and crashed him back against the bar and held him there. Another yob squared up before the other Esher blade.

"Come on 'ave a go . . ." He roared and rounded off with a four-letter noun.

The other two yobs stood leering by with their right arms clamped firmly round the shoulders of the two terrified girls who, incredibly,

33

seemed to have gone even paler than usual.

To make themselves feel better over any inadequacies or indignities in their lives, the yobs were obviously determined to give the Esher blades a beating. They were taut and poised.

Unprovoked anti-social behaviour has always produced one of my strongest emotions. A cold fury that worthless persons should disturb the majority and a zeal to be my community's champion and avenger, that is if the odds did not look totally impossible. Or perhaps, in those days, I was just glad of an invitation to take part in dangerous but challenging sports. Later in life, to my annoyance, I have occasionally funked, when I could have put deserving cases through an instant Bad to Good Citizen Conversion Course, because I felt it might bring repercussions on the status of public servant, or my family, or whatever.

In my youth, however, there were no such inhibitions.

"I say, would you chaps like a drink?" I said to the yobs in the wettest and most foppish mannar I could muster. My right fist was unaffectedly in my jacket pocket and was quietly gathering up a quantity of heavy loose change. It was my only trick and it could only be used once in any location, but it had served me well in my dance-hall bouncer days.

After a moment of disbelief, contemptuous grins broke out over their faces. In addition to the ultimate beatings they would give, and possible slightly enforced sex that they might have, they might also get some free drink. They could play a sort of cat and mouse. Their evening was probably looking better and better. They were relaxed, confident and enjoying themselves, as I hoped they would be.

I should really have proposed that they and I went outside to duel. However, military tactics is, unfortunately, a science of ungentlemanly conduct.

After a few more languid, effete and servile gestures while I positioned them, I slammed my loaded right fist, assisted by the kinetic energy of my fourteen stone, "masher" tailoring camouflaged, body into the biggest yob. It probably folded him with surprise more than anything else. Without pausing, I hit the other would-be beater with both fist and knee.

One of the would-be lechers hit me with a not too severe blow on the side of my thick head. As he, and the other, then hung back, I did not give them any more attention for the moment, as the two big yobs were about to leap vengefully to their feet. In a fair fight, either could have beaten me easily – but I had every intention of winning with the absolute minimum of hurt to my side. I, therefore, lashed out with all limbs anywhere and everywhere.

I made out to the two would-be lechers that it was all over, so that they too, would be unprepared when I hit them. They merely tried to protect themselves and did not fight back, so I stopped.

"Get out! Get out! All of you!" shouted the barman agitatedly to the battle area in general, which the yobs, now all vertical – but shaky in two cases, obeyed.

Chronic remorse now swept through me. They were only ordinary blokes like me out to have a good time, I thought. Perhaps I have more in common with them than this moving transport worshipping lot, even if I do live in the latter's neighbourhood.

Round the incident off by being real cool, I reminded myself. Keeping my shaking hands in my jacket pockets, I approached the counter just as the landlord strode imperiously round from hosting the rich merchants of Kingston in the Saloon bar.

"What's going on in here?" boomed this worthy patriarch of Titan chest, shoulder and girth.

Knowing that the incident was now out of sight and that what is considered hooliganism when conducted by poor and badly spoken youths, can be written off as high spirits when carried out by the well dressed and spoken, I leaped in before the confused barman could gather his thoughts and tell on me.

"I am *so* sorry," I said, endeavouring to look and sound like the epitome of the straight-bat-playing, public spirited Englishman – even so modest that he apologises for his very virtues.

"I was forced to remonstrate with a group of ah . . . ah . . . *fellows* who were threatening your customers."

I bowed in the direction of the other clients of the early soirée, two drunks and an old tart, who nodded respectably or at least did not say anything to let me down. There was no support from the Esher bright young things who appeared to be still in coma.

"Had it not been for Taffy here," I said, indicating the barman, "I don't know what would have happened. The way he used his authority! I was only glad I was able to assist in some small way. May I get everyone a drink?" I rounded off to the room at large, nearly causing three cases of whiplash in one area.

After forty years in the trade, the "guvnor" was far too wise to be deceived by the likes of me. However, having satisfied himself that there was no damage to his property and that the attention of the police had not been drawn to his premises, and having given me a final frown, and ignored my offer of a drink, he returned to the pink-shirted, correspondent shoe wearing and peroxide blonde groping gang in the Saloon.

The spotty cravat and cavalry-twill swains and pallid shepherdesses were returning to life with a vengeance and all enthusing at once.

"I say, thanks," said one of the chaps.

"Gosh thanks awfully," said the girls speaking for once and looking quite animated and interesting and making me realise that they probably did do more than just use up smallish amounts of oxygen, food and toilet paper.

"You did jolly well," said another chap.

They had mentioned earlier that they were going to a party at a country house and so started to buy bottles to take with them, which had been their reason for entering the bar in the first place.

"Whatever you do, don't invite him." I just heard one of the males say to those near him. "He's obviously a trouble maker."

"Sorry. We're away," said someone.

"Bye."

They all said individually as they scurried out. Outside I could hear the chaps calling authoritatively to each other.

"Don't forget we've got to pick up Bumsey and Elsie and Mike and Janis, and Tats and Anna. I can take another two in the MG. Tats has got the DB5. Can you get another in your Sprite?" and the like. Engines revved and roared, girls squealed and then there was silence – apart from the large old clock ticking above the bar and Taffy's sotto whistling as he polished glasses and put them away.

My right fist ached and the knuckles were cut. My white cuffs were soiled, my tie needed re-doing and there was an ache above my right ear.

The day after the next I had to swear an oath before God and in the name of my Lady Sovereign that I would protect my countrymen even unto death. I wondered if liking all sections was an absolutely essential prerequisite.

Good grief, I thought, those girls would probably be giving themselves to those insipid bodies before this night was out. I closed my mind to the ghastly vision.

"Another Saturday night and I ain't got nobody," sang out the juke-box from one of its popular numbers of the period and one that I always seemed to notice more when I was on my own. The record was from the yobs' pre-paid collection.

Briefly, I contemplated telephoning Denise but, at the time, I felt that everything had been said that should be said.

I should later go up to the East End, I thought suddenly. This last night of my early youth would be spent in the Cockney homelands of my heritage with the culture and traditions I loved. I would find an old public bar with a jangling piano that thumped out cheery and raucous Cockney songs or tinkled melodic and sentimental old Cockney ballads. It would be an evening of knees-ups, rude jokes, hooting laughter, simple and happy companionship and vulgarity. Several times, I had ended up at closing time skipping down an East End lane in giggling company and with my pockets full of bottles on my way back to a scullery. My Cockney rhyming slang inner conversations have, over the years, brought me much cheer and comfort in places of fear and stangeness.

By the time I should return to my country, twenty years later, Cockney "villages" and their lifestyle would have been erroded for ever.

I bought the barman, the drunks and the old tart drinks and chatted for a while. I discovered that Alf had served in the First World War, Jock had been in the Second, until severely wounded at El Alamain, and Hilda used to be in a theatrical company that entertained the troops in various remote and fly-blown parts of the Empire.

Finally, after noting by the clock that sufficient time had passed for the recouperated, and probably reinforced, yobs to furiously reappear, I bade an affable farewell to my new friends, cast an anxious glance round the gloom outside the door and jogged off towards Kingston bus depot.

"The plugs are always missing from Service wash basins," said my father, while we were alone for a few moments during my belated and hurried final preparations before being driven to Hampton Court Station.

He handed me a small object wrapped in tissue paper. It was a concave rubber-lined chromium disc. A personal plug capable of containing, what might be one's limited portion of hot water, no matter what the calibre of the plug-hole.

It would have taken much care and concern to have thought of such an unusual gift and much time to have found it. It was typical of the strength of quiet love and care for his family that I have come to know exists behind my father's outward aspect of a typical urbane, genial and slightly absent minded type of Englishman.

My father is a man of vision and good education who could have been many things. Loyalty, however, is his overruling virtue. So he spent much of his life in a dull but financially secure profession, so that there should never be the slightest risk to his mother, who was widowed early, and later to his young wife and two sons. During the Second World War he was a Royal Navy Gunnery Officer of great panache – so I heard. I think he enjoyed this occupation more than most others in his life. Not the fighting, as he is the gentlest and most cultured of men, but the ancillary chance to learn of lands and peoples far from the tourist track.

While other men worried about the tactical situation to their front and looked to their lives, I am sure that for much of the time, my father's eyes were cast upwards in awe and delight at the ancient Greek and Roman remains that bordered the battlefields around the Mediterranean sea.

Along with my metal Vietnam issue mirror, the plug has never left my sponge-bag, except when in use, to this day.

"Don't forget to hang your towels and underclothes out to air as soon as you get there," said my mother from outside the railway carriage window, assuming that the military would lay on a special five star Nissan hut for her son.

"You silly old thing," she finished, which is a very profound term of endearment from her. She gave my hand on the window edge a squeeze.

My mother, an occasional actress, with interesting good looks is a rather theatrical and witty woman. Her observation also makes her a very enjoyable raconteur. She should have had a daughter to give her company as the three men of her family do not always give her the attention she deserves. When she was young, and I was just a very little boy, I remember more than one male visitor to our house seeming quite mesmerised by her gypsy eyes.

"Cheers," said my studious and generous younger brother. He is five years younger than I. When he was in his late teens and I in my early twenties he was a super pal. In earlier years, regrettably, the age gap and the insensitivity of the very young meant that I had sometimes ignored, belittled or bullied him. His generosity of spirit, however, always won through. He smiled at me fondly then as he still does to this day.

I contemplated these three most tolerant people in the whole world and first started to realize how lucky I am.

My father gave a thumbs up as the train pulled out.

"Good Luck!" He called, a wry smile about his mouth and perhaps a touch of moisture about his eyes, "I think you'll need it."

And he was as right about that as he is about most things.

———————

The Adjutant brought his sword to the recover before the inspecting General with a flash of stainless steel and an élan that seemed as the very epitome of martial gallantry. He then indicated to his horse that he wished it to about turn and face the parade again. The magnificent white charger, however, being as aristocratic amongst its species as its rider, was disinclined to be thus inconvenienced. It obviously far preferred its current direction: rear end towards the chill wind that swept the Commissioning Parade that December day. With a sharp and ruthless combination of rein, knee and spur, therefore, the Adjutant quickly re-established his supremacy in the matter. The sudden movement of the horse's ears manifested its profound shock at this treatment and it seemed to execute the change before it realised it. It also twitched its tail upwards as if some more spectacular gesture of defiance and protest had crossed its mind.

Fortunately, however, it did not carry it out.

The youngish Guards captain's visage or part of it, as the top half was totally extinguished by a short Shako-like cap, was now towards the parade. His finely chiselled aristocratic features declared, unquestionably, a lineage going back to Charlemagne. From beneath the short near-vertical peak of his cap his steel-blue eyes looked out as determined and menacing as the gun-slits of a concrete bunker. A few blond Greek god statue curls protruded from the back of the cap. His Butcher boots were bulled to shimmering cylinders of black glass and his back was as ramrod-straight as a Prussian Lancer's.

The moment was now come when the inspecting General – accompanied variously by the Brigadier Commandant, the Colonel Second-in-Command, the Adjutant and his horse, the Company Commanders, the Platoon Commanders, the School Regimental Sergeant Major and the School Drill Sergeant – would inspect the parade.

The General moved imperiously down from the saluting rostrum and the entourage gathered, and fell into step in order of seniority, in his wake. The tall stick orderlies slow marched in parallel ahead of him. The canes under their left arms precisely horizontal. The brass buckles and ornaments of their broad white cross-belts and back cartouche pouches glittering in the wintry sunshine. The magnificent *flotilla*, with a jangle of sword belts, medals and spurs and a kaleidoscope of blue, scarlet, silver and gold, moved majestically along the fronts of the forward platoons.

During inspections, when the whole parade, apart from the inspecting party, are stationary, the band usually goes into a medley of teashop quartet style, gentle and well-known traditional airs to entertain the spectators. Unfortunately, all military Bandmasters and Directors are frustrated swing orchestra leaders and, unless strictly controlled, never miss a chance to step outside their terms of reference and fanfare their egos with third rate Benny Goodman or Stan Kenton arrangements. I have seen many parades embarrassedly subjected to jarring and inappropriate renderings of "St Louis Blues", "Manhattan Skyline" and the like.

Mercifully, however, on this occasion someone had reminded them of their heritage and lovely Victorian, and folk, tunes wafted across us.

As I was in the centre of the rear rank of the rearmost platoon, I did not consider myself a person of special significance to the occasion. When we had marched on across the parade-ground in column of route, I had taken the chance to surreptitiously locate all the pretty, seated and thigh revealed grown-up sisters. However, the chance to pass the time in contemplation of that view was now denied me by many layers of several hundred broad blue-clad backs.

I think, therefore, that I was studying cloud formations. I had to look up anyway for, apart from it being a punishable offence not to do so, the vertical peak of the number one dress military cap made it impossible to see if one did not have a haughty upwards tilt to the chin.

"Chest out! Shoulders back! Neck on the back of the collar! Look up!"

Sergeant Major Cameron, our Company Sergeant Major used to bark. "Don't look down. You'll find nothing there but punishment!"

I had learned over the preceding six months to go into a sort of trance-like auto-drill. Outwardly, I was standing straight and tall and doing foot and rifle drill movements with robotic precision. Inwardly, however, I was chatting to myself, reminiscing, amusing myself with jokes or making future plans of some sort.

I cannot now remember what cloud shapes I had identified as I quietly hummed "Greensleeves", or "I Dream of Jeannie with the Light Brown Hair" in time to the band. No doubt something representative of my interest at the time: the overflowing foam of a newly filled mug of beer, a female buttock perhaps?

The clouds and sky were suddenly gone. A General Staff gold embroidered cap had blocked them out. From below the "scrambled egg" peak, two hard blue eyes fixed mine. I started to wake up and realise that halted directly before me was a tall frock-coated figure. At his waist was a gold sash and Marmaluke scimitar. Across the left half of his barrel chest was a shimmering mass of coloured silk ribbons and shifting metal of gallantry decorations and campaign medals from the Kyber, via World War Two, to Korea and Malaya. His dazzling narrow-toed boots had long silver spurs protruding from the heels and he was indeed the very model of a British General, modern, "Major" or otherwise.

All senior officers have some sort of personal criteria for their random parade chats; men with moustaches, medals or blond hair; the smartest, the scruffiest, the tallest, the shortest, one per row or every twentieth. Who can tell?

This General had already paused many times for cheery encouraging words when his mysterious system had inexplicably chosen me. He had asked me a polite question which in my inattention I had not heard. Genially, he now awaited an answer.

The awful lengthening pause was made even worse by the fact that the band stopped. The whole world for some nightmare reason, it seemed, hung upon my answer to a question that I did not know.

Behind the General's left shoulder, the Brigadier Commandant's face was becoming even more impassive than ever. A sure sign of strong emotion in Britons of his ilk. The scarlet sashes, spiked moustaches and pace sticks of the Guard's Warrant Officers seemed to tower over me. My fine Company Commander looked dismayed. My Platoon Commander and

Sergeant were getting ready to commit a wholly justifiable and satisfying murder as soon as the parade was over. The Adjutant, and his horse, even looked at me, which was something they did not often do to the lower military classes.

What the hell was it? Something about a Regiment. That was it! They always ask what Regiment you are going into upon commissioning. He had in fact, so I later discovered, asked me what Regiment I had been in. Assuming that, like many Mons Cadets, I was an ex ranker.

"The Royal Regiment of Artillery, Sir." I rattled off in parade ground response style.

A hit! I had scored a hit! The General had himself climbed to his present high position via the ranks of the Royal Regiment and his personal crusade was for a more egalitarian modern army with ever more chaps going through the ranks. So I had, wrongly on one count, combined two concepts that were guaranteed to give him pleasure. He beamed with genuine happiness. The Brigadier Commandant became positively deadpan with relief. The rest of the group seemed to shrink back to normal. The mounted Adonis became distant again and, with a clatter of accoutrements and a scrape of metal boot studs, they passed on.

To a spoilt and lazy person, Mons Officer Cadet School was a traumatic experience. From the moment that I first arrived at the Guardroom and announced, "I'm an Officer Cadet," and the duty Guards Corporal said, "I couldn't give a fxxk, Sir," the style for the future seemed to have been set.

I quickly discovered that the Officer Cadet is the greatest military loser of all time. He is not commissioned, so Officers and Senior NCOs treat him as a Junior Rank. However, it goes without saying that the troops will not accept him, as he may become an Officer. Someone in high places, with a wry sense of humour, had directed that all Non Commissioned ranks call the Officer Cadet "Sir." Full reign, however, is allowed over the tone in which the "Sir" is employed and what precedes it.

But of course, it was on the drill square that the very finest Senior NCO wit and eloquence was displayed, although swearing always stopped.

"If you get this drill movement wrong just once more, Sir, I'm going to push this pace-stick through your ears and drive you round the parade ground like a motor bike."

Officer Cadets or not, drill training language has always had a style of its own. When executing the halt, the attention or the stand at east, the final foot movement was always to:

"Drive the heel of the boot through the square!"

Most amusing, in retrospect only, was one day when the School Drill

Sergeant, a Warrant Officer, gave us the Present Arms order with his usual magnificent Guards' style delivery:

"Genral Salu-ert! Presaynt . . . (low key) WHAARMS!" (a short sharp high pitched insane scream). We obviously failed to carry it out with sufficient zip and crash.

"As you were! As you were!" He roared.

"When you do arms drill, I want to hear noise! Noise! NOISE! I could make more noise than that with me dick on a dustbin lid!"

Above all, however, perhaps the most important final ingredient to drill was to give it "bags of swank".

Mons OCS was very much an outpost of the Guards' Depot and the stamp of this Victorian army, within an army, was very much put upon it – to its benefit. There were, however, some Instructors from other of the more dashing "teeth arms" units: the Cavalry, the Royal Horse Artillery, the Royal Tank Regiment and the Parachute Regiment to name but a few.

My Platoon Commander came from the Royal Horse Artillery and I have often, for his sake, hoped that he became an international salesman upon leaving the Army. He would have become a multi-millionaire. I think he sold the artillery to his entire Platoon, myself included, most of whom had previously selected other regiments and corps.

We seemed to flash through our Officer Cadet days as though blowlamps were permanently played on our backsides.

It was a route march at the double with rarely a halt. It was non-stop from the drill square to the weapon training centre, to the small arms ranges, to the exercise areas, to the gymnasium, to the assault course, to a meal, to supervised evening kit or barrack block bulling, to a classroom, to a moment or two of sleep. We could change outfits faster than strippers and fall asleep on a rock pile if left alone for a few minutes.

Some thirty per cent of our original number, for various reasons, were not with us by the end. I was only still there because of a few generous gestures by my instructors. I like to think that they quite enjoyed the company of this comically clumsy oaf, who never failed to provide a subject for the exercise of sarcastic wit or an example to illustrate to the rest of the Company how to do it wrong. I like to think too that I was worth persevering with because they could see I cared about the real *raison d'etre* of the profession and, when the time came, would care for men.

Formal punishment could be earned quite literally at the drop of a hat, and especially of a rifle, or any slight military oversight or lack of concentration or comprehension. This meant being formally paraded before the Company Commander and, after a short ceremonial procedure of military law, involving much marking-time on his Axminster, being awarded a certain number of days of restriction of privileges. As we had about the same rights as galley slaves, I was always mystified as to the privileges that we had to restrict. What in fact happened was that one paraded at the Guardroom every hour on the hour through much of the night and was inspected. As a result of this, one could be charged again and get still more restrictions of one's ever lessening marginal privileges, with even more opportunities to earn even more charges and so on.

When I finally graduated from Mons OCS, many of my companions expressed extreme surprise that I had not been invited to buy my company commander a new office carpet.

Despite, however, and perhaps even because of, our restricted lives, humour, and other things, could occur.

Beezley telephoned one Saturday evening as I sat watching the NAAFI bar's television set with a glass of beer in my hand.

"Got two absolutely super girls!" He said. "Told them all about my heroic Officer friend . . ."

("I'm not commissioned yet," I said.)

"Anyway they're dying to meet you. So don't let me down. I know a pub near you. The Queen's Hotel or something. I'll meet you there in about half an hour and, by the way, the dark ones mine." He hung up. I had a great disinclination to go. I knew Beezley's girls. They were always gorgeous, fashionable and wealthy, as indeed was Beezley. I had always doubted my credentials for that world and particularly during my basic military training days. Service girls, Army daughters and Aldershot good-time girls had been sweet enough to me but then almost all the men they met were required to be close cropped and ultra conservatively dressed. I had been certain, however, that no South Kensington or Belgravia Venus would want to be seen anywhere near the likes of myself after the first horrified glance.

I did the best I could with the civilian clothes I was allowed at Mons and depressedly strode off to the hotel.

What the hell, I thought. At least I should have a few drinks and jokes with old Beezley and take the mick out of the two stuck up tarts and the names they would unquestionably drop. As I would be on a losing wicket from the outset, why not go on the attack. Go down with all guns firing.

As it took me over half an hour to walk to the hotel, Beezley was already in the Lounge Bar with one stunning fair haired girl only. I was quite relieved. I was now to be only a peripheral drinking member and, after a bit of a chat could leave them, as they would obviously wish to be left and catch the late TV film and the last knockings in the NAAFI.

"Judy had to dash off and see an old Aunt or something who lives near St James or somewhere," Beezley said.

43

"Apparently she promised her mother she'd go and see the old faggot. She said she'll drive herself down later."

I doubted it but beamed at them and accepted a drink from Beezley. The girl was as I had anticipated but she was not to be my concern. I made a few light quips about the military and got a few smiles. After a few more drinks, Beezley started to increase in volume, as was his wont, and started bellowing phoney military orders about the bar, which was fortunately nearly empty. This reduced the girl to hysterics.

"Form a square! Volley fire by numbers!" He roared at the top of his voice. I thought that we were about to be invited to go to another pub as the landlord walked in. However, he escorted a tall, dark girl who was not just pretty, but truly beautiful.

"Here we are," he said genially.

"She's been getting lost through the bars. Nearly caused a riot in the public." He winked at her and went out. I stood up and was introduced to her.

"God, you look awful," she said. "Just like my brother when he was at Sandhurst." Still I like the feel of it." She said, running her hand agreeably over my short spikes.

After that, the evening just flowed beautifully on. I decided that I was hopelessly in love even before I brought her first drink to her. I just could not seem to say a wrong word. We seemed timeless soul-mates. Had there ever been chestnut hair more shining and lustrous in the history of the world, a body that moved with such grace, or a more intoxicating blinding smile. I had but one ambition and that was to cast myself into those enormous and sparkling hazel eyes.

Suddenly and heart-rendingly, I noticed that the clock had sped round to half-past ten. Eleven o'clock was curfew for Officer Cadets at the main gate. I had to go if I was to make it on foot.

"Stay a little longer and I'll drive you back," Judy said. I was totally besotted by her every aspect and needed no more encouragement to throw all caution to the winds. Mons Officer Cadet School, the British Army, the combined Services and the British Empire could have fallen apart about me and I should have neither cared nor noticed.

We were inadvertently sitting in the Resident's Lounge and so the landlord was generous over closing time. The blissful evening went on.

Eventually, Beezley and his young lady said that they ought to be getting back to town and Judy and I were alone and walking hand-in-hand together like old friends to her gleaming sports car. I described how if we circumnavigated Aldershot and approached Mons from an unusual direction, we could miss all guards and check points and would be able to get onto a little track that ran behind the garrison rubbish dump. It passed some old disused stables, went through a small wood and ended right at the fire doors at the rear of my barrack room.

As we went through the small wood, Judy slowed the car right down and, what with that, the hand that was on my inner thigh and the beautifully soft, warm breath and tongue in my right ear, I formed the impression that she was trying to intimate something. I turned to her. She switched off the lights and engine and we fell upon each other.

A while later, and still partially entwined, her expensive chariot had borne us on again along the remaining short distance to the terminal by the fire doors.

Unbeknown to me, however, during the time that I was temporarily absent in paradise, my fellow block residence, Terry, John, Jock, Paddy and a few others from our room, were staggering back from some scruffy and cheerful local where they had passed their evening. They had returned to our room for a final drunken chat and had then realized that they had forgotten to make a stop at the block bathroom as they passed.

What need, they had then obviously thought, to trail lengthily and riskily, in the case of some of them, back along corridors when just outside their fire doors was a discreet and convenient little natural facility.

The hydrodynamic display from the top of the concrete steps, that the headlights illuminated, as Judy and I rounded the final tree, must have equalled the fountains of the Tivoli Gardens in its volume and intricacy.

In a milli-second, Judy sprang from my side and, after another aghast look at the scene just in front of, and partially on, her shiny radiator, started frantically putting her car into reverse. I leaped out undecided on whether my priority should be to stop that lot or reaffirm my unending love. I decided on the latter but, after a few rapid sounds of crashing gears, some quick manoeuvreing and a roar of engine, I realised that I was waxing lyrical to the empty night air. I also forgot to ask for her telephone number.

In a fury I strode over to the concrete steps.

"Oh hallo. It's you." They all said cheerily and beerily as they swayed in unison.

"You Clods!" I screamed. "There was a young lady with me in that car!"

"Cripes! Sorry!" They all said and began hastily cramming themselves back in.

"Oh, its too late now!" I said "She's gone."

Which, a thousand times alas, she irrevocably had.

Having been charged with a military offence while at Mons OCS, and probably in the Services generally, it is essential to then correctly follow through the ensuing, ceremonial and traditional sequence. An Officer Cadet could be charged for any reason. Usually it was some aspect of his appearance or behaviour that would pass unnoticed in civilian life; or even for no reason, except that someone needed charging to encourage the others or you needed charging because you were getting too cocky about things.

The sequence of events was not difficult. You were charged and, during a charge-hearing session, were marched, in your best uniform, minus your hat and belt, with the superior who had charged you, and perhaps an escort, into your Company Commander's office. He would be seated behind the desk in his exquisite hand tailoring and wearing his hat. He would affect not to notice anything, despite the fact that his furniture was leaping about with the boot-stamping and his windows were nearly being blown out by the Company Sergeant Major's roars. When all movement and noise finally stopped, his stationery re-landed on his desk top and the Company Sergeant Major announced you, he would look up solemnly and take up the charge sheet. There would also be a Bible on the desk. This would not be required and was for ornament only.

He would then read out the charge sheet and ask you if your details had been correctly entered and if you understood the charge. No matter what, you said that they were and you did. You never looked at him, but concentrated on the point where the wall and ceiling met directly above his head. Next he would announce to you the name of the charger and witness, usually your Platoon Sergeant, and ask if you required him to give his evidence on oath, i.e. enquiring whether you did not consider his word, in the normal way, dependable enough and if you wish him, therefore, to swear on the Bible. Unless you were feeling exceptionally suicidal that day, you would not be able to bark out, "No Sir!" fast enough.

The charger/witness would then give his evidence most tersely and succinctly, with a sort of Bofers gun rhythm and would round off with a short sharp "Sir!" You would then be invited to question the witness (i.e. his truthfullness) via the hearing Officer, if you wished. As this falls into the same category as being invited to stand in front of a moving train, your "No Sir!" would be yet another monument to fast and decisive thought. It would be without importance if the charger/witness had got you confused with someone else and what he said bore no relation to your case, or even if he had quoted tracts from "A Pilgrims Progress." There is but one response for those of sound mind.

Next you would be invited to make a statement, should you feel that there were any mitigating facts on your side. This was another easy question for the non-masochist. However, you were theoretically free to say "Yes Sir!" and come out with a string of lame excuses or, far worse, some time-wasting relevant facts.

At last with feigned regret in his voice and to all round relief, you were pronounced guilty and given a reasonable punishment as a reward for helping to keep things quick and untaxing.

Then, with all the usual shouting and crashing, you would be marched out. Your hat and belt would be returned to you. You would receive a quick and, often, not unkind pep talk from your Sergeant Major. You would complete your punishment and all would be well. A short while later you would win another chance to go back to the beginning again.

I had become so well practised at the sequence that I had to be careful not to prompt the Company Commander if he fluffed his lines or answer before he had asked the questions.

We regulars had been happily and routinely going through our weekly playlet when catastrophically my Company Commander went on leave. He was temporarily replaced by a Household Cavalry Officer who must have been away on Staff appointments for quite a while, as he had obviously become totally out of touch. He had a sort of aristocratic clergyman look and was followed around by half a dozen Whippets.

The Monday of his arrival, I had breezed noisily in for my usual appointment. My personal details and understanding of the charge had, of course, been fine. The witness's unsworn word had, naturally, been as the gospel. It went without saying that I was not able to question such exactness and no, I had not had anything worth saying to prevent the full weight of well deserved and righteous military punishment from falling upon my wretched self.

Appallingly, at this point, the Major deviated from our script.

"Come, come now," he said.

"You must have something to say?" The Company Sergeant Major, the Platoon Sergeant and I were not able to believe our ears.

"No, Sir!" I repeated determinedly.

"Now look here." He went on, "This disobeying a lawful command only refers to carrying out a wrong drill movement." The CSM and the Platoon Sergeant seemed to have been simultaneously shot in the back. "As Officer Cadets, you are supposed to be of good education, I cannot imagine you doing something as silly as this deliberately. You must have something to say about it?"

"No, Sir!" I repeated desperately.

"This is absolutely absurd." The aristocratic twerp wittered on, "Of course you have something to say. I absolutely demand that you say something!" I wondered if I could have pretended to faint, have fallen amongst the Whippets and then have fled in the commotion. The two Scots Guardsmen, though magnificently at attention, had seemed to be

47

leaning towards me, determined not to miss a word that I might have let fall.

"Er well, I'm absolutely guilty, Sir," I said.

"There was a high wind across the parade ground that could have helped me mistake the word of command but, of course, I'm guilty as charged, Sir."

My uniform seemed to be cooking me and its deep collar strangling me.

"Well now, why didn't you say that before?" He said. "This puts an entirely different light on it. Charge dismissed. March out Sar' Major!"

You just do not know the sentence you have passed on me, I thought, as I was marched out with my two seething companions.

It took quite a while of fairly intense physical activity and many extra manual labouring tasks, but eventually I was forgiven for being a "Smart Alec barrack room lawyer".

Mons OCS also ran field training exercises. At first, it seemed to me that the purpose of these could only be to promote masochism for its own sake. The whole object had initially seemed to be to get, as quickly as possible: hypothermia, blisters, fatigued nearly to death, encrusted with mud, insomnia, malnutrition, smelly socks and underwear, bruises and soaked to the skin. Eventually, I realized that the intention behind the old Russian military saying "Hard on the training area, easy on the Battlefield" was the goal we aimed for. However, there were times when a bit of good luck and/or cunning made one's way a little easier in the field.

For the first half hour, after the rest of my Platoon had left me guarding the dug in defensive position on the hill overlooking Frensham ponds, I stared lynx eyed and aggressively over my rifle into the mist and damp. It is usual to leave sentries in pairs so that they can guard each other's backs, survey all points of the compass and stop each other from going to sleep. However, as the intention was to have maximum participation in the patrolling and ambushing activity that was to occupy much of that night, I was left as a token only. I would be able to catch up with the training on another day.

It was early on a November evening and, as soon as it got dark, it started to rain. I knew, of course, that there were not really any hostile foreigners lurking in the Surrey bracken, so after about half an hour, I fear that my concentration started to wane. I wrapped myself in my supposedly waterproof cape and sheltered in my wet clay dugout. I popped up occasionally, of course, just to make absolutely certain that no storm-trooper, communist guerilla, Zulu warrior or whirling Dervish had inexplicably free-fallen onto my position.

It was on one of these occasions that I saw the lights go on and give

48

away the fact that behind the fringe of trees at the base of my hill was The Frensham Ponds Hotel.

I instantly dismissed the treacherous thoughts that had flooded into my mind and stared with additional defiance out at the ever increasing rain and blackness.

At the exercise debrief on the Friday, the volume and confidence of my sentry's challenge to the returning Platoon, considering what a long and thankless watch I must have had got brief passing praise from the Instructors. Of course, I affected to ignore Terry when he said:

"God you were lucky. I was leading the patrol back and not old Ingles. I could smell the rum from about fifteen feet."

I always thought it to be so totally unrealistic that no one ever got "killed" during our never-ending battles with the School's "enemy" party, a hapless Platoon of the Cheshire Regiment. Each time we went through tactical manoeuvres, of various types, with a blaze of blank ammunition but no-one fell down. The Cheshires, when it became time for them to lose, as usual, merely stopped firing and remained just standing or sitting in their positions while we did our various follow up actions.

"Two hundred rounds remaining. No casualties!" was always the sort of post action reports from our Sections.

Charles Hutchinson, another friend and destined to join the 9th/12th Lancers, and I, decided that this could not go on. Thus, during the later field exercises, when the directing staff were not looking, we became quite good at simulating ghastly and sudden death. We flung ourselves backwards clutching our brows to suggest being shot through the head. We pitched forward as if doubled up by a machine gun burst. We flung our arms out starlike to show that we had been shot in the back. We developed revolting slow and noisy deaths from multiple and horrific wounds as well as instant falls. We recovered quickly, of course, in order to participate in the next event. It produced much infantile humour for our friends and ourselves.

At last my big chance arrived. Our Company defensive position was to be attacked that night. The scenario was that our Platoon would be over-run and annihilated. The other two Platoons could then practise putting in a counter-attack and win back the strategic feature and our bodies. We were ordered to stop firing and play no further part once the "enemy" arrived on our position. Naturally, this was not good enough for me.

Right on cue the "enemy" swept onto our position. During the final phases of their arrival, I fired off my last burst and then clasped at my chest with a hoarse scream. Next I staggered gasping about the position, the epitome of the strong and valiant warrior who, with maximum histrionics, fought against even death itself. Finally, and with a last despairing cry, I hurled myself over the parapet of the small sandy cliff on the edge of the position. Trying to emulate a Hollywood stuntman, I crashed through a small tree, bowled furiously down a long slope, flattening small bushes and clumps of bracken, turned a couple of cartwheels and a near somersault and finally landed with a shower of dead leaves and a satisfying thump on the soft damp earth.

I lay like one horribly broken by his violent and horrendous death and smugly anticipated the popularity and humour that my military establishment mocking gesture would win. Out of the corner of one dead staring eye I saw the highly polished boot, then I saw the other boot and the base of the shooting stick.

"What happened to you?" the Brigadier Commandant, who had chosen that particular spot to watch the training from, said. I had fully resurrected rather rapidly.

"I was dead, Sir," I said lamely.

"Hmm. You certainly looked it," he said fairly genially.

I quickly decided to revert to total immortality for the remaining Mons' battles, as to do otherwise could earn me some Guards NCO punishments. The pain of these would not, of course, have been as that of actual death. However, it would have been considerably more prolonged.

Generally, however, the six months, or so, of Mons hurried by. We slimmed down, hardened, became super fit and learned how to organise and economise on thought and action to produce results fast in response to an order. We straightened up, increased our stature, literally and metaphorically, and learned how to be immaculate in military or civil dress.

"Bulling has been abolished in the British Army, so I am told." Sergeant Major Cameron often said to us.

"But then it's not a word I've ever really used or understood. What I know about is Self Respect! Pride in your Appearance! PRIDE IN YOUR SERVICE AND YOUR COUNTRY!" He had always finished with ever increasing volume.

We had all known how right he was, and every evening, weekends included, we spent long hours turning toecaps to a flawless sheen, putting razor-like creases in trouser legs and tunic sleeves, turning hard brushes on the tops of our caps until they resembled a beaver skin topper, and blancoing our white belts and turning the brass buckles to pure gold. To prevent the buckle from marking the belt and vice versa, it was advisable to insert toilet paper between the two until the blanco hardened. One of our members regularly forgot to remove the toilet paper before going on parade. He was the one whose bayonet would always fall off. The community spirit had, therefore, taken over the collective preparation of his kit and had also threatened to pound him if he did not stop earning the Platoon extra "riftings". However, if we thought that CSM Cameron would like us to have put a crease in our shin bones and have blancoed the whites of our eyes, we would have done it, for as well as being our very strict father he was, unquestionably, our hero.

In basic military matters, I have always felt that if I could ever be even only a percentage of CSM Cameron, Sgt Ingles and the other Guards SNCOs, then I should have exceeded my wildest dreams. I still try to turn myself out smartly for their sake. In every war that I have visited, I have daily washed, shaved, polished my boots and done the very best that I could with my campaign ravaged kit. If I ever did become as lapse as some I have encountered, mostly from other military backgrounds, I could believe that Sergeant Major Cameron's impressive manifestation would wrathfully materialize before me. It would be merciful then if the enemy would kill me quickly, for I should surely die most horribly of shame before him.

If ever the necessarily contrived and inconsummate world of the peacetime military confused me, which it mostly did, as to the basic military principles or points of honour to be considered before embarking on a particular course of action, I remembered his simple, clear and true philosophies and I would ask myself what he would have done. Things usually seemed obvious then and I became cheerful and confident again.

We also learnt how to turn a fifty year old barrack hut, still in its original and unrenovated condition, into something that might have won "Good Housekeeping" magazine prizes. Modern house-wifely cleaning machinery was forbidden to us, but with a few men towing a large broom, with a polish laden duster under it and with a few more men standing on it, we were able to produce a sheen on the ancient brown lino that would have made it impossible for anyone in stockinged feet to have remained vertical. We polished the brass window fittings until they were like white gold and converted the fire buckets to silver. The glass of our windows shone and our woodwork was either scrubbed clear or waxed to a rich lustre, depending on its function. Our daily bed layouts, from our "bed boxes" (a precisely squared and arranged "box" of stripped bedding) to our gleaming mess tins, cutlery and button sticks, were monuments to the arts of pressing, starching and rubbing. Even the metal studs on the soles of our "display" best boots were polished. All things everywhere were uniform and lined up.

Unfortunately, we still had a particularly mortifying experience following our first barrack inspection. After our houseproud efforts gained us grudging praise from the Company Commander, we all received a host of extra duties when our cleaning equipment was unexpectedly inspected, as, not surprisingly, it had fluff or polish adhering to it. That night, we pondered the problem of how to clean without transferring the dirt to the cleaning utensils. Finally, John had hit on it.

After first ensuring that the Quartermaster Sergeant was out, we plied his storeman with Mars Bars until he agreed to exchange our old cleaning equipment for a new set and let us have, in addition, some old items that were so worn that even the Quartermaster Sergeant declared they could be thrown away.

Our new cleaning kit was then locked away between inspections and no-one, unless he had felt like facing a lynch-mob, would have dared sweep, polish or dust with any of it. Thus, the subsequent inspecting officers were able to examine our scrubbed handled and shampoo advertisement haired brooms and fresh gleaming yellow dusters with obvious pleasure.

The barrack block had, of course, been prepared, with a lot of extra work, using nearly bald brooms and shredded cloths that spent inspection mornings residing in a thicket behind the hunt.

Our relationship with our pot-bellied barrack room stove had been another area where conflict between inspection standard cleanliness and practical convenience had to be resolved. The sub-zero night-time winter temperatures on the other side of the wooden wall inclined one to wish to light a coke fire. However, the stringent morning inspections, that required to discover an externally and internally scrubbed stove and not one microscopic fragment of coke on the surrounds, tended to render operation of the stove impracticable. So expediency, and the constant lack of time, also solved this one. We slept with our greatcoats and as much other clothing as possible, on our beds. Some people even wore their gloves and balaclavas. The stove was taken to bits, washed and left clean and the coke buckets, except for a token appearance at inspections, had shared the thicket with the old brooms and ragged dusters.

Organised sport had, of course, filled most of our non-military training time. My breath managed to gain me a place on the School rugby team, where I was an enthusiastic, but gauche, centre three-quarter. Most of our competitive matches, of any sport, were always against the other junior officer factory from a few miles down the road, The Royal Military Academy, Sandhurst. There they spend two years as Officer Cadets, as they are enrolled straight from school and nearly two thirds of their time was taken up with purely academic study. Mons Officer Cadets were slightly older because they either came from the ranks, had already gained academic qualifications or had a previous profession.

Odd groups of Sandhurst Officer Cadets used to drop by occasionally to show off. Apart from white gorget patches on uniform collars, Officer Cadets are outfitted like Private Soldiers. Sandhurst Cadets, however, used to be issued officer style George boots and brown belts in addition, so these used to be mandatory wear for their visits. Albeit, it was hardly necessary for them to try to draw attention to themselves by displaying kit that we did not have, as their scarlet banded caps (denoting membership of a military agency with "Royal" in the title) already gave them obvious distinction beside our plain dark blue ones.

Mons was not on the route of anywhere they might need to go to, so these chances to feign humorous disbelief at our First War Nissan hut architecture, and other aspects, would have been contrived. Mostly, however, we did not mind them as it gave us the chance of a little banter. "Hey, has someone crapped on your belt?" and "Only poofs wear ducky little boots like those." An obvious favourite, of course, was to suggest that Mons achieved in six months what took Sandhurst two years. Their reply to this was, naturally, to mutter about quantity rather than quality.

It was said by Sandhurst Cadets that Sandhurst produced Generals, eventually, while Mons produced Second Lieutenants. Certainly, the official intention was that we should clear off after a few years of Second Lieutenant or Lieutenant and not linger to risk blocking the narrower Captain and Major promotion pipes, as these and the more senior ranks were intended as the exclusive prerogative of the more lengthily and, therefore, more expensively produced Sandhurst Officer. The role of Mons OCS had always been to turn out the vast numbers of the lowest ranking officers, the Platoon or Troop commanders, that Britain needed to fill out the wide base of the military pyramid. There would not be a place for most of us in the ever narrowing upper part.

A few years after I left Mons, a Government would arbitrarily reduce Britain's role to a size more in keeping with the smallness of the spirit of the times. Soviet influence would, as predicted, replace ours nearly everywhere, Mons would be cut off from those that it had devotedly prepared to serve and would be no more.

The end of our spartan life started to seem nigh. There were the final field exercises, including one in Libya, which gave us a glimpse of how far reaching British military influence still was, and the final written exams and test. Then the instructors started to talk about, and even prepare for, the final Commissioning parade.

Even if we were not able to believe it would ever happen, there were signs that most of us, who had got this far, would probably actually hold Queen's Commissions and would burst from the chrysalis to make the incredible instant metamorphosis from the most rudimentary of military embryos to the ruling caste. We started to be spoken to as though we had not been a sub-species and we were even tolerated in rationed early-evening packets in the Officers' Mess. We also became a little bit social officially.

For some silly and illogical reason, I was finding the whole thing killingly funny right from the outset. Perhaps it was the way Sergeant Major Cameron was taking it all so seriously.

"Right, listen in, youse!" he roared. "Six volunteers are required to represent the School, with Credit at a social function!"

The social function was a hunt ball in Hampshire. I amused myself still further by imagining the background to it all.

Some old Dowager, no doubt the widow of our Commandant's CO of thirty years earlier (when he had been a nervous young "snotty") had probably demanded six of the "most eligible young men" for her high born young "wall-flowers". We, now the senior Company, had obviously been detailed to provide.

Sergeant Major Cameron was selecting the volunteers very wisely. He was picking all the smoother members of our titled collection. There was Officer Cadet Lord this, Officer Cadet Sir someone-or-other, and Officer Cadet the Hon so-and so.

As there was absolutely no possibility of my inclusion in this group, I was unwisely relaxed and started to lose the battle to keep a straight face. I was in the front row just by the Company Sergeant Major. He had accumulated five sotto-muttering volunteers and was pondering the final team member, when I suddenly exploded with snorting noises into uncontrollable open mirth.

"What are you bloody laughing at?" He roared, and, no doubt, to make an immediate and positive response to this insubordination, said, "You can go too!"

This brought me to an abrupt and astounded silence. After we had been dismissed, I went over to my five aristocratic associates-to-be. They were not at all pleased at the prospect of enforced mingling with county people they did not know and of being deprived of their usual weekends of blue-blooded London supper parties and trysts.

"It might be good fun!" I said, probably confirming myself as a random, vulgar opportunist of no orderly social pattern. They all crushed me with artless looks of suave disdain.

I managed to borrow a set of tailed evening dress and we all lined up with the Guard and the prisoners early on the Saturday evening as CSM Cameron wanted to inspect us. I put on a pair of white gloves and it was unfortunate that Cameron had inspected me first as he charged all the rest for not wearing any. The evening seemed to be off to a bad start.

"What are you wearing those damn things for?" one of the others had asked furiously.

"Are you going to serve the soup or something?"

As it was duty, a mini-bus and soldier driver were loaned. We got to the area of the country house but were unsure of its exact location.

Being the one who unquestionably had the commonest touch, I said that I did not mind going into a pub to ask the way. I managed to do this several times before the lengthening delays in my reappearances and the fumes found me out. However, we finally got correct directions from a cyclist and drove up to the imposing country pile.

We all had a very good time. The hospitality was superb, the people were friendly and the young ladies had been mostly attractive and jolly. The others said afterwards that I should not have marched them across the drawing room, following our arrival, and halted them in front of the old dowager. Not that she seemed to see anything odd about it. Most of the young set at the party larked about in the vast and lush eighteenth century conservatory which, in retrospect, might almost have been an augury of jungle experiences to come.

But suddenly, there we were on our Commissioning Parade, a vast gathering of spectators, which included my parents and brother, and everyone in their very best military or civilian finery.

Amongst the varied magnificence of uniforms. I could see, at the front, a row of scarlet frock coats denoting the aged iron-men of the the Royal Chelsea Hospital. As we were about to advance into a military world where technology neutralizes many of the human physical and manly virtues, they could look back to the days when such things were all. Their medal ribbons told that they had started in a red-coat army that had been so often victorious against outnumbering hordes with little sophisticated weaponry but much discipline and courage.

It is said that Nell Gwyn, a King's generous hearted cockney tart, used her charm to persuade her Royal lover to found a home and to care for the final dignity and well being of his abandoned old soldiers who had been her companions in poverty in the streets of London.

Prostitutes and Soldiers, the two oldest female and male professions respectively, often seem to give each other a special consideration as there is quite an affinity in their roles. Both are paid to do, with their bodies, what others will not, or cannot, do. Both are revered, romanticised and generously treated when urgently needed and are insulted and shunned when not.

The inspection being over, the inspecting General strode back to the saluting dais, gradually shedding his train en route as they fell out to their various places for the march past.

We were put into close order. We shouldered arms with a flash of white gloved left hands and rifle slings and a single thunderous crack. Our right-turn was completed by one mighty crash as tens of thousands of metal studs slammed as one onto the parade ground. The rest of the parade seems now to form a sort of surrealistic dream in the memory. Spectators told me later that it was flawless. Almost as if many hundreds of bodies had suddenly become one. A single, many limbed, but perfectly synchronised, animal.

Above the throb and thud of brass and percussion and the rhythmic rattle of the drums could be heard the nobly barked orders. I was proud that I marched in company with my magnificent Guards instructors. The tall and elegant, Stanley Baker look alike, Sergeant Ingles at the Platoon's front and the rock-like Sergeant Major Cameron at our Company's flank, his great pace stick exactly parallel to the ground and the tassels of his sash swaying with the march.

We quick marched past to the jaunty tunes of glory, "The Grenadiers", "Highland Laddie", "St Patrick's Day" and the others. We Left Formed. As one, we snapped our heads and eyes towards the immaculately saluting General on the "Eyes Right". We gave it "bags of swank". We broke into the ponderous, formal and stately Slow March to the tune "The Duchess of Kent" and our massed ranks, this time in relentless heavy glide, again passed before the General.

I heard later that old Servicemen fathers had not tried to hide the emotion of restirred memories, that mothers had stared openly with adoration and pride at their sons, and that grown up sisters had flushed at the passion and strength of that scene.

Finally, our columns of Platoons were converging into one great phalanx six men across. The band played "Auld Lang Syne" as a slow march and our even mass of blue, scarlet and white and serried forest of glittering bayonet blades, swept majestically from sight.

For the very last scene of Mons OCS we were all in a great marquee full of uniforms and stylish ladies' hats, sipping sherry. Everyone congratulated us on our parade. We swore that we would all keep in touch. There were the two great bear-like men, Company Sergeant Major Cameron and old Instructor Sergeant Major Alred, suddenly hatless and human and trying not to weep down their broad scarlet sashes and barrel chests full of campaign medals, as they wrung young hands and flung their great kind arms round young departing shoulders.

"Right then. Your first commissioned job," said my fleshy, bespectacled, and rather owlish-looking, Battery Commander on my day of arrival at the British Army of the Rhine (BAOR) artillery regiment.

"You can lead the Battery back to the regimental lines, then the other officers and I can go on ahead by land-rover, get showered and changed, meet you, and be ready to have things quickly tidied away as soon as you arrive.

"You are here," he went on, tapping the map with his finger.

"Dannenberg is here and the camp here." He prodded the map a couple more times with the pudgy digit and then stood back bearing about the last friendly smile he was to give me.

"Any problems?"

With a pencil, I lightly circled both our location and the regimental base and took a quick look at the space on the map between the two points. There seemed to be a reasonable number of different coloured wiggly lines indicating roads of various widths.

"No, I don't think so, Sir." I said.

He got into the front of the land-rover and a group of superior looking chaps, wearing hunting cravats with their combat kit and little bun-like officer pattern (purchased) berets, got into the back. The land-rover bounced off down the black mud and puddle filled track between the pine trees.

I had joined the Battery on the last day of a two week field training exercise. I now stood, clutching the map, at the centre of a very large circle of incredible looking, warlike machinery and troops to whom I had been rather superficially introduced. They studied me silently and unblinkingly like a group of simple, semi-hostile, natives, prepared to give the new green missionary a brief chance to make an ass of himself before turning him into a spear pin-cushion.

"Well, lets get on to the track then," I said in the general direction of a group of Senior NCOs. To my delighted relief, a hive of activity broke out. NCOs called orders, Gunners ran and the self-propelled tracked guns, limbers, armoured personnel carriers and other gigantic vehicles came roaring out of their hides and formed an orderly column on the dirty track. Without any guidance from myself, they were all pointing in a single direction. I frantically orientated the map and discovered that, by good fortune, this happened to be the most expedient for getting back to the garrison.

"Your APC is ready, Sir," said a North country driver, indicating a huge squat tracked vehicle at the head of the silent and waiting column.

With mounting excitement, I strode over, watched by several hundred pairs of contemptuous eyes and clambered with reasonable agility up its slippery metal sides. I dropped through the square hole near the front, ricocheted round the metal protrusions within its bowels and then climbed back up on to the Commander's platform and stuck my head and torso momentously out of the aperture.

It hardly seemed worth progressing any further as an army officer as my wildest dreams had been fulfilled. Here I was, a twentieth century Alexander, about to lead my valiant troops and awesome war machinery to some noble destiny or other. When someone handed me a pair of Rommel-style goggles, my cup ran over. With a gesture unequalled by stout Cortes or the hero of any waggon train film ever made, I indicated "Forward."

"Are you going to tell them to start engines, Sir?" said the Barnsley accent, reverberating from the hollow insides of the vast and weighty cast metal termite.

"Don't worry, Sir," he went on, as I turned round to shout.

"I can do it over the radio."

With a deafening roar and a considerable amount of black smoke, everything exploded into mechanical life.

We set off, tracks clanking, through the black mire, with engine noises that were a mixture of throaty bellow and ear-drum boring whine and a motion like a lifeboat caught in a suicidal sea.

At the junction, I told the driver to tell the twenty odd vehicles behind me to stop. About a third were tracked (the colossal SP guns and APCs) and the rest were gigantic trucks (artillery ammunition limbers and supply vehicles). They had rubber tyres that stood nearly as high as a man. I studied the map of the Luneburg training area. The shortest distance between two points being obviously what we were after, I soon selected a route.

I indicated right, with a splendid arm movement and with my troops grinning in delight we continued. They had obviously thought I should not be so skilled at map reading.

I was amazed by the unwieldiness of these giant vehicles as we passed through the centre of Saltzen during the lunch hour. The office workers all stopped to stare, which made extra difficulties as the German police had to divert the civilian cars onto the pavements because our width took up both sides of the street.

I thought the SP gun drivers were terribly skilful in the way they managed to wrench their way round the roundabout in the central square by operating their tracks alternately. I felt that the loss of the town's litter bins, parking meters and road surface was a small price to pay for the fact that the barrels missed the department store windows.

Traffic lights and a level crossing kept annoyingly separating my convoy but the German police were marvellous and no-one seemed too upset about the excavation of the herbaceous borders and the flowering shrubs. Albeit most burghers stayed pudding-faced, the school boys were driven wild with delight. They must have thought it was all part of some sort of carnival and started singing a jolly song in unison. The word "doofer" cropped up repeatedly in it. I pretended to conduct them. However, we finally separated ourselves from the remains of the High Street and I passed on with a few regal hand waves to the unresponding citizenry.

I was filled with respect for German stoicism. After all, they probably had to put up with this sort of thing every other day as their magnanimous British protectors moved around. Still, I thought, it is but a small price to pay to prevent Russian colonisation.

The rest of the journey was along reasonably straight and uncomplicated residential and rural roads, although the expressions on the faces of oncoming car drivers who happened suddenly upon our dark green, twelve foot high, mile long, many thousand ton metal serpent, remained fascinating. Fortunately, the grassy banks they obligingly pulled off onto were not too steep either upwards or downwards.

Eventually, we happened upon the Regimental lines and I told my driver to take the usual route to the Battery park. We swept majestically onto the square in front of the battery block and, without a word from myself, all vehicles curved in to form an immaculately dressed line from my left. The beaming faces of the troops must have been a reflection of the pride they felt over such a neatly executed journey.

I looked for the Battery Commander's party and, to my amazement, his vehicle came sailing through the gate *after* my group. I could see his round red orb and glinting spectacles looking at me from the murky interior

Give it the final touch, I thought. I called "detachments front" and they all leaped from their vehicles, still chortling with pleasure at being home, and came to attention in front of the radiators. I doubled over to the BC, vaulted to attention before him and gave a smug and snappy salute. Won't he be pleased, I thought.

I was, therefore, ill prepared for the blast from his shaking jowls that nearly sent me back somersaulting across the square while the other officers looked on snootily and the chaps silently doubled up.

"Range Roads" were specially hardened ribbons that meandered across the training area and made, at great expense, specifically to keep heavy military vehicles away from the population. Yes, it did say "range road" in very small writing on the map, I agreed. I also courteously accepted the month's worth of extra duties I was given.

Being the Regimental Orderly Officer was a great space filler for the newly commissioned officer. It enabled the new young arrival to get to know the regimental real estate and population and to practise taking responsibilities and decisions over small matters and also prevented the more senior Junior Officers from having to put up with the bore of him socially.

"You are the Commanding Officer's representative outside normal working hours." Adjutants and senior subalterns would say grandly to try and awe you with it all. You were in fact the titular head of, and scapegoat for, the regimental guard piquet: "but I informed the Orderly Officer," even if it had been most fleeting reference, was always guaranteed to redirect the recriminations. If anything remotely serious happened you were to seek guidance from the Adjutant, duty Field Officer or even the CO himself.

You arrived to many scheduled Orderly Officers, probably about two per week. Every opportunity was also afforded you to earn extra Orderly Officers. These could be awarded, or recommended for award, by everyone senior to you. They could be awarded for actual recorded crimes, like being late for things, or for such unwritten vagaries as doing something that someone felt was "unofficer-like" or "not on". The more the new arrival did, the less all the other Subalterns would have to do.

Once again, as with my Mons charges, I came near to breaking all former Imperial records. My total by the end of my first week with the regiment was truly impressive. There was the misuse of Saltzen high street incident on day one that got me thirty days – and from which, incredibly, the Regiment had recieved no complaint from the civil authorities. The second day I missed a period of officers' instruction. The notification for this had been circulated verbally before I had arrived. The fattest regimental toady's porky hands and knees could hardly get him to the Adjutant fast enough to sneak on me afterwards. This added another seven days.

I committed yet another fairly serious crime towards the end of my first week.

The Divisional Commander, a Major General, was to make his annual visit to us and no one knew what to do with me. The officer I was to replace had not yet gone, so I was surplus to the regimental structure. Finally a plan was worked out. I was to be in the Officer dress of the day (best Service Dress and Sam Browne) so that I could be a useful "extra" to help pad out the further reaches of the mess ante room and the dining room table during the lunch. Apart from that, I was to have a very covert role. I was given charge of all the soldiers serving in the Regiment's cells. We were to form a sort of mobile titivating force that would walk ahead of the inspecting party, putting an overlooked dab of dark green paint here, picking up a previously missed cigarette butt there and wiping off newly landed bird droppings, and so on. It was a clever idea, for not only did it provide a bit of extra insurance for the excellent presentation that everyone had been working hard for, it also got all the undesirables into one packet and out of sight. In fact, my main instruction was that on no account was my little command to be seen. This was another very good idea, for although I was a collection of razor-creased khaki and shining brown leather (belt, boots, gloves and stick), martial aspect was sadly lacking from my three troops. Soldiers under sentence are not allowed hats, belts, gaiters or boot laces. Their main garments were ill-fitting green overalls. One was the sort of chap who, when a bar room free-for-all breaks out, you study very carefully to see which side he is on before declaring your loyalties. He was a sort of King Kong and his taut coveralls stopped just above his Titan calves. Another, a ferret-face type, looked as though he stole babies' rattles and his coveralls swamped him in a great green concertina. The third appeared to be a mad anarchist. Even the prisoners' crop could not stop his hair from standing out round his wild-eyed face, and his coveralls were patched and holed as though he had had a "premature" with a bomb kit. By and large, I decided, we were a group well worth hiding.

All went smoothly at first. We scurried along, sticking to cover, about five minutes ahead of the inspecting General and the escorting Regimental hierarchy. My chaps, armed with brooms, pails, dusters, dark green paint pots, brushes and rubbish bags did a splendid job. Inconsiderate falling leaves were snatched up. Dust, so lacking in a sense of occasion as to land just prior to the General's visit, was quickly whisked away. Instant superficial repairs were carried out where minor damage had been previously overlooked. Everywhere, we patted, smoothed, brushed and straightened.

Finally, we had completed all parts of the main regimental administrative area. The inspection programme was going well to time. All that now remained was the gun park and workshops area. This was located in a satellite camp about a quarter of a mile from the main site at the end of a straight linking road.

After a final pride-filled glance round, my chaps and I, in step and in a neat little squad, doubled off down the gun park road.

We had got about half way along when, by good fortune, I looked back. To my horror, the motorcycle outriders and the long bonnet of the first staff car were turning into our road. I searched around in desperation. On our right was a continuous fifteen foot high barbed wire topped security fence that guarded the fuel compound. To the left, the road was bordered along its entire length by a six foot brick wall.

"Over the wall!" I screamed.

The chaps flew over. My tight tunic and belt could have slowed me but King Kong reached back and snatched me over. We had made it just before any of the illustrious ones could see us.

We were in the garrison rubbish tip. It was not a particularly disagreeable place. However, most important of all was that its encircling walls hid us from view. We had done all we could and had carried out our instructions to the letter. The gun park would not have the benefit of us but hopefully all would be well and, with luck, the General would be in such a good frame of mind after the gleaming regimental lines, he would give it no more than a token glance.

One of my troops led the way to a small clearing at the centre of the refuse hills. Someone courteously drew up an old dustbin for me to sit on and flicked the lid with a brush. It was a sunny and warmish day, the smell was not too bad and it was a comfortable enough haven.

"You chaps can smoke if you like," I said, knowing that they were not supposed to have tobacco but probably did. They grinned appreciatively and made their roll ups. We all relaxed and listened to the steady purr as the fleet of cars passed on the other side of the wall.

Suddenly, there was a squeal of brakes that was followed, in succession, by others. Next came the sounds of car doors opening and slamming. Finally, leather footfalls sounded on the road. We tensed.

"What's over here, Geoffrey?" said a deep old Etonian accent.

"That's the POL (petrol, oil and lubricants) compound, Sir," said the CO's voice.

"And here?" said the General's voice, obviously having turned to our wall.

"Uh, over here, Sir?" said the CO stalling.

"Rubbish, Sir", said the Adjutant's voice.

"Pardon!" said the CO's voice.

"Oh yes Sir, rubbish" said the CO's voice authoritatively.

Footsteps approached the wall and red-banded dress caps could now be seen hovering above it. I grew numb with horror.

Two expensively gloved hands appeared on the top of the wall and a dress cap with a General Staff badge on it, followed by a distinguished elderly face, rose above as the General stood on tip toe. Four more heads popped up in sequence: the CO, the Second in Command, the Adjutant and the Regimental Sergeant Major. They stared stonily at us.

I leaped to my feet, called my chaps to attention, their brooms held smartly at their sides, and gave a snappy salute. It caused no reaction. The row did not return my salute and, after a few more moments of hard and silent look, they all turned away. All that is, except the Adjutant, who remained a moment longer, his face white with fury. Finally, he too hurried back to his vehicle. The doors opened and slammed again and the convoy moved on.

"I mean, did you think you were being funny?" the Adjutant said later that afternoon.

"Perhaps you thought the General would laugh or something? I *weally* don't know if you are just stupid, or are deliberwately *twying* to sabotage things and make fools of us all!

You did not do as you were told. I mean what were you doing in that bloody place? You had absolutely no business to be there! Oh don't bother to tell me! I don't want to know!"

He concluded affairs by awarding me yet another sennight's worth of extra orderly officers.

Our Adjutant was an officer I came to respect and like as, behind his immaculate adjutant style, one gradually discovered that he was inflexibly honest and caring about people and principles. He was one of the smartest and most elegant officers I have ever encountered. He was ex-Coldstream Guards and terribly pukka and correct, yet could be down to earth as well, especially in humour. He had a sleek ex debutante wife with an incredibly astute and rather waspish wit which was superb for cutting the poseurs down to size. She was unembarrassed and unmerciless with officers or wives who tried to conceal their respective unmitigated career self interest or meanness of spirit behind insincere clichés. They rented a beautiful old German country cottage rather than live in the married Officers' upmarket "Coronation Street" in the camp housing area.

My admiration of him was not reduced by the number of extra orderly officers I earned off him over my first commissioned eighteen months.

On one occasion I was jogging across the gun park. I was late for something as usual and I spotted his tall and stately figure in the centre of the park examining the activity going on at its different points. His tailored officer pattern service shirts were such a pale cream as to be nearly white. His swagger stick always seemed longer than everyone else's. His brown George boots had the deep and lustrous mahogany sheen of a concert grand piano and his jaunty, gold braid embroidered scarlet and blue "fore and aft" cap set off his aristocratic head.

At the sound of my approach, he turned and studied me. I smarmed routinely as I passed but he remained unsmiling. He swivelled to watch me go by and start to retreat. He allowed me a further fifty metres before he called out:

"I'll see you in my office in fifteen minutes!"

I was perplexed. What could I have done this time?

"Officers don't *wun*." He said at the subsequent one-sided conversation. "If an officer is seen *wunning*, people immediately assume there's a flap on. You could panic the *twoops!*"

That particular incident rated a gift of three, as I remember. I got another three a short while later.

A very senior officer was again to inspect us. As usual, the guns and vehicles had to be sanded down, resprayed and the battery crests replaced on the sides of the gun barrels and the vehicle doors, respectively. Other duties, leave, sickness and courses seemed to have taken a heavy toll of my gun troop and we were falling behind on the sanding down. One morning I had resolved that it would have to be all hands to the pumps.

I had managed to find an old set of coveralls in a gun bay and was out in the sunshine with the rest, furiously rubbing at a wheel with a piece of sandpaper. An exquisite shadow blotted out the sun.

"My office. Fifteen minutes!" he said.

"What were you doing impersonating a Soldier?" was the clipped opener at this particular session. "Did you think you were *impwessing* your men?"

He continued; "The small amount of *differwence* your work will make is not worth the *fwacture* it will cause to the world they have come to accept as normal. The *twoops* are very conservative. They like the officer to do his job and leave them to do theirs. They expect you to give *diwections*, *encouwagement* and *pwaise* or *wecwimination*. Go outside your expected *wole* and you *wisk* making a fool of Officerdom itself!"

To this day, I believe my Adjutant of many years ago. The greatest snobs in the British Army are the Soldiers rather than the Officers. They are quickly affronted when the structure of life seems not to follow the slightly hackneyed pattern they expect. I think they still prefer traditional situations where their Sergeant is a bit of a bully, their Sergeant-Major is a slightly distant sort of fatherly martinet and their officer, regardless of the level of his origins, has the courtesy to act the Sahib for their sake.

This seems not to have been passed on to the current generation of Service officers. They turn up at all ranks functions in the same jeans and tee-shirts, and with the same behaviour as the troops, and I believe that they disappoint them. I think that British Servicemen still prefer a traditional "character" to rally round, who appears off duty in the standard double-breasted blazer or Harris Tweed and his old school tie or some such outfit. Then do they feel that all is right with the world.

Many years later, after my return to mainland British military service, I was on a multi-Unit tank firing range. While socially mingling by the tea urn to the rear, I was within earshot of a group of Senior NCOs from a number of different Cavalry regiments. They were demonstrating their pride in their Troop Commanders by recounting their aristocratic excesses.

Each Sergeant could hardly wait to better the last with how many more sports cars his man had written off or how many more debutantes he had impregnated. Obviously there would have been no respect had the Officer not had some idea of his military job. However they were so additionally grateful that he had the decency to support the system and be the junior officer of the Regiment that their fathers and grandfathers had told them to expect.

Thus it was, however, that near continuous "extras" took care of most of my early period with my regiment. No social function, bar or maiden could be at risk from me, it seemed, as I led my fairly monastic and ordered life.

I always felt that it was a shame that, short of court martials, the award of extra turns to be Orderly Officer was, it seemed, the only way to punish a junior officer. Several principles appeared to be compromised. If the Orderly Officer really is meant to be "the CO's representative outside normal working hours," then it should be a duty avidly sought after and in which great pride is taken.

The award of extra Orderly Officers also ensured that the military establishment actively assisted in the undermining of the young officer's already precarious status and standing with the troops. If a duty is to be official, it must be promulgated in the Unit's Routine Orders. One could always tell, by the whoops, when the crowds at the notice boards had found the amendment to the month's Orderly Officer duties:

"Delete Lt Brown. Delete Lt Jones. Delete Lt Robinson. Insert 2/Lt Smith. Insert 2/Lt Smith. Insert 2/Lt Smith."

2/Lt Smith's fall from grace was made public, so that he could probably be cheeked a bit without risk and the officer corps as a whole had broken one of its own golden rules by parading its fallibility before all. I once suggested some alternative systems of local punishments for erring Junior Officers to the Adjutant. He never used bad language but, by his silent stare, I knew that, had I been capable of receiving telepathic messages, I should have been told to go away in extremely abrupt and crude terms.

The other problem with being Orderly Officer, in my Regiment, was that the duty had to be done in Royal Artillery Number One Dress. This is a magnificent Victorian equestrian military ensemble with a high gold-embroidered patrol collar and tight cavalry pants that pass under the insteps of spurred boots. It looked absolutely magnificent but was not really the ideal outfit for climbing in and out of tall military vehicles, sorting out drunken Junior Rank social functions or tearing up flights of apartment steps to get to the wife beating.

Being frequently the Orderly Officer in a large garrison town was quite an education for a young man. It was not so much a military education as a highly concentrated experience of human lowliness. The young unmarried

Officer, scarcely out of his teens, strove to be: policeman, social worker, father-figure and diplomat. The dreary drunks, feeble fights, petty thefts, neglected and wayward children and sleazy marriage problems seemed, after a while, to be forever re-enacting their predictable courses.

The Orderly Officer can, however, sometimes find himself on very unfamiliar ground.

I propped the drunk against the door frame of the tower block of Soldiers' married quarters, whereupon he instantly sagged into a pile on the ground. My tight patrols did not favour the struggle it would take to try and get him vertical again, so I left him.

With a white-gloved hand, I pressed the bell beside the name that he had taken ages of disorientated staggering from block to block to guide me to. His body had been overlooked when the social event had been removed from the NAAFI private functions' room some hours earlier.

By coincidence, I had been passing on my return from the Guardroom as the barmaid had run agitatedly out. She had been sweeping up and had found him. I had telephoned for transport to take him home. The locally employed German civilian driver had said that he would not take a drunk home unescorted. So, as I knew the Orderly Sergeant and his men to be busy with another matter, I had rashly decided to go with them. All had been quiet at two o'clock in the morning and it was not far.

My ring did not bring an enquiring voice from the two-way communication system nor an electric buzz as the door was released. Instead, I heard a casement window opening high in the sky. I clanked across to the centre of the yard and looked up towards the distant metal-curler framed silhouette that protruded from the dark square far up the building.

"Uh, good evening, Mrs Green!" I called.

"It's the Orderly Officer!"

At this moment her husband attempted to stand, lost his balance and, hopelessly out of control, careered across the square and cannoned into me. He blinked upwards as he tried to focus on his remote spouse.

"Yer can fxxx orff!" she screeched at him.

"And yer can take that ponce with yer!"

"Come, come now, Mrs Green", I reasoned. "Where's our sense of humour? I feel sure you don't mind your husband occasionally having a little night out with the chaps!"

Neither his intoxication nor my tight ceremonial uniform inhibited the agility with which we both flew across the yard to escape the shards of porcelain and other substances that followed the explosion of the chamber pot hitting the cobbles.

It was not particularly cold for the time of year, so I left my greatcoat behind and, with the snow muffling my spurs, I set off just before dawn, from the Officers' Mess and headed for the Guardroom. The Adjutant allowed the Orderly Officer to draw lots for when he turned out the Guard. All the counters in the tin were for timings between one and five o'clock in the morning.

I placed a boot toe on the top Guardroom step and was suddenly struck in the face by the upper parts of a naked, and extremely buxom woman travelling at considerable speed in the opposite direction and was sent flying backwards into a snowdrift.

The naked woman was pursued across the regimental square by the Orderly Sergeant. About half way across he gave up the chase and returned to pull my bewildered form from the snowdrift.

I was taken into the Guardroom between the Orderly Sergeant and the NCO Marching Relief, found a chair and given a cup of tea. After allowing me a moment or two, the Orderly Sergeant recounted the events leading up to this most unusual incident.

A youngish woman, I cannot remember if she was British or German, of above average sexual needs, was in the habit of calling at the Guardroom and serving the duty Gunners to the mutual benefit of all parties. She would walk through the village and the garrison lines wearing only winter boots and an overcoat. The Orderly Sergeant or his Bombadier NCO Marching Relief would be unable to see her enter the building and dart down the corridor to the guards' dormitory at the end. The duty room was L shaped and, although the Duty NCO had a superb panoramic view of the Regimental lines from the long windows, along two front walls, he could not observe the external door, his duty room door or the passage that connected him to his standby troops.

The only times an NCO needed to be concerned with the room at the end of the corridor was when he inspected it and signed for its furnishings and equipment at the start of his tour or handed it over to his successor at the end.

Thus, a prowler sentry, having finished his shift, would report back to the Duty NCO. He would then be dismissed to the dormitory and told to send his relief out. His relief would then spring, or be dragged, from his community efforts, would button himself quickly and neatly into his uniform, report to the Duty NCO and start his duties. The relieved sentry could then take his turn with the room's additional facilities.

Naturally, the six or so Gunners that used the room at any one time kept to a strict oath of silence on their good fortune, and life went peacefully, and satiatedly, on.

On the night of my astounding experience, all had at first been going as usual until one of the troops had either been too greedy or too prolonged and there was an unnatural interval between one sentry and the next. The Orderly Sergeant had, therefore, strode impatiently down the corridor, flung open the dormitory door and switched on the light. A tableau vivant of extreme lewdness had greeted him.

The female person had nimbly extricated herself, had pulled on her coat and had flashed past the baffled Sergeant. He had recovered just in time to seize her collar. Without breaking step she had slipped out of her garment and had flown on down the passage to arrive in the doorway just as I was bending forward in the act of climbing the step. The memory of that devastating sensation remains with me to this day.

Gradually the other Junior Officers (Second Lieutenants, Lieutenants and Captains) spoke to me and, occasionally, without criticism. Everyone wanted to tell me "The Form" of things and give me the benefit of their "experience" however limited this was.

"Speaking as an Officer of more than twice your service . . ." one bottom-faced Second Lieutenant actually said. He had been commissioned five months and I two.

I was new and young and anxious to do the right thing. For the first three months I (metaphorically) sat cross-legged at the Senior Subaltern's feet, as he held court before his toadies each evening after dinner and waited for pearls to drop upon me. I searched keenly for the image to admire and emulate. It had seemed wonderful to be sunk in a great leather armchair, in my Mess, in my Regiment, sipping a port after dinner and laughing at the cruel and sarcastic wit of my seniors. Sadly, however, I realised all too soon that they were mostly a poor lot.

None had distinguished themselves, or even been present, at any active service event that might have justified their military lording. Outside of the day to day peacetime administration of their troops, their sole occupation seemed to be holding, alcohol assisted, in absentia evening trials of other junior officers. After much humorous belittlement of his performance, the subject would, as usual, be pronounced "unofficerlike." It was a sentence from which there was no reprieve. What was "officerlike" was the image they fondly believed that they had. They were deceived in this, however, as the inner-circle were really little more than an unenterprising and dubious collection of current military jargon regurgitators. Virtues were made of inadequacies. They did not leave the garrison area and participate in German life because the Germans were "arrogant" and/or "vulgar". It had nothing to do with the senior subalterns' parochialism, lack of effort at languages or inability to adapt or communicate outside the limited environment that they had latched on to. They abstained from vice, i.e. women. The fact that their ugliness in all mediums ensured that they were at almost no risk was not relevant. Sexual intercourse itself was probably "unofficerlike".

If we went out, it was by mini-bus, passing attractive and interesting looking German *gasthauses* and places of youthful entertainment en route to another British Officers' Mess where there would be a near identical Senior Subaltern and Subordinate Judiciary set. We could then have matching evenings to the ones that we usually had. Once, as we passed a beer and dance hall that looked particularly lively, I suggested that we went in and nearly got myself an on-the-spot life sentence.

At the end of those three months, when I realised that no one remotely resembling the hero I sought was likely to emerge, I abandoned them. I learnt German, initially from a short tape recorder course and from then on by what the Germans refer to as "the pillow method" and departed into the high quality recreational life of West Germany. However, I, of course, played sport for the regiment and attended all of its main social events. For the next three years I provided the inebriated nightly ante room court with a near constant subject. I cannot imagine how many concurrent unofficerlike terms I must have been unknowingly serving.

In other ways too, the ante-room social leaders' reactions followed a predictable pattern. They expressed their selfless concern that the polite and well-groomed German girls that I brought to Mess events meant that I was leading a life of sexual abandon and the girls were probably all East German spies. Some made a habit of open insulting speculation of my Aryan companions' morals but gulped their beer and watched steadfastly as these fine-boned flaxen haired and statuesque maidens passed. None of the mistakes I made and the things that I said failed to be passed on upwards.

Obviously, the constant barrage had some effect. The poor peacetime COs who tend to become trapped administrating from their offices, rather then being out commanding, had to believe that there could not be this much smoke and no fire. So some ambiguous generalities were included on my annual reports.

One could have become embittered but I could not, I was enjoying Germany too much. Finally, I got steadily cheekier. In addition to the constant scrutinizing and reporting of my every detail, and the extras, the oligarchy also cut me dead in the end. They would not speak to me unless it was absolutely essential. I used to respond to this by little bursts of chirpy, inane small-talk as they passed silently and superciliously by – their glassy eyes determindley fixed on the middle distance.

I have sometimes wondered if there was any sincere public spiritedness behind it all to make me a better officer. I only know that at the time I believed it to be a sadistic space filler for the frustrations of military egos and energies in the warless vacuum. A bitter resentment of any junior who would not admire them, a leftover of a House Prefect bullying instinct. I was well capable of smacking their silly heads but Mons had taught me too well to respect an established order, regardless of the individuals of which it was currently composed.

The Senior Subaltern eventually fell from grace with the Royal Artillery and joined the Catering Corps. I sometimes imagine him with a pinny over his uniform, mincing about a kitchen and pompously pronouncing the pies "uncomestiblelike" or some such rubbish. His principle Lieutenant developed into a comic drunk and was persuaded to leave the Service, and his two most vitriolic and vituperative agents became very senior officers with OBEs.

Fortunately, there were a few other rejected or semi-rejected junior officers who gave me company. I also enjoyed a measure of friendship with some of the Majors. Not my own, alas. I tried hard to please him at work but he did not seem pleasable by me. However, it was in this strata that I came much nearer to finding my elusive Hector.

Some of our senior Majors were Second World War, Korea and Malaya veterans. They tended to be without the pettiness, insecurities and desperate competitiveness of those untempered by combat.

When I was first commissioned an Officer might not get married, without his CO's permission if he was under the age of thirty. Unlike these days, when nineteen year olds enter Service commissioning academies already distracted by marriage, about three-quarters of our Officers were unmarried. The CO's permission was unlikely to be with-held by the nineteen-sixties but people tended to ensure that they had no need to ask. Most Officers endeavoured to fall in love in a controlled manner.

If one married below the official age limit there was no entitlement to a Service married quarter, marriage allowances or any other special considerations. It was merely a hobby. Also, all single Officers, except for Quartermasters and Lieutenant Colonels and above could not be permitted to live anywhere other than an Officers' Mess. Presumably, it was considered that Quartermasters were too old and Lieutenant Colonels and above too responsible to deteriorate into unwedded scandalousness and sordidity if permitted to live outside celibate military walls. This was, on occasions, an overly optimistic assumption. The rest of us, it had been decided, would be immediately transformed into Abdul the Bulbul Emirs the second we were out of official sight. The relaxing of the rules in the seventies seems to have borne this out as both un-wed junior officers and junior ranks of opposite sexes now "live in sin" in rented civilian properties.

The mandatory living in the Mess rules were a little unfair on the very respectable elderly single Majors who had to organise their dignified and stately lifestyles in competition with the noisy and inconsiderate subalterns.

Major 'Punjabi' ("I was a 'Piffa' y'know") Farquharson and Major 'Tun' ("well, of course, in Burma we always . . .") Rumbold were as marvellous as the celeocanth. They were unmarried Imperial Officers who had served an empire more mighty than those of Caesar or Kublai Khan. In addition to complete set of Second World War medal ribbons and those of post war conflicts like Malaya and Korea, they had pre war ribbons as well, from North West Frontier, Waziristan and Iraq.

One day the unthinkable happened. A newly commissioned Second Lieutenant made formal request of the CO to get married. I happened to be standing behind the two Majors at morning coffee in the Mess on the day the news hit the Regiment. The friends of nearly forty years always seemed to drift together, perhaps for all-round defence as they became ever more leftover.

"I say Old Man, do you know that I've just heard that young Reid has asked the CO for permission to get married?" said Farquharson.

"Hmm", said Rumbold.

"What do you think's the matter? Isn't he happy in the Mess?"

I decided that entering the Dannenburg dine and dance restaurant that Saturday evening was a mistake. It was the occasion of my first desertion from the ante-room Home Counties facsimile and escape into West Germany. I had gone out on my own as I knew that if I had found another Briton to go with we would have spoken English and I was grimly determined that, no matter how halting it might be, the local population were to have my embryonic German inflicted on them. It was not that it was not a nice place. The Germans always have neat and tasteful decor and thoughtful lighting and the clientele looked immaculately behaved. No-one stared at me or looked hostile either. Indeed I had the same crisp white shirt and just-out-of-the-dry-cleaners fashionable suited look as all the males present, and Officers were permitted considerably longer hair than Officer Cadets. It was the communal togetherness of the young Germans that made me feel like a gatecrasher. Also, I had noticed that the place consisted entirely of young couples. One obviously did not just go about picking up girls. Neither could one loiter and leer at a bar as it was only permissible to operate from a table.

I was just about to smile pleasantly at those near the door and dart back out into the street when a genial, but officious, green-waistcoated waiter came over and started to steer me across the open floor to a table. My heart sank. There were no totally unoccupied tables. I should be put, as an odd male, amongst resentful couples. One fast drink, I thought, and out. And then he sat me opposite Waltraut.

I was sitting with the prettiest, and only unattached girl in the place on the last vacant chair. She was small and very blonde and wore a little black dress. She had gigantic dark blue eyes. A couple also sat at the table.

"*Guten Abend*", I said, and gave little short bows of the head to all. They returned my greeting with distant politeness but seemed not to mind my presence. All three chatted together amiably. I gave the waiter my order which, miracle of miracles, he understood and tried not to gape at Waltraut.

A popular number came over the music system and a number of couples started to dance. Dare I? I thought. She is bound to refuse; then I shall have the chronic embarrassment of eating my meal with them. I can always pay for my meal now, not eat it and saunter out with any fraction of dignity that may remain, I thought.

"*Fraulein, möchten sie bitte tanzen?*" I said, checking the route to the door out of the corner of an eye.

To my incredible relief, a smile of spontaneous pleasure broke out over her face, even though she neither replied nor looked at me. She excused herself from her two companions and allowed me to lead her onto the dance floor.

The route to becoming loving friends very quickly started. She lived in Luneburg and was visiting a married female cousin, the couple at our table. She was amused and delighted by my German efforts and this humour spread to others about us. Soon other tables were in fits and mocking me in a kindly way. As the drinking progressed I played up to this by deliberately and obviously putting incorrect nouns in sentences, that were close in sound to the correct ones, which made the sense comical. It was all very heavy and simplistic but seemed to suit the native sence of humour. The waiters stared mystified at our hooting half of the room.

It was a glorious evening, but the memory that lingers is of Waltraut: her sometimes shy, sometimes animated, pretty face with affection already starting to brighten her lovely eyes, the scent of her, and of holding her on the last slow dances.

Later, when we were alone, I notieced that a Dresdener doll hand that I held wore an engagement ring. She held the ring and the finger in it, and shook them with her other hand, in a sort of mock anger. I never discovered if this meant that things it might refer to were either dying or dead. She then brought my ponderoulsy constructed "Wouldn't-wish-to-be-a-cad "German wafflings to a halt by a V1-like launch of her small and perfectly proportioned entity.

"Du doofer," she whispered sweetly as we erroded the myth of the lack of spontaneity and passion of Northern races.

Luneburg was not really so far from our country garrison but I did not get around to buying a car during my first six months and then I was so locally tied by the dreary extras. Waltraut came by train to see me at weekends and once I went to her in her compact and imposing city. I fear, however, that administrative and logistic drawbacks caused me to drift after some weeks. What a shallow youth I was, as she was such a treasure. Waltraut, as a name, is apparently mainly used in South Germany and Austria. In German TV sitcoms it is often the maid's name. However, my Waltraut would definitely have been cast as a cute poised and independent daughter of the house.

She patiently suffered my German so that it improved and she equally patiently taught me the conventions of a society that, unlike our own, retained strong tradition, a structure and sense of order in all levels and age groups. But most precious of all, she gave her exquisite self.

When I was in particularly fond circumstances with local girls during my time in Germany, I occasionally used to wonder what the reaction of our respective fathers would have been if, during a shelling exchange, someone had told them that their children would love each other someday.

Marianne, a fashion model, followed quickly on. She was tall, elegant, athletic and spectacularly structured with aristocratic straw-haired Nordic beauty. She would unquestionably have been snatched up for master-race breeding a generation earlier. Her usual serenity contrasted strangely with her sudden clothes sheddings at Summer night lakesides. I have truly seen Venus both arising from, and entering, the waves. However, she was too beautiful to be wasted on one man alone and passed on after about two months.

The sloe-eyed and secretly smiling Ursula proved, to my mortification, that engineering a meeting with, seducing and then departing from members of the opposite sex was not the sole prerogative of myself and other males.

There were others with whom the friendship, though often highly memorable, lasted no longer than the mid-Friday evening meeting, in a Hanover discoteque, to whispered and tip-toeing Saturday early dawn farewells from their parents apartment block. Often, when I went out on a Friday evening, I would hang a uniform and accoutrements in the back of my car, so that I could change in the, as yet unmet, young lady's residence

73

prior to my early departure.

Sometimes I only just made it in time for the Adjutant's "Fall in the Officers!" on working Saturday mornings. I would make early bustle in the vicinity of my near-permanently scowling battery commander, so that I could later snatch the odd nap in one of the less frequently used stores.

Finally, I met Ulrike whom I wanted to marry, but we were put through the unkind test of frequent and sudden military separation and were found to be wanting. She was one of the prettiest and most sought after girls at Hanover University. Male students constantly tried to separate her from the memory of her absent soldier lover by extolling the unrelieved brutalities of the profession. It was a fashionable, easy and, ultimately, successful ploy. Meanwhile, temptation kept mercilessly cropping up in my path.

She had a Slavonic style of beauty with dark, delicately sculptured and hypnotic features. She also had the brightest of personalities and would have made a lovely life-time companion. But, for better or worse, she was spared me and Western causes, whether they liked it or not, were to have my single devotion for many years.

I filed into the Officers' washroom, to the left of the Mess front foyer, with the other Junior Officers. The Senior Subaltern Committee had not yet arrived, as they did not like to be as prompt for morning coffee as the rest of us.

I started to study my hungover face in the mirror and noticed the thunderflash on the chest-high glass shelf in front of me.

Explosive tend to play a fairly regular part at Royal Artillery parties, mainly because the character of our battlefield task, ensures that we live constantly co-located with it. There are exploding warheads, propellant charges, fuses, primers, detonators, demolition explosive and training explosive natures. A thunder-flash falls into the latter category. It contains about the same amount of explosive as a hand-grenade but is encased in cardboard rather than cast metal. However, its blast effect is considerable.

Most COs and Senior Officers turn a Nelsonian eye to any cordite, or other noisy party guests, as long as the Mess is rebuilt before they enter it the following day. The amnesty definitely ends with the party.

My Regiment also had an impressive collection of some of the actual eighteenth and nineteenth century mortars and cannons that our subordinate batteries had used at Malplaquet, Minden, Waterloo, Sebastapol, Lucknow and other violent places. Thus, the subalterns could, late at night, practise ceremonial kneeling gun-drill in their Mess

74

uniforms and fire half-bricks from the front path and packets of golf balls across the Mess lawns.

It used to intrigue me that although a Mess uniform, with all its intricate tailoring and detail, was an Officer's most expensive outfit, the primary objective seemed to be to wreck it as soon as possible after purchase. It was mandatory to wrestle in it, play indoor rugby in it, throw food and drink at each other while wearing it, climb walls and buildings in it and generally carry out as many activities as possible that would stain or tear it. My mess uniform visited a dry cleaners and a tailor after every outing. The first time I proudly wore it was the night that the Captains and Majors tried to throw all the Subalterns into the fish pond. A group of us escaped by barricading ourselves in an upstairs sitting room and holding an independent party. Unfortunately, as I made my unsteady way back across the gardens to my block later I fell into the pond unaided.

"Hello!" I said to the washroom in general and picked up the thunder-flash. It was in a slightly precarious condition as it had been prepared for activation. Its striker, a large match-head was exposed. The evening before, of course, we had burnt holes in the parquet flooring and blown window frames out as usual. However, the long-suffering Mess staff and the various local artisans that we had collectively hired, had put the place to rights again. The thunder-flash was unquestionably out-of-bounds at ten o'clock that following morning.

"Well, we've got to get rid of this pretty quick!" I continued to the shiny-tiled room of young men.

"I'll take it to the range and let it off," I stated.

"Or perhaps I could just mash it up, tip the charge out and throw all the bits in a dustbin by the kitchen?" I said, re-thinking the possibilities aloud.

"Throw it down here," said Roger, the scion of a wealthy and longstanding Tyneside business, taking the thunderflash from me.

Roger currently destroyed a new sports car every month and was being simultaneously sued by several young ladies for emotional stress and scars. He always owned up to everything, expressed genuine sorrow and cheerfully distributed generous cheques. However, I felt uncertain about his fine judgement.

"It'll block the pipe," I said.

"Rubbish," he replied.

"This camp was built by the Kaiser and you know how much the Germans eat."

I was still not sure and would have spoken more but, to my total horror, he struck the two parts of the striker together and dropped it hissing into the toilet bowl. He then pulled the chain, before I could stop him or snatch the thunderflash back.

"What have you done?" I gasped.

"I never realised that you meant to flush it away lit. It'll fracture the pipe!"

"I shouldn't thinks so," said another junior officer, looking out of the window.

"I reckon it will blow that man-hole cover off in the car park."

"Not if we all stand on it, said yet another.

The fuse of a thunderflash lasts about thirteen seconds.

"Quick!" I shouted.

All ten or so of us rushed out of the washroom, out of the front door and down the path. The first four to arrive stood on the man-hole cover and clung onto each other. The rest of us clambered onto them, forming a rough sort of human pyramid. All our collective weight was concentrated on the small circular area.

There was a great muted roar from the bowels of the earth. The ground shook as with a volcanic tremor and the man-hole cover danced and tried to lift. When silence returned we dropped off our pile. All seemed well. The good solid German sewage pipe had held.

"You clot!" I hissed at Roger. "God! We were lucky to get away with that!"

It had, however, been a more eventful thirteen seconds than we had realised. During the time that we had rushed out of the washroom and stood on the manhole cover, one of the senior Captains had entered the washroom and enthroned himself.

Fortunately, it was his wont to first spend a while on a meditating phase for, when the thunderflash exploded, the only outlet for the over-pressure, as we were on the man-hole cover, was back along the way it had come.

Suddenly the water geysered up between his legs and his shirt tails were blown up around his head.

When we re-entered the Mess, he was staggering about in the foyer, ashen faced and with his trousers round his ankles, in a state of shock. Quickly we seized him, rushed him through the Staff areas and out of the back door to his room. There, we laid him down and ferried brandies across.

Ever after that, if he entered a cubicle and someone saw, they would rattle the man-hole cover. He would then fly furiously out, as he thought the thunderflash had entered the system that way.

Thunderflashes never seemed to favour me. Almost every time I threw one, to simulate a grenade during a training exercise, it would be caught up by a springy branch and be returned, tennis-match style, to explode at my feet.

One of my most disagreeable experiences with this aggressive and noisy object happened during the final field exercise of my Mons Officer Cadet days.

Every sixty minutes precisely throughout the night the enemy of the School Demonstration Platoon did something to make us Stand-To. They fired single blank shots, noisily cocked a weapon or made a fiendish Asian enemy style call. The intention was to get our sentries to keep calling us out so that we should get no sleep. Premature departures from the School meant that I was the only person in my two-man trench. Apart from the fag of having to dig it on my own, it also meant that I had to occupy it alone and no-one else was there to pass the half-hour long Stand-To periods with. It also occurred to me at about one o'clock in the morning, after about six Stand-Tos that there was no one around in the pitch darkness to appreciate the speed and devotion with which I darted from my little bivouac tent to my grave-shaped trough. For higher tactical reasons, therefore, I decided to conserve myself for more significant events and excused myself from more unnecessary departures out of my fairly snug little bundle of grey blanket.

I dozed off and missed quite a few inconsequential bangs, clicks and shouts of "Hey! Blitish Johnny!" when suddenly the whole Demo Platoon attacked and over-ran our position. The proximity and quantity of shouts and blank firings woke me up, and I peeped out of the narrow front aperture of my tent. There were lights, noise and confusion everywhere. Then I noticed the enemy platoon commander, and his party, about ten metres in front of my position.

My big chance to be the hero, I thought gleefully. I had been issued with my first ever thunderflash that afternoon. The Demo Platoon would assume that everyone was correctly Stood-To in the outer perimeter trenches and would not expect me to be still in the centre of the position.

I would shout "Grenade!" and throw the thunderflash near the Platoon headquarters and "destroy" them. I fumbled quickly through my blanket and found the pyro-technic. I looked quickly out again to make sure they were still there, then I ignited the thunderflash.

I let it burn for a few seconds to give a near simultaneous and more startling explosion on landing. The moment came. I swept aside my tent flap with my left arm. My right arm was drawn back into the throwing position. Unfortunately, I also accidentally swept the centre-front pole away and the tent collapsed onto me. The more frantically I struggled to get out, the tighter the canvas wrapped itself around me. I became totally trapped at the centre of a tight cloth cocoon in company with a terminally fizzing explosive device.

"Good heavens, what on earth was that?" the Platoon Commander apparently said to those around him, following the muffled report from behind. They peered about, shrugged their shoulders, gathered up their victorious troops and made a tactical withdrawal from our position. My fellow defenders did not find me until dawn. They frowningly separated my unhappy remains from the small smoking pile.

Bivouac tents turned out to be surprisingly expensive to replace too, as I discovered when one of our arch enemies, the Company Quartermaster Sergeant, came along, in person, to my barrack room to smugly present me with my bill.

I would have thought that pornography would have been "unofficer-like". However, it presumably was not, as the self-appointed protectors and shapers of the younger officers' lives used to go in for it. In fact it represented the senior subalterns' only foray into German life. Every few months they would go to Hamburg to places that sold normal beer, at one thousand per cent inflated prices, accompanied by the spectacle on stage of paid German, and other, women doing every sort of sexual exposure and action.

I stood on the edge of the pavement about half-way up the Reeperbahn early one Saturday night, while a dozen young born leaders argued around me. They all wanted to go to different places. I seemed to be the only one who did not care. I was just pleased to be out after one of our routine and rather overly laboured exercises on the ubiquitous North German pine and braken coated heath. The street was full of terribly interesting looking international people and there was quite a good coverage of pretty girls. Most were off-duty typists and salesgirls, albeit there were a few more lacquered ones, who, presumably, were a more involved part of the dazzling neon scene.

Everyone, except myself, seemed to know of a pornographic club that was the best in town. I was not particularly keen to get fleeced in some sleazy joint in return for depressing shows, but I wanted to feel part of the team and awaited a majority decision. The shouting and gesticulating group of Haris Tweed jackets were getting some curious stares from the passers-by.

In those days, there used to be a little hot dog stand every few metres along the street. These handy and good value entrepreneurs also used to sell bottles of beer. There was one just to my left. To assist the decision-making, I offered everyone a beer but the discussions were far too heated for anyone to pay any attention to me so I carried on sipping and enjoying the scene on my own.

Crowds of Germans kept coming in and out of a pair of large double doors behind me. Curiosity got the better of me and I strolled between my ebbing and flowing group and peeped inside. A fabulous sight greeted my eyes. It was a vast cathedral-like beer hall. A traditional oompa band played cheery tunes to a jolly throng. Balconies were bedecked with fair maidens and impressive matrons in national costume, dispensed foaming tankards in all directions.

"I say! I say! Look in here!" I called excitedly to the others. "Let's go in!"

My very junior status commanded no attention. No one even looked at me, so I went in on my own. The choice of seating was very important.

I quickly checked around and there was the place. A group of female friends on a night out with a spare gap on their bench.

"*Darf ich bitte?*" I said indicating the seat in a polite, but friendly, manner, making sure my foreign accent came through.

"*Och! Ein Komischen Englander!*" They said laughing.

"*Ja! Bitte setzen sie!*"

They were a bevy of blonde princesses from a German fairy tale with big and beautiful eyes and bodies and laughing smiles. I happily waved a finger of my upraised arm to attract the waitress' attention.

About half-an-hour later, Nigel strode crossly in. The girls and I had our arms about each other and were swaying in time to the music.

"We've been looking for you for bloody ages," he said. The others were all for leaving you. I just came in to tell you we're going to "The Safari." You coming?"

"I'll follow on," I said. "Sorry if I held you all up. Like a drink?"

But he was already striding out red-faced and tight lipped.

"*Ihre freund?*" said one of the girls.

"*Ja,*" I said.

"*Blurtmann!*"* said another and they all dissolved into giggles.

About nine o'clock the girls started anxiously conferring. It seemed they were all to have dinner at the home of the parents of one of their number and were already late. There were more slightly tipsy sniggers as I gave quick kisses all round and they gathered up their afternoon shopping bags and started to move off, but not before I had managed to surreptitiously elicit a couple of telephone numbers for future reference.

I stood at our table and waved them to the door. I also threw flowers from the decorations and skimmed beer mats after them. I succeeded in rendering them helpless again as I feigned unrequited love and made exaggerated courtly English bows of farewell. Suddenly, however, I

---

* Very vulgar for an unsympathetic type.

79

noticed that one of the terrifying waitresses was looking at me, so I sat down quickly.

I carried on drinking the exquisite draught Bavarian beer, chatting to anyone who would put up with me, eating a few sausages and lah-lahing in time to the rhythmic music – while I tried to pick up the words from those about me. Finally, I nodded off.

I was prodded awake by a cleaning lady. Behind her and looking equally stern, was one of the colossal middle-aged bouncers (ex-stormtroopers?) they traditionally seem to employ in beer halls in his odd uniform of a London city-gent rig of black jacket, pin-striped trousers and pale grey tie.

*"Entschuldigen Sie. Bitte"* I said, and produced my wallet and started examining the pen marks on my beer mat to see how much I owed.

Their expressions relaxed marginally. I was obviously not a troublesome drunk. The beer hall had just been emptied so I found my waitress, who was clearing up empty beer mugs and glasses at a furious speed, and settled up. I attempted a cheery *"Auf wiedersehen"* to the staff table but it faltered before the unsmiling gaze of that mighty collection of Valkyries, so I hurried out.

Earlier that evening, I had seen one of them deal with some drunks. A chap had staggered down an aisle between the tables and had bumped into her. It was as though he had collided with a cathedral pillar. He had tottered helplessly back. Continuing his momentum she had spun him round and propelled him, with the same single movement, straight through a pair of handy double doors. A fat customer at an adjacent table had flung back his head and laughed openly at the sequence. Without pause she had spun her impressive frame round and delivered him a male heavy-weight-style right-hander to the jaw that catapulted both him and his chair into the crowd behind.

When I got into the street outside, I was astounded to notice, by my watch, that it was after midnight. I asked a nearby pimp the way to "The Safari", resisted his inducements to examine his own business enterprises and hurried off. About half way to the strip joint, I met the others on the way back.

They sounded quite animated about the interesting scenes of human debasement they had witnessed but complained bitterly about the absurdly inflated drink prices. Another prolonged argument about where we were going to go seemed about to get under way when, miraculously, someone spotted a place just across the road from where we stood in which, apparently, record lows in degradation could be seen. We all crossed and went in.

It was a large low ceilinged place, decorated in a red velvet sort of

French Second Empire style. There was a minute stage at the end of the room where, presumably, it all happened. We had obviously come in between the acts. Hard-faced male and female staff moved amongst the customers. While we waited for the astronomically priced drinks to arrive, I realised that for once, I had put myself voluntarily in a place of pornographic display. I resigned myself to sitting through it, however, to try and be part of the company. There were plush armchairs for us to sit on, set before large circular tables with beaded cloths that reached to the thick carpet. I fell asleep, even before the drinks arrived, slid from my chair and rolled into the palatial marquee beneath the table.

I woke up, having had an excellent night's sleep and was totally perplexed as to where I might be. It all came back quickly enough, of course, as soon as I peeped out of my table-cloth. Although my friends had gone, there were still plenty of people in the dive. However, the shows seemed to have finished. My companions would not have been able to leave had the bill not been settled, so I stood up and strode quickly out into the near daylight street. There was a belated shout from behind me, so I darted through a deserted shopping mall. It was nearly five-thirty. While all manner of sexual, and ancillary, inventiveness had been going on on the stage, I had been innocently dreaming of my Thames-side, Surrey boyhood. I was disappointed that my group had not bothered to wake me and take me with them.

I had a wash and brush-up in a public convenience, got a coffee at an early shift food cart and wondered how I was going to get back to Dannenburg. I had come into town a shaken passenger in Roger's latest sports car. By the time I had emptied my cup, the sun was fully up on a quiet and unimpressive daylight Reeperbahn. I decided to go and look for Roger's car – just in case it was still there. Incredibly, I found the car park and his car was still in it. Knowing that Roger never locked the folding roof, I opened it, vaulted the side and went back to sleep on the passenger seat.

Roger cheerfully appeared a short while later. He and the others had been to several, ever more luxurious, houses after leaving me. They had not meant to leave me; they had just forgotten me, he said.

On the way out of Hamburg, Roger stopped for two attractive girl hitch-hikers. I got into the small compartment in the back of the sports car, so that they could all squeeze across the front. The girls had looked delighted with the chance of a ride in an *"Englisher Sportwagen"*. In near record time we got back, dropped off the shaky and ashen-faced girls and went to the Mess.

I was the only one of the very junior officers at breakfast, as I was the only one who had, inadvertently, had a normal night's sleep.

"Hamburg! *Och Du Frecheitlicher Junge!*" shrieked Gertrude, our large and motherly mess waitress when I announced that I had passed the night in the city. Her large, kind face beamed, she winked a conspiratorial eye and nearly fired me off my chair with a nudge from her mighty elbow. The Majors and senior Captains lowered the tops of their newspapers briefly to survey me in disgust.

As the years passed and I started to approach the end of my Short Service Commission, I became more and more grimly determined to try and please old "Wurst", the German word for sausage and the Battery Officers' name for our gelatinous commander. I wanted to please him because I felt that it was something that a subordinate should try to do and also because he was basically a good chap.

His near permanent irritability was probably caused by his ill-ease with subordinates (his forte was as an instructor in technical institutions) and the fact that he was very hen-pecked at home – we suspected. The main problem, however, was that he seemed to be one of those unfortunate persons who really does not have a sense of humour and takes every line uttered, including contrary statements made as broad attempts at humour, as being the speaker's intention. For example, if, on one of his infrequent furloughs to the mess, a junior officer said:

"God! I don't feel like getting my guns' log books up-to-date tomorrow for the end-of-month check! I think I'll go absent for the day instead, get smashed and fornicate myself to death!"

Wurst's head, no matter how far away across the ante room he was, would whip round. He would then probably give the bewildered speaker, who in fact had no intention of shirking this duty – despite its tedious nature, a lecture on the importance of keeping military records up-to-date and setting behaviour examples to the troops. Explaining that the intention had been to make a joke would not change anything as jokes in general, and particularly jokes about military paperwork, did not seem comprehensible to him. However, having delivered his lecture and, if the junior officer were one of his, made a mental note about the Officer's "attitude" for an annual report, he was just as likely to tell the officer to being all his books to him the next day and he would do them.

My inability to resist trying to make humour by exaggeratedly stating totally obvious falsehoods, of course, constantly set my standing with him further and further back. He could not seem to divine when people were not being serious.

There were several ways in which I gained myself no favours with either the BC or any of the career officers. My raspberry-blowing two-finger waving Short Service Officer response when the peace-time military world got too intense about itself was one of them. My general cheek was another. At the time, I saw no harm in constantly referring to Regimental Headquarters as "regimental hindquarters", or the Ajutant as "the asterisk", or the Orderly Officer as "the orderly orifice". In retrospect, however, I can imagine that such things would jar. And also, of course, poor Wurst was as alarmed as everyone by my unnatural behaviour in going native.

Perhaps if I could have accepted my incompatibility and had stopped trying, I could have been only an average failure.

I fired myself from the rear door of the armoured artillery command post and landed at bow-string attention and with quivering salute at the BC's feet as he lumbered onto the gun position. It was all going rather well, I thought. It was a good piece of real estate with plenty of natural cover to conceal the guns and other vehicles. The troops had enhanced things still further with their camouflage efforts. I had the local defence works established and manned, a routine going and I knew we had been reacting well to the simulated fire missions coming over the radio. All in all it was pretty slick, I decided.

Wurst was looking at my boots. I also looked down and, to my surprise, there were two extremely vulgar four letter words written large and clear in orange fluorescent map-pencil on each toe-cap. The bored troops riding in the vehicle sometimes did it as we travelled. They sat with my boots at about eye height on my commander's foot-ledge. My top half was in the fresh air above the vehicle as I led the way.

"Well you obviously can't think of anything useful to do with your time!" he roared, despite the fact that the words were upside down and back-to-front from my side.

"You need some action around here!" and he started banging on the side of the command post with a metal piquet.

"Gas! Gas! Gas!" he shouted.

It was the NATO warning signal for an attack by chemical agent. To set the example by the speed of my reaction, I snatched my gas-mask from the haversack that remained constantly attached to my chest, except when I had to stick myself through the narrow hole in the command vehicle's roof, drew it over my face and replaced my steel helmet in a matter of milliseconds.

When I managed to re-focus on the BC through the scratched, steamed and dingy eye windows, instead of appeasing him, I seemed to have driven him into a frenzy. After an outpouring that bound up many concepts of my military past and unlikely future, I was given a provisional appointment for my personal calendar, i.e. the corridor outside the CO's office as near as possible to the split-second of the return to camp. The purple visage then swept from my limited and mystified view.

When I took my gas mask off a short while later, all became clear to me in more ways than one. The fluorescent crayon graffiti authors had struck again. Across the smooth black rubber that had covered my forehead and cheeks were the most foul, but terse, crudities personally tailored to the Battery Commander.

His stout shape had inspired some imaginative analogy and there were unkind and probably untrue, suggestions as to the substances of which he might be constituted, bodily parts he resembled and even an accusation of porcophilia.

For the umpteenth time, I looked nobly, but anxiously, from the sideless concrete bridge to my front to the vast acre of rank upon rank of mighty tracked metal monsters to my rear. My responsibility was truly awesome. I strode over to my Landrover wherein sat my driver for the occasion; Gunner Scrubb. (A name and vision that shall cause at least one of my death-bed despairing hollow groans.) At this point, I was fortunately unaware that my relationship with Wurst was about to hit bed-rock. Earlier, in the late afternoon, he had given me a briefing that had left me in no doubt as to the significance of the duty that I was about to be assigned.

My Regiment was attached to a United States armoured Brigade at the United States training area in North Bavaria. A vast exercise was to commerce early that evening. At a precise moment, the first vehicle of this mighty force was to cross a "start line" and initiate the enormous deployment of the iron-clad hoard from their peace-time location to their "battle" areas. The only British unit participating (ie: ours) had been accorded the honour of leading this great putch. Our Regiment would, of course, be led by its historically most senior Battery (ie: mine) and my Battery would, naturally, be led by its Command Post Officer (CPO) (ie: me). So it all boiled down to the fact that thousands of bi-national troops and vehicles would wait upon me. The more senior Junior Officers were already in the training area conducting the reconnaissance and planning of the gun positions in readiness for our arrival. The crossing of "start lines" on the split second ordered is a matter of great moment to military planners.

I doubted that Wurst was very happy that I had, by coincidence, been cast in this historical role but probably felt, as I did, that the circumstances were such that nothing could go wrong.

The entire force was parked together of a single gigantic sandy vehicle park that was surrounded by a sort of wide and deep dry "moat". The only exit/entry point to the park was the flat concrete bridge to my front. The "start line" was the point at which the bridge joined the far bank (currently about nine feet from my Landrover's front bumper). All I had to do, therefore, was to tell Gnr Scrubb to drive forward at the precise moment that the exercise was to commence and I could not fail to cross the deployment "start line" on time. All other elements, both British and American, would follow me in the designated order. It would be an impressive example of military precision. The range road that led to the deployment areas also started on the far side of the strip of concrete. I should, of course, have been leading the multitude from my APC but peacetime safety considerations dictated that military convoys be led, at night, by a tyred vehicle with lights as this would be marginally less devastating for a civilian driver who strayed onto the military roads and met us.

Dusk was starting to fall so I took another look at my watch, which was synchronised with the Adjutant's. He controlled the Regimental command post. Just to be on the safe side, I reached into my vehicle and picked up the radio handset.

"Hullo zero, this is one-zero, send time, over!" I called.

I could hear the exasperated expressions in the background as the signaller gave me my fourth time check of the last hour. We counted down the seconds.

"Time, nineteen-thirteen now, over," reported the signaller.

I checked back. My watch was the same as theirs, as indeed it had been on each of the four previous exchanges. However, you cannot be too careful, I thought. I was slightly hurt by the intolerant tones coming over the air. It was alright for them, sprawled about on the benches of their APC, swilling tea and dragging themselves to death. I was the one accorded the sacred mission and should be indulged a little.

I turned to my Gun Sergeants who stood at the helms of their self-propelled guns and gave them another "thumbs-up". They replied a little wearily, I thought, for people who should be "like greyhounds in a slips".

Fifteen minutes to go.

"Start engines!" I yelled, making a circling movement with an outstretched forefinger above my head for those who might not have heard. Everything thundered into mechanical life, except one that merely made repeated starter-motor whirring noises. I started to dash forward my heart in my mouth but, with much spluttering and black smoke, it started. We were nearly off.

I thought of asking for another time check, but pictured the Adjutant's face if I had, and decided against it. I gave the vehicle commanders and drivers and final "thumbs-up". However, it was too dark to see clearly what digital gestures they made in reply. I then leaped into the passenger seat of the Landrover ready to start count down.

It was at this point that a United States Army staff car glided to a halt at the other end of the concrete bridge. It seemed to be several hundred metres long and look as as if it could have seated about six people, in parallel, across each row of seats. It completely blocked my path.

As soon as its suspension had finished rocking majestically, an incredibly smart Lieutenant-Colonel in a loose-fitting dress uniform, patent leather shoes and dark glasses (despite the gathering gloom) got out and strolled over to me.

"Our General wants to get round the guys before they move out." "Say, can you move this thing outa the way?" he said.

I glanced at the car's bulky and impressive occupants behind the Polaroid glass and then at my watch. We had two minutes. Quickly, I sprang out of the vehicle, manoeuvred Gunner Scrubb and the Landrover out of the entrance to the tank park and waved the staff car through. I gave it a cracking salute and was courteously waved to in return.

My Landrover was now to the right of the bridge and the front was about six feet back from the dry "moat".

A minute to go.

I decided that as we were so close to the "off", there was absolutely no point in doing any interim movement. When I gave the word, Scrubb would obviously do a tight "S" manoeuvre, bring us onto the bridge, over the start line and another mile-stone in fine saga of the Anglo-American military fraternity would be chalked up.

"Five, four, three, two, one . . . Forward!" I called breathlessly to Scrubb and stabbed a forefinger towards the windscreen.

I looked up from my watch just as we went over the parapet. We fell upside down for about fifteen feet and crashed onto the wide flat floor of the ditch where our canvas and tubular metal roof was crushed onto us and trapped us in the vehicle.

Mercifully, I remember little these days of the demented nightmare of the ensuing quarter of an hour. I think I recall total bewilderment, the sounds of the lifting equipment getting the Landrover off us and the anxious calming voices, and restraining arms, of my Sergeants as I screamed:

"I'll kill him! I'll kill him! Let me get at him!" into the night air, as I was pulled back up the side of the ditch.

Scrubb was spirited away, so that he could survive to continue his lifestyle as a lethal simpleton for another day, and I was assisted onto the cast metal bonnet of an armoured car from which I could continue (or start) my belated mission. We were about seventeen minutes late.

Predictability, at the first cross-roads, a vast, dark sphere, topped by two glinting square lenses, stood silhouetted against the swirling mist and watched us fixedly as we passed.

What could I have said that would have been either believable or acceptable? Nothing. I had let down the Battery, the Regiment, the British Forces, and the Nation.

*"Guten Tag!"* I called to the rather damp and dishevelled chap who was walking through the woods parallel to the Landrover on which I was leaning.

He did not reply, but looked furtively at my group of troops and I and hurried on.

What an odd sort of bloke, I thought. He was wading through the snow with the trousers of his light grey suit soaked to the knees, in cheap, battered and sodden shoes and an open necked shirt. I even felt the Harz mountain chill through my army parka. Not very polite either, I considered. My German was perfectly clear and my greeting was both audible and friendly. Still it takes all sorts, I decided, and was prepared to overlook him. People who lived near the Iron Curtain probably would become introverted and nervy.

"Just a minute!" said the British Frontier Service Officer (BFS) looking up sharply from the map he was studying in company with a group of *Bundesgrenzeschutz* troops behind me.

"Who's that?"

He walked quickly up to me.

"Search me," I said. "Just some local wandering about, I shouldn't wonder."

"Well, where's he come from?" he said, looking about us.

The penny started to drop. He could not have come from behind us, from the German Federal Republic, as we would have seen him as we passed through the open countryside. Was it possible, therefore, that he had come from in front of us, i.e. from the communist German Democratic Republic?. Only fifty metres away were the red, black and yellow hooped posts of the border. These were followed in rearwards sequence by: the escapee shooting-gallery ploughed and mined strip, the layers of barbed and razored wire fencing, goon-towers, dog runs and a fifty kilometre deep and heavily patrolled belt where strollers could also be shot or seized for long prison terms.

*"Entschuldigen Sie bitte . . ."* I started to call politely after the damp and shuffling figure.

*"Oi! Kommen Sie hier!"* roared the BFS Officer, an ex-Welsh Guard RSM, rather less politely.

The poor, hunted looking figure hobbled slowly and apprehensively back towards us. I noticed that his youngish face was nearly as white as the surrounding countryside and he was shaking uncontrollably. This seemed to be mainly caused by the fact that he was frozen to the marrow. However, he was also quite inordinately nervous in the presence of armed troops.

"*Zind Sie aus dem Ost zone?*" I asked him. The fact that I posed such a question must have made it clear to him that he was in West Germany. He seemed suddenly to look quite emotional and tried to speak but his blue and trembling lips would not form words.

"Willkommen in der Budesrepublik," said a blond and smiling Bundesgrenzeshutz Officer and shook his hand.

The man clasped the Officer's arm and fell weeping against him. We all put our arms round him in support and a great coat was draped about his shoulders. He was then helped into the front seat of a vehicle and driven back to the German barracks to be warmed up, fed, identified and found a place in the fold of free Germany.

The story of his escape was a stirring one but the courage and fortitude shown was not untypical of that displayed weekly along the inner German border by ordinary persons wishing to exercise their natural right of free movement.

He had taken about two weeks to cross the fifty kilometre forbidden border buffer zone. The fact that he was lightly clad and carrying no belongings caused the *Volkspolitzei* and *Volkesarmee* – curious titles as it is the *volk* they shoot, bully and imprison – to suppose that he must be a local worker not far from base, as no-one in their right mind would be going far in a North German Winter without masses of protective equipment. He had, thus, edged his way towards the border pretending to be maintaining forestry, electricity sub-stations or whatever. At night he had slept, freezing, in the derelict buildings of what had once been farms before the DDR regime had forcibly evicted their traditional inhabitants to clear the zone. The night before we met him, he had reached the wire, towers, dogs and mines of the actual Iron Curtain itself. He had managed to avoid detection by the tower guards and had set out across the ploughed strip. As the Communist leadership never told its people anything that might upset them, he had been unaware that there would be mines. Fortunately, he had decided on a Winter escape and the depth and consistency of the packed snow had prevented his weight from setting off the pressure-plate mine detonators.

From dawn onwards he had wandered aimlessly. Hypothermia had started to set in seriously and had sent him into a sort of walking coma. He became so disorientated that he could not have told which side of the border he was on. Hence his odd behaviour when he had met us.

However, just when one started to get depressed that regimes as lowly as those of Eastern Europe should have existed at all, there was always the odd incident that would restore one's faith and cheer one up.

Right up against the wire of the segment of border that my Regiment patrolled was a beautiful old *schloss*. It had remained boarded up and empty, of course, since the Soviets had imprisoned their post war zone of Germany. To have even approached it from the Eastern side would have meant instant death. However, the Communist ruling caste decided that that *schloss* was too fine an asset not to be used by themselves. It was decided, therefore, that it should be a leave centre for high ranking party trusties. Only those whose Communist lineage was of the purest and most irreproachable should be let near this noble facility – so near to the lure of the insidious West.

Over some months we observed with interest as East German workmen, considerably outnumbered by their all-officer guard force, renovated the lovely old building.

Finally, the great day arrived when it would receive its first package of Communist nobility. A more hand-picked group, apparently, there never was. Whole families were screened down to the very youngest thinking age children. Eventually a totally faultless group was found for the inaugural long weekend.

Their bus pulled up at the *schloss* main door and the whole lot, at the double and clutching their unopened suitcases, tore off the bus, through the ground floor and burst out of the nailed up back door and into the West.

There was also a popular tale (or legend) along our bit of border about our local publican. It was said that he had had a few drinks one night, had staggered off over the border, spent a few hours with his aged mother, who was trapped in their original village on the other side, and had then staggered back without being captured, shot, blown up, or torn apart by dogs.

I always volunteered for any regimental border patrols, as I felt that they were the nearest one could get to giving the tax payer any return for paying you and be something of a real soldier in Germany. Although there was no war as such and now there never will be, I was glad of any unease or inconvenience that could be caused to those nasty mafia regimes as they went about their repressive work.

Few other officers seemed to share my views; they seemed to think that tinkering about with sophisticated and expensive military equipment, that would grow obsolete and old without ever being used in action, in barracks or practising with it on the training areas for when the great pie-in-the-sky World War Three arrived, was what a Western military man was all about.

Perhaps I was too lacking in vision that I could never see what might be as being the threat upon which my eyes should be fixed and my energies and enthusiasms prepared. I only know that, as I looked around the world of my soldiering era, I could see ways in which the Communist enslavers were already at work. That is why my usual distraction could be transformed to inspired industry by a border patrol in Germany, and why later I was glad, in principle, to be gathered up by a couple of localised anti-communist wars of my day.

I feared that the others risked becoming like the highly trained actress who saves herself for The Great Epic Starring Part and spurns the very thought of appearing in soap commercials or bit parts in B movies. She may finally find herself old and close to death and, not only has the long awaited great event not happened, nothing has had the advantage of her study, nor has she ever been what she set out in life to be.

After all, the soap commercials and bit parts do keep the basic skills sharpened so that should The Great Epic Starring Part eventuate, as long as one widens ones horizons a bit, one could be all the more ready for it.

I also used to wonder then why the populations of Russia and her colonies in Eastern Europe and Central Asia were so servile and never rose up in universal rebellion against the autocratic dominance of the gang leaders. Finally, of course, they did. However, it still seems amazing that for over forty years repressive regimes that were obviously universally hated from their outset were allowed to go on.

I heard of another border incident when I was visiting West Berlin. A new British infantry regiment had just been posted in a few weeks earlier and the officers had decided to throw a sort of house-warming party in the Mess. It was to be a theme party, one of those typically silly British come-as-you-were-when-the-ship-went-down, pyjama, sheet or towel type dressing up events. By about eleven o'clock on the particular Saturday evening it was positively throbbing. Heavy fairies and chortling elves skipped and twirled gleefully on the dance floor. The euphoria of the comic costumes and the duty free drink had charged the air with abandon.

It was at this point that an entire *Volksarmee* border guard section, of about twelve men and their officer, decided to escape to the West. As they were all in it together there was no one nearby to shoot them in the back, so they organised a power failure on the search lights along their portion, snipped their way through the wire, darted across the minefield path they had previously left for themselves, vaulted a ten foot wall that marked the actual border and dropped down into the West. By coincidence they had landed in the garden of the celebrating Officers' Mess.

Compared to East Berlin where, in the sixties, the rubble of World War Two still littered the streets and all was drab and tatty, it must have seemed another world. Fountains played amongst classical statuary and manicured lawns and flower beds. The escapers priority was to find someone to surrender to. This was going to prove more of a problem than they could have imagined. The nearest and obviously inhabited building was the Officers' Mess, so they jogged across the lawn and went in through the open doors.

Another impressive sight must have met them. Compared to the seedy public buildings encountered by most lower ranking Communist state residents, here was rich dignity and style. The corridors were lined with plush carpeting and the walls were covered with gold framed military oil paintings and polished trophies. The main public rooms in this particular Mess were on the first floor and, after a bit of wandering around the empty corridors, the incredible din from above drew them up the great sweeping staircase and into the wide doorway of the vast party room.

For men of dreary, frugal, sheltered and regimented communist lives the vision of that chamber must have been stupifying. Just as they must have been on the point of deciding that what their political officers had always told them about the depraved West was true after all, and been about to rush back into the minefield, someone had spotted the thunderstruck group. They were wearing jackboots and the flattish East German pattern steel helmets; they were festooned with ammunition pouches, goggles, binoculars and other military accoutrements and carried Soviet AK 47 sub-machine guns.

"It's the local police . . . probably come to complain about the noise", someone apparently hissed to someone else.

This was passed quickly through the jigging throng and accepted.

"Try to jolly them up a bit . . . bring them into the party," came spreading back through the ranks.

The prettiest girls were despatched to the task. Slipping their arms through those of the still dazed and gaping soldiers, they spirited them into the meleé. Drinks and canapés were pressed upon them.

"Have you met Lavinia, Celia, Nigel and Rodney?" chaps kept saying, as they were swept from group to group.

When they had gathered their wits again, the East Germans started to try, with increasing desperation, to get someone to take them seriously. It was only when they were getting nearly frantic that it was decided that, as foreigners are wont to do, they were getting far too serious and boring about themselves and the Orderly Officer was fished out of a bar.

Orderly Officers may attend social functions but may not drink excessively. Being more clear-headed than the rest, he decided, upon seeing the Communist troops, that perhaps there were some aspects of the situation that needed slightly more in-depth examination.

The East Germans were taken down to the guardroom, their weapons were temporarily locked in a toilet cubicle, the regimental guard plied them with tea, the Royal Military Police and the West Berlin civil authorities were called and, no doubt with great relief, they finally managed to defect.

Unfortunately, there were Berlin occurrences with less happy endings. During my visit to Berlin, a drunken Russian soldier was picked up out of the road by a Royal Military Police patrol. He was an off-duty guard from a Soviet War Memorial.

After the completion of formalities, the erring Russian was passed back to his countrymen at a Check Point. Through the cross-border military grape vine, a week later, we heard that he had been put to death. It is just as well that British Servicemen are not executed for undiplomatic drunkenness. We might soon start running short of people at all levels.

I was always sorry that I had but one visit to Berlin. Despite a fair amount of mentally tiring work interpretingI had a very enjoyable time in that great city of odd situation.

I also observed the truth of the Victorian philosopher Winwood Reade's statement that:

"There is nothing so natural as the natural inequality of man."

The Russian officers of all ranks who were on occupation duties in the mass of East Germany looked simple rough types in hairy serge uniforms and crudely made and poorly repaired boots, while those on staff appointments in east Berlin had exquisitely tailored khaki worsted, finely tooled leatherwork and the style of the Czar's army.

The American girl looked very young, very pretty and, somehow, very lonely as she sat looking out of the large plate-glass windows of the American Officers' Club in Bavaria. The way she rested her chin in her hands increased the impression of a rather forlorn little girl. She had short natural blonde hair and a neat little white dress.

As we approached her table, she turned and her face spontaneously lit up with brief pleasure. It was like a moment of sunshine on a grey day. Affectionate greetings were exchanged between my friend Mat, his wife Cindy and the young lady. Then I was introduced:

"I'd like you to meet Cassie," said Mat.

We made polite exchange and I shook her exquisite, but firm, hand.

Mat (Captain Monet, United States Special Forces) and I had met up on a Bavarian mountain top a week earlier as we had led our respective groups of troops on mountain walking fitness trips. We had all stopped to chat and had got on so well at all levels that we had decided to temporarily amalgamate and complete the exercise together. He, and his troops, had been superb companions as we strode along or cracked jokes over beer mugs in high altitude music box style hotels. At the end of the trip, I had pressed some Scotch whisky from my base store upon him and he had insisted that I accompany his wife and himself to the Officers' Club the following Saturday evening.

"Cassie's the wife of Scotty, my best buddy," said Mat.

"Scotty and I go way back. Why, we were born on the same block, went through high school together, got drafted together, went through "rookie" training together, both decided to go for commissioning and went through Officer Candidate School together and then both wound up in the same unit – except he's in Vietnam right now."

It was my first encounter of any sort with that distant and – it was generally considered – largely American war, that had been gathering momentum during recent years.

Cassie was seated at the table reserved for us. I had not previously known that I was to be provided with a partner for the evening. So, I was very pleasantly surprised that I should be in the company of one so beautiful.

We had our pre-dinner drinks at the table and then our most generously proportioned, fine-flavoured and uncomplicated American meal. They all obligingly fell about at my idiot British humour and the girls thought that my accent was cute. Mat and I, who had already developed a mutual style of repartees during the preceding week, had Cindy and Cassie in fits with our recounts of mountain route march incidents. Cassie came gradually alive like a long neglected Spaniel that is unexpectedly taken out and played with.

After dinner, a small ensemble struck up with some internationally popular dance tunes. The Duty Dances, I suddenly remembered, as I am not a naturally enthusiastic dancer. So with all the polite expressions, small bows, and chair movements and other old world courtesies that were once such an expected feature of my race I whisked Cindy away into a German waltz. As soon as it was over, I escorted her back to her chair, thanked her and sat out the next number with another drink and more enjoyable conversation. The moment the orchestra leader raised his violin to his chin for the dance after that, I was on my feet requesting the privilege of Cassie's company in the dance.

The slow and waftily romantic strains of *Georgia* drifted across the room. I was slightly put off by this, as I did not feel that this was really the sort of tune one should dance to with a married lady. However, we had already advanced a good way onto the floor and risked causing an obstruction to the couples who had already taken off.

I decided that I should have to try and make some sort of slow waltz of it, so I placed my right hand on the rear of Cassie's slender waist and reached out my left to hold her right hand at a distant mid-point between us. She would, of course, rest her left hand lightly on my right shoulder.

However, with her usual solemn expression, she put both her arms round my neck and rested her soft and fragrant face against mine. During the ensuing five minutes, the normally unrelated emotions of shock, embarrassment, joy and wild sexual desire rotated furiously as I had my ears bitten and breathed into, was very thoroughly and passionately kissed and had my body, that had adopted a sort of near motionless parade ground stance from the onset of the surprise, groped and fondled.

The experience of being the subject of totally unexpected female initiative on the dance floor had happened to me only twice before – unless one counts dear little Brenda from Thames Ditton when we were only nine. One was a cool flame-haired girl in a leopard skin dress in a London night club, and the other was an equally cool, but national costume clad, girl at a Bavarian Saturday afternoon beer-and-dance. On each occasion when the music ended and the girl strolled unconcernedly back to her seat, I was left behind, a jelly of ecstasy, in the middle of the dance floor – and never more so than on this occasion.

I struggled to recover quickly, however, and hurried after Cassie. Circumstances were rather different than on the previous two occasions. With a polite smile, I slid Cassie's chair under her small round bottom, hastily excused myself and raced off through the throng to where Mat was at the bar.

"A word in your ear, if I may?" I said discreetly, while glancing furtively around.

He smiled pleasantly at me as I drew him a short distance from the crowd at the bar.

"Look," I said. "I think dear old Cassie probably gets a bit lonely – husband away – that sort of thing. Er . . . I mean that slight incident on the dance floor just now . . . er nothing meant by it, I'm sure. Um . . . I wouldn't want you to think that I was trying to . . . er . . . instigate anything."

"Say! What? Are you the lucky one!" said Mat putting an arm round my shoulders. "Gee! There wasn't a guy in high school who wasn't crazy about her!"

He thumped my back encouragingly and rejoined the cheery group at the bar. I was aghast.

But . . . Best buddy! . . . Same block . . . The draft . . . Officer candidate training . . . I was going to say, but he had gone. I was shocked by the extent to which America seemed to be the land of the free. Five years later with a UN peacekeeping force, I was to meet Scandinavians and discover just how far sexual convenience can be taken.

I returned to Cassie, who snuggled up to me, put an arm round me, kissed my ear and slipped an affectionate hand onto my inner thigh. It was as though we had been long-term lovers. It was difficult not to respond to her as she was one of the loveliest girls I have ever seen. If I had suggested a walk beneath the Summer stars I do not think we would have made it past the first grass verge – possibly not even past the front door mat. I held her perfect face in my hands and kissed it. There was an imminent risk that we might even consumate our friendship there and then in the restaurant.

It was painful decision time. Never an easy task for one as weak-willed and self-indulgent as I. She had a man who daily faced death in a far and ferocious war. I did not then know that one spent one's in-theatre furloughs falling over beautiful and available Asian girls. I had spent almost no time in my life analysing aspects of the concept of honour but, however much I might forget the lessons of my upbringing, I knew that my current circumstances would be covered by a rule near the top of page one of any tome on the subject.

The band came to the rescue by playing some rousing and jigging pop tunes. I whisked the startled Cassie onto the dance floor again and we jerked and girated to every number. I never normally bother with formless pop dancing, so I thought up all kinds of comic leaps and twirls that ended up being emulated by the whole group of laughing dancers.

I made some pretext of needing to check my troops or something and fled just as the time of departure looked imminent. For a moment, I thought that Cassie looked surprised and very hurt. Alone later, I sighed much with my confused thoughts.

I was ignorant of all aspects of war then and could not know how different separation-by-war is for man and woman than all other separations. The soldier on the field of battle knows that at any time he can be killed or maimed with terrible violence and pain. The partner at home feels a helplessness, as her husband is not away on a business trip but has been ordered by his nation to a war and cannot arbitrarily return to her when she needs him. She will, of course, feel loneliness but also an uncanny fracture of a domestic and family life that is normally seen as a right by all. These sensations bring about a gnawing and crushing uncertainty to both parties. There are sudden awful, dark visions of what the future might be: widowhood, orphans, or having to constantly nurse a helpless and disfigured cripple, accompanied by poverty, charity, pity, and more types loneliness; being an incapacitated ex-soldier who must try to behave like a hero.

More than ever at these times, one can feel the need of another human being of the opposite sex to physically hold to you, not for the pleasure of sexual sensation in particular but to feel their normal life, draw comfort from their living warmth and counter the fearful emptiness. If, however, the one ycu should hold is far away, then whom do you hold?

The home front is nearly as fraught with mines, of a sort, as the battle front. This, and other unsuspected knowledge, awaited me.

My honourable behaviour of that night, however, has been frequently countered, and heavily paid for, by agonies of regret and sleepless pillow biting nights over the dream of what could have been with the golden and desperately desirable, but forbidden, Cassie.

"How fantastic!" I said (in German) to Herr Brinkmann, the magnificent, aged employee I had met one evening while visiting a Headquarters mess. "To think that you knew the Kaiser."

Herr Brinkmann's white-cropped bullet head jerked slightly and he fixed me kindly, but censureously, through his round and rimless bottle-base lenses.

"I could not *know* the Emperor, Herr Leutnant," he said gently. "I was his valet."

"Oh, I see," I said.

"But didn't you get to chat to him as you sorted out his boots and helmets and things?"

"I was a shirt valet," he replied.

"You mean he had one chap just for shirts?" I exclaimed.

"Oh no, Herr Leutnant," he said, smiling reassuringly. "There were six of us, under the direction of a Corporal."

"Six!" I gasped.

"I am sure the men of your Royal house have more," he said, a little formally.

"But the Kaiser was a most frugal man. He would never permit an able bodied man who was needed at the battle fronts to serve in his household. I was conscripted as a cavalryman, but because of my eyes I could not learn to ride. It seemed that I would serve my time in the stores, but I did so like to keep them neat. Then one day I was called before an officer and told I was posted to the Emperor's staff. Just like that. Oh, such magnificence, such order!"

There was a long pause while he remembered and I tried to imagine a lost German palace.

"*Entschuldigen Sie bitte*, Herr Leutnant," he said quietly and turned to go. "Thank you for enquiring," he said pausing and patting my arm. Then he made an imperial bow and shuffled off across the gloomy hall to gather up the many pairs of British officers' boots and shoes that he had to polish before the next dawn, a very old, straight-backed man in a servant's black waistcoat.

On my last night as an Officer of a Royal Artillery Heavy Regiment, I was invited to join a dinner gathering at the Second-in-Command's house. It was, as always with things that he had anything to do with, a very stylish and enjoyable affair. The sides of the long candle-lit table were lined with sparkling ladies and dinner-suited men. Both the Major and his wife were the children of Generals and the father of the latter sat at one head of the table and had me on his left.

I hardly ate for listening to his stories. He was only seven years short of his century, but in manner was like a man of half his age. He had served against the Dervish horde in the Sudan, in the Boxer uprising, the Boer War, the First World War, the Third Afghan War, the uprising in Iraq and Transjordan, in several expeditions against the Pathans and, incredibly, he was recalled for specialist duties in the Second World War. I hung upon his every word.

Someone at our end of the table quoted some well known military cliché that expounded some martial virtue or other.

"Yes that still remains true," the General said generously.

"In fact my great grandfather told me, when I was a very little boy, that it was first stated to the other staff officers, and himself, by Wellington at Waterloo."

I was transfixed. Just for moment, I (who would be and insignificant bit-player on the back-water battlefields of contemporary history) was only two conversations away from His Grace, the Iron Duke, and the world history pivoting field at Waterloo!

It is about the best military memory from my time with the British Rhine Army.

The British Rhine Army was unquestionably a useful deterrent to the slight possibility of conventional invasion by the Russian empire. It was useful as a sentry, guard dog or burglar alarm is useful. Each new day of peace that dawns over North West Europe may well be a monument to it. However, its role had a damp squib effect on my youthful enthusiasm to serve my community in a way that I believed I should. I had taken up the mantle of soldier and I would not just stand around in it. I would be the fact of it, or put it down again.

British garrison duty in Germany after 1945 had some parallels with British garrison duty in India during the two centuries preceding 1947. In both situations, otherwise fairly ordinary people could have a slightly superior lifestyle against a cosmetically military backdrop. In India there were servants. In Germany, and other contemporary garrisons, there are the cheap duty free drinks, cigarettes, cars, petrol and domestic electrical appliances.

Preparedness for war can only be maintained, of course, by imagining, training, practising and pretending in peacetime, but I found it all too much a case of all dressed up with nowhere to go.

I had been becoming increasingly saddened by the cruel communist invasion and infiltration of South East Asia during the last few years of my Rhine Army service. Her Majesty's (Australasian) troops confronted them and it was there that I ought to be. It seemed odd to me that anyone, who was both a trained soldier and a true believer that humans should not have totalitarian regimes forced onto them, could feel they had the right to be anywhere else.

My problem, however, was that Wurst and the fast failing senior subaltern team had dictated a final report for the CO's signature that would have made it difficult for me to go for a job as a car park attendant. It was a masterpiece of generalisation, ambiguity, innuendo and subjectivity. It guided and encouraged full scope to the reader's very worst imaginings. It taught me well for the rest of my service, in many forces, the importance of being precise, specific, objective and a little generous, when playing with another's life, and the gift of his labour, by the writing of a professional report.

The Adjutant heard of it and risked his excellent career prospects by confronting the CO. The CO did some investigating and interviewed me again.

"Well what I have written, I have written." He said apologetically perhaps. However, the report was not recalled from the Ministry of Defence.

I applied to both the New Zealand and Australian Armies to be a private soldier. I was keen to serve the New Zealanders. I had a slight family association from earlier pioneering days and they were such a hale and hearty southern British branch. The Australians too are a race of character and style. I had had some fine friends from amongst the extremely beautiful, and generous, Australian girls who filled parts of London.

They they both made up the noble ANZAC (Australian/New Zealand Army Corps); the heroes of my 'pommie' boyhood. Australian Army pay was apparently nearly double that of the New Zealanders.

Both countries extended me the honour of a favourable reply. The Australians offered to fly me to Australia as a soldier; the New Zealanders invited me to make my own way to New Zealand where I might be commissioned as a Lieutenant.

As I contemplated my impending New Zealand Army service, I resolved to serve them faithfully and as well as I could, and perhaps after a few years when the Indo-China wars might be ended and my usefulness over, I should drift off somewhere or the other and find myself an interesting job. I had no idea that this lovely land would bring me a richness of life that I could not have imagined and would divide my heart equally, and painfully, down the middle for love of the land of my birth and the one that was to first send me to fight and would sentence me to a lifetime of anguish that these two green lands must be twelve thousand miles apart rather than just off-shore of each other in the same island group.

I have every reason to be grateful to the British Army. Its record proves that it ranks amongst the finest in the world. I believe it strikes one of the best balances between disciplines and flexibilities possible. It trained me well. Subsequent shortcomings in my military performance have been caused by my personal defects alone.

I am grateful for my first meeting with British private solders who, despite their drearily predictable tendencies for petty theft of military kit (coyly referred to as 'souveniring' or 'perking') and getting boringly drunk every time the chance was presented, were unexplainably loveable, were loyal when treated correctly, were witty company, and had a great depth of collective strengths. I was to see them and the Australasian members of the triplets, as steady under fire as ever their family members were in the many thin red lines of the past.

I relish the memory of my first encounters with British NCOs and Warrant Officers. They are the main engines of the British forces. They have acquired over their years many subtle skills that enable them to achieve beneficial results in the face of official obstruction and still ensure the preservation of their species. Even a poor quality officer, if he is deemed sincere, will have their protection. An insincere one risks finding himself suddenly and unexpectedly alone, with his follies, in the path of a furious, and oncoming, superior.

Meeting British Officers was an inspiration. The warriors, of course, have been an inspiration – even though I have never managed to emulate them. However, it is to the peace-time military careerists that I must be most grateful of all, for they inspired me with a near-desperate determination to distance myself as much as possible from their world. It was they, more than anything else, that sent me on the road to adventure.

I must also be grateful to the British government of the day and the shame they inspired. Anxious to devote more time and resources to parochial and domestic concerns that were more comprehensible and materially beneficial to their voters, they were ratting as fast as possible on old allies and global events where Britain's experience could have exercised beneficial influence.

Alone, therefore, I had to make amends for the shortcomings of my

99

colleagues and countrymen! I felt so terribly sorry for them all!

One steamy monsoon afternoon about a year later, I escorted an Australian Army nurse, who had made a short visit to one of our fire bases in Vietnam, along to the helicopter landing area.

"You were once in the Brit army, werncha?" she said.

"Yes", I replied. "The Royal Regiment of Artillery."

"There's one of your guys just arrived on exchange at our camp back in Aussie," she went on.

"Yeah, he's from that too."

And then, incredibly, she mentioned the name of my old senior subaltern's pompous, pontificating and patronizing second-in-command.

"I'm going back next week. Yer got any messages for 'im?" she shouted above the racket of the approaching helicopter.

Now this has to to be something really good, I thought, something to cut him to the quick. Something along the lines of:

"I have called the fire in battles – of that pattern of gun that in Germany you lot only ponced and posed around – and other types too. You all called me thick peasant – but who's the real soldier now?" etc, etc.

"He's a funny old-fashioned Pom, just like you," she said and smiled a broad, big-toothed and friendly smile. She had large bright blue eyes and freckles across her sun-tanned cheeks and, when we took our jungle green hats off to prevent them from being drawn into the rotor of the descending helicopter – she revealed golden corn-coloured curls.

"Oh, tell him all the best from me," I said, as I lifted her slight, green-denim frame into the aircraft.

We waved to each other until her little doorway in the sky had completely disappeared into the misty blue haze above the brooding green.

My eyes had filled with tears. I should so awfully have liked to have seen him – just for a while.

# ⌜PART TWO⌝
## THE ANZAC AT NUI-DAT

*Lieutenant General Bernard Law ('Monty') Montgomery DSO, Commander of the British Eighth Army, on a visit to his New Zealand Division, vexed:*
  *"I say, don't your men salute their Officers?"*

*Major General Bernard Cyril ('Tiny') Freyberg VC, DSO and 2 Bars,*
  *Commander of the New Zealand Division:*
  *"Oh, if you wave at them, Sir, they usually wave back."*

New Zealand Army Folklore

During the time that girl-chasing and partying had permitted me to study for my 'A' Level English Literature exam at college, I remember reading "An Anthology of Elizabethan Verse". It was filled with very pretty, but fanciful, courtly love sonnets written by young Elizabethan blades. The Elizabethan engraving at the front of the book was a rather attractive composition entitled "Young Man Amongst Roses" by Nicholas Hilliard. I was never, of course, as good-looking, or as finely dressed   as the slightly flaccid, musing and tights-wearing young man in the picture, but throughout the Autumn after I left the British Army I used to adopt his pose a lot.

I doubt that at the time I was thinking specifically of him, or that my ponderings on young ladies were as pure. However, leaning against a small tree surrounded by lovely flowers, as he was, is a very agreeable situation.

What with terminal leave and quite a backlog of untaken annual leave, I had several free months back in England before I would be fully discharged from the British Army and could go and join the New Zealanders.

At first, of course, I was overjoyed at the chance to concentrate full-time on drink and romantic adventure but after a few weeks it all began to pall. Also, my mother was starting to show signs of mutiny, even though it was reasonably good-humoured for the present.

She would say things like, "Shall I ensure that there's plenty of hot water for your bath tomorrow morning? Or will you be falling in the

Thames again?"

She would then go into fits of laughter before my scournful gaze.

On another occasion she said, "I am building up a terribly interesting collection of things from the times when you borrow my car. I have got a lady's umbrella, a necklace, three unmatching earrings and some garments. Some of your lady friends must have felt quite a draught on their way home."

Once when I was driving back at dawn from an unexpectedly prolonged tryst, I was suddenly aware of a furious tapping on the window beside me. I had fallen asleep at the traffic lights and the angry morning rush hour had piled up behind me.

I became a gardening labourer in Hampton Court Palace gardens, which were but a short cycle ride from our house at the time, and reverted to a part-time social life which was generally agreed by all to be the correct order of things.

My days were now filled with creative exercise in idyllic surroundings. I took quite a pride not only in my edging and weeding but also in my gardener's uniform of flat cloth cap, donkey jacket and hob-nailed boots. However, I suppose my uniform was a bit officer-like. My cloth cap was more the sports car enthusiast type than the standard large and floppy check pancake of my colleagues and, although my donkey jacket was issue, my boots were brown instead of black.

My gentleman-ranker status and my work style filled the head gardener with suspicion at first but, after we had chatted about his army days for a bit, he relaxed and I was assigned my own area – an exquisite walled garden of flowering shrubs.

The others would plod steadily through the day at their own assigned tasks. However, I would become periodically intoxicated by the beauty of the scene and would lapse into my "Young Man Amongst Roses" stance. I would make up for these interludes by furious bursts of work and by the end of the day I had done as much as anyone.

I enjoyed the patient and philosophical people that gardening attracts. Both the old traditional gardeners and the young apprentices were delightful company and Diane I came to love.

She was a shyly smiling, and slightly built, amenity horticulture apprentice. She took to joining me on my lunch-time bench and we would discuss her interest in horses. One day when there was a chill wind, we moved to her green house. We came to share our sandwiches and, after a few weeks, each other in the twilight beauty of that green, earthy and scented place.

I would give directions and history lessons to startled French and German tourists in their own languages. All animal life, in my garden, became unafraid of me. Squirrels would come up beside me and unconcernedly rummage in my lunch bag. Birds would perch on my outstretched toe-caps, as I sat, or would stand on my hand to take bits of sandwich or pork pie from between my fore-finger and thumb.

"Well now, why do you want to join the New Zealand Army?" said the New Zealand Army Colonel, looking and sounding exactly like a mainland British Colonel.

I mentioned my faint New Zealand family connection and said I had always wanted to see the place. We were high above London near the towering top of New Zealand House. I could just see a corner lion from Nelson's Column.

"How do you feel about serving in Vietnam?" he said. "Under the ANZUS Pact we're with the Free World allies. There's no end in sight at the moment.

I said that I felt that the Republic of Vietnam should be helped to repulse invasion and did not mind going at all.

"We reinforce our units over there on a trickle system," he went on. "That is to say, one at a time."

I knew what he meant. Rather than keep withdrawing whole military units after a year or so of service and replacing them with another of the same type, you kept the same unit, and its equipment, there and gradually replaced its personnel. To achieve the staggered effect, some of the people who arrived at the beginning had a slightly shortened tour, while others stayed a bit longer than the standard year in theatre. The gradual replacement system was cheaper, administratively economic, and ensured a continuity of in-theatre experience. However, I drifted into an absurd reverie and imagined soldiers being singly delivered by aircraft or ship and wandering off alone and randomley into a jungle. The Colonel was outlining pay and conditions of service. Such things, of course, have no relevance to democracy's Janissaries.

"Well have you got any points for me?" the Colonel said, having rounded off his kind explanations.

"Er, no thank you, Sir," I said, hastily transporting myself back to his office. "Oh, except that I am so sorry that I shall not get the chance to wear the 'lemon-squeezer'."* I said without thinking. He watched a group of fluttering pigeons outside the window.

---

* A Scout-style hat, with a pointed crown and regiment or corps coloured pugaree, of nonchalantly dashing aspect and the traditional New Zealand Army head gear since the beginning of the century.

"Yeah," he said in a pensive and slightly sentimental tone.

"The old 'lemon-squeezer' made you welcome anywhere," he continued slipping gradually into a touch of New Zealand drawl.

"In two world wars it made the Kiwi soldier instantly recognizable. I can't imagine how someone was allowed to get rid of it a few years ago. It was really only because of war that the rest of the world got to know us and we had no finer ambassador than the old 'Baggy'.[*] Populations that had never even heard of us before found that we had all the virtues of the British and a few of our own too. They found that the old Kiwi was a friendly, straight-dealing sort of a joker – able to turn his hand to anything – innovate from almost nothing, always keep going . . . Jeeze, I'll never forget . . . One time in Crete . . ." He looked up and grinned. "Oh well, I guess I'd better not get started or you'll be stuck here all day."

I should have liked nothing better than to have been stuck there all day.

"You'll manage all right," he said.

"Just be yourself. Don't ever try to make like a fifth generation Kiwi. We like the old Poms all right, as long as they take the time to get to know us . . . adapt a little maybe."

It was sound advice. In the nearly eleven years, and the three campaigns that I served the New Zealand Army, I never changed my English public school accent or in any way attempted to do them the insult of roughening my image, or whatever, out of any misguided belief that it might better suit a national style. That noble and generous spirited people gathered me up as their own – as I was.

The Chelsea Pensioner and I greeted each other with the polite pleasure that had become our wont over the last week or so. His weekday 'blues' uniform and peaked pill-box cap and the regimental buttons on my fashionably waisted and flared blazer made it obvious that we were military colleagues of a sort. I would make a small inclination of the head and mouth a smiling 'good evening' and he would do a combination of companionable grin, wink and twitch of the head. We did not speak as we were both always there on business and would not have wished to have been distracted. However, I believe we found comfort in the presence of an ally – albeit we remained unintroduced.

We always met in the same place and at the same time. This was outside the bar door of the extremely fashionable pub in the King's Road, Chelsea, at a few minutes to opening time. Having replenished my latest

---

[*]  Short for 'Baggyarse' in view of the generous cut of a Soldier's issue trousers.

mode influenced tailoring, after studying some of the exquisites drifting up and down the King's Road and sat for a while in the window of a teashop with an unimpared view of all the passing girls, I would hurry down the road to the bar door as soon as instinct told me that it was five minutes to six. We would stand like sentinels on either side of the door, stare up and down the road and rock pensively on our heels.

The sound of the bolts being drawn on the inside would induce a sense of resolution in the air as though a set battle had suddenly become imminent. The Colour Sergeant and I would then turn towards the door and go briefly, but silently, through the courtesy of an 'after you – no after you' session. My obvious subaltern-on-leave look no doubt prompted the old NCO to make the initial gesture. However, his gold chevrons and crown and three rows of coloured silk war ribbon, left no question that his seniority must prevail.

I would follow him into the traditional pub Victoriana and sixties primary colours, decorated bar and we would part company. His station was down at the bottom curve of the counter near the door where he could not be missed by anyone entering, while mine was on the raised area at the rear where anyone entering could not be missed by me.

The pub had become a mecca for the sixties "beautiful people." The place would soon start to fill up with boutique owners (indeed the pub was almost a beer boutique), male models, fashion shop assistants, pop stars, photographers, actors and the like. I waited to prey on any neglected female companions and charm them off to other locations. The fact that about seventy per cent of the males in the room were either homosexual, drunk or drugged or weedy, or a combination thereof, tended to make this process less of a labour of Hercules than it might have been for someone as unfamous, or as fundamentally out of touch with popular trends, as I.

My friend would buy himself a half of the cheapest beer while we waited for our respective customers. He would sip this as the place quickly filled up with top mode fairies and elves.

After a couple of rounds of popular, strong, expensive and unpleasantly coloured alcoholic concoctions, the vain and absurdly dressed population would get quickly flushed and louder. While I bided my time like the jackal tailing the desert lost herd or the shark circling the unsound life-raft, my comrade would already have set up shop. The curiosity of one of the males would soon get the better of him.

"Hey Dad! What did you get that one for?" he would say indicating a ribbon above the old soldier's left breast pocket that had caught his eye. "Were you first in the NAAFI queue then?"

This would, of course, render his particular circle helpless.

"Very droll, Sir, very droll," the octogenarian would say gently. "But I can tell you know your military history, Sir. Now there's not many people who would know that was for the Sudan War, but you spotted it straight away."

The rudely and stupidly laughing group would stop perplexed.

"I'll never forget at Omdurman," he went on, "the Dervish horde surged towards us. The sands of the horizon were black with them. You could only estimate them by the acre."

The trendies had been given no chance to make more clichéd anti-military jokes and were becoming intrigued.

"Steady lads! Form a square! Deploy the Gatlings forward!" He would call dramatically.

I shouted out before anyone more senior had got their wits about them. What a carry on! But they all looked to me.

"Oh, bless you, Sir, that's very kind to an Old Soldier. A small – er, large brandy. Thank you, Sir."

As I was saying . . . he would continue, "Oh dear. Now look at me, Sir, getting so carried away I am on account of the honour of your interest, I drank that one down before I had a chance to wish you good health. Oh well that really is kind, Sir, another one. Thank you very much, Sir . . . Well they came on and on though the howitzers tore 'em to bits and our volleys brought 'em down like skittles . . ."

Soon the group had temporarily forgotten their usual absorbtion with fleeting fashions and short-term pleasures as the mighty saga of their previously unrealised Imperial history came to life before them. As the evening wore on, they, and other unlikely collections, would be taken spellbound through deadly skirmishes in Afghan passes and terrible sieges in Mesopotania. They would glimpse a lost world of death before dishonour where vastly outnumbered Victorian soldiers deployed with parade ground discipline before the massive charges of suicidally brave native warriors.

They would sense the dust, sweat and the taste of controlled fear. They would feel the tension as the thunder and screams of the ferocious and merciless horde grew ever more deafening as it swept irrevocably closer. They would almost hear the shuddering crash of the British volleys as they hurled their wall of tearing metal. They would have a terrible vision of the valiant dead and writhing piled on the ground – and the stately old warrior would drink enough brandy to have killed off the average pack horse.

He filled me with pride and admiration for my calling. It is just a pity that at the time I did not think to plan ahead for my own eventual retirement. He might have been prepared to take on apprentices.

I was sad by the way I missed the faithless Ulrike. I was not so much sad

106

because I missed her a lot. I was sad because I felt that I should miss her more. Was I so shallow, I thought, that I could not be devastated by the loss of the woman I had wished to spend the rest of my life with? Would I never burn with an all-consuming and eternal passion like the ardent lovers of epic verse? My remarkably slow, character maturing progress and the sexual abundance of my youthful era were not encouraging to such a situation. The Swinging Sixties were probably not a great deal more promiscuous than earlier eras, but people were more blatant and talked about it a lot more. I used to think what a strange misnomer it was that the fashionable term for it was the "new morality", for surely casual, loveless and quick mating was the manner of our near-animal pre-historic ancestors and, therefore, a very old morality.

Not that I was complaining about the situation at the time. During my military tour with the British army, in particular, what a super, free brothel the 'permissive society' was for a soldier on leave. Unlike the civilian male, the soldier tends mostly to appear in his community for short periods. (An average leave is about two weeks). He has no time for anything resembling a normal courtship and so must try for some form of more immediate companionship and comfort. This would formerly have involved buying something that was poor quality, absurdly over-priced and probably unhygienic. By then, however, the majority of normal, and often very pretty, girls of all classes were usually quite speedily available.

But Ulrike's sloe-eyed and cheekily smiling Slavonic face did have a disturbing habit of appearing, despite the attention that I (and all males who could make some faint effort at charm) could get from the pretty-haired and leg revealing girls that packed the entertainment places of every town in the land – and particularly London.

During the weeks of my last farewells to my London youth, I had some unusual encounters. Apart from dear, petite Diane, kneeling on the bench amongst the potted azaleas, there was Rita, an Italian girl on holiday who spoke not a word of English. I speak no Italian. We obviously liked each other, when we met at the dance, and should have loved to have chatted. Finally, by the end of that evening, and for several more evenings until she returned to Salerno, our desperation to communicate in some way led us to the only possible solution. She was a spectacular, natural blond and I sometimes felt sad that she was not dressed and sitting opposite me at a restaurant table, laughing at my jokes.

There was also a girl from Gottingen. One night, having totally misunderstood a young lady's directions as to how to get to her apartment, I inadvertently rang an incorrect doorbell. A pretty nightdress-clad German girl opened the door and, after a brief laugh together about me getting lost, she kindly invited me in and unexpectedly retained me. I often wondered if I would have recognised her if I had ever passed her, clothed, in the street.

However, the strangest encounter was with a very aristocratic young lady indeed. Following our chance meeting, when we were both with different unrelated groups at a smart London restaurant, I was appointed a sort of unpaid steward-with-special-responsibilities. She was doing the current debutante season and, as I was obviously unsuitable to be seen with, I was given a key to her apartment and instructed to let myself in each evening after I left the pubs at closing time. I could then doze in the bath until this statuesque and sinful ice princess got home from ball or banquet an hour or so later. Having bid her evening-dress clad escort a demure good-night on the porch and closed the door, she would slide out of her silken finery and join me wearing only the dazzling and priceless jewellery of her fingers, arms, neck and brows.

Totally unexpectedly, she was the only girl who seemed truly sad when the time of my departure came. For once, I called in the daytime – uninvited, outside my official hours, in a suit and with some flowers – to wish her goodbye. We knew almost nothing of each other's lives. I had only ever seen her authoritatively sensual or coolly disdainful. I had not really noticed before that she was very young. Incredibly, her titled head was suddenly resting on my starched collar and I could feel her soft and warm face, hair and tears. She begged me not to go as she wanted me with her and I might never come back.

These days I sometimes see her still classically beautiful face in gossip columns or society magazines. She is wife and mother to a handsome family and the mistress of vast wealthy estates. She moves with, and is related to, the highest in the land. Does she ever remember the common soldier she once wept for or ever wonder if the fire and steel Vietnamese war dragon rent and tore the body she once clung to?

The 'sixties were a carefree and happy time – so long as you remained no more than a tourist.

———————————

The interval between my departure from London Airport one prematurely hot April day and my arrival at the war now seems very short. However, a lot was packed into it.

I flew to Singapore. Is it possible to design a more excitingly feminine dress than the westernised Chinese girl's fitted, high-collared, short-sleeved, slit-skirted, silky Cheong-Sam? I had also not previously realised that female feet could be objects of such delicate porcelain-like beauty.

After a night in the airline's hotel, I moved to the New Zealand Army lines at Nee Soon. Singapore was still an impressive ANZUK outpost populated by smart, dark green clad Australian, New Zealand, Malay, Singaporean and metropolitan British troops and their families. Almond eyes, round eyes, small noses and long ones all seemed to consider each other fellow locals. It was a beautiful, easy and slightly decadent lifestyle.

Sadly, I joined the Singapore garrison at a time of some strain between the young single officers and the married officers and (especially) their wives. However, on this occasion, it was not my fault, as the reason for it all had occurred a week or so before my arrival.

The British Commonwealth officer status community held a large garden fete to raise money for local charities. One of the most significant events was a baby show. The proudest parents lined their babies up in prams across a section of lawn. In front of each baby there was a collection box. The intention being that members of the public would put money in the box of whichever baby they deemed the cutest. Thus, the baby with the most money would be the winner and the charities would benefit from the sum of all the boxes.

Most of the Commonwealth subaltans, predictably, gravitated to the bar tent from the outset of the fete. Regrettably, they must have spotted the baby show through the door flap. A couple of them, therefore, caught a taxi down to a local *kampong* and hired a monkey. They then acquired some baby clothes, including a bonnet, and a pram, and dressed the obedient and docile monkey in the former and sat him or her in the latter.

Feeling that they should show their candidate some support, they loaded the monkey's box with money. Throughout the afternoon a chortling and ever more unsteady stream of junior officers staggered across the grass to keep on filling the monkey's money box – with the unfortunate result, of course, the the monkey won.

To some people their peerless children are but extensions of their own egos and there apparently was some quite remarkably hate-filled sense of humour failures.

There was talk that I should go straight from Singapore to an artillery battery in Vietnam. To the surprise of the local New Zealand staff, I requested to see New Zealand first. I had this alarming vision of myself at a last stand, riddled with shot, saluting and, as the enemy poured over the defences, gasping with my last breath:

"God bless New Zealand – wherever it is and whatever its like!"

I went to New Zealand for a few months and almost immediately loved it as if I were made of its earth. I prepared for my approaching time in Vietnam and enjoyed the ". . . for tomorrow we die" spirit of the Royal

New Zealand Artillery Vietnam reinforcement depot at lively sub-tropical Papakura.

When one is introduced to one's British officer commanding for the first time in the mess, one is usually given a polite, friendly but restrained, greeting and a few hackneyed phrases of military advice for one's time with him. However, my New Zealand commander at Papakura had merely paused briefly to give me a great cheerful thump before continuing his reminicence to the bar of an unnatural and ancillary sexual act performed on him by a Japanese girl during his leave in Tokio from the Korea war. He was a rough, jovial and charming bear of a soldier who had served in the Second World War and all the British Asian conflicts that followed. He had been awarded the Military Cross following the battles of Imjim and The Hook. I had immediately, and irrevocably, added him to my private list of personal heroes.

My first forty-eight hours in New Zealand were fraught with the risk of death through every kind of excess. I was gathered up by my instant and enduring fellow junior officer friends: Grant, Dick and Tub, from the moment that I landed at Whenuapai (pronounced Fen-oo-a-pie) air base one Friday evening. We drank in the mess and every bar in the Papakura area and went to a party at someone's house until breakfast time. I collapsed in my room after this but was dragged out a few hours later to go and spend the whole day drinking in the local branch of the Returned Services Association – an elite New Zealand war veterans' club. I was spellbound as I listened to veterans of the Boer War, First War, Second War and all recent wars. We came out in the early part of that Saturday evening and returned to the Officers' Mess which was full of young ladies whom Tub had kindly arranged for us. We went from the mess to most of the smart bars in central Auckland. When they shut we all saw our respective young ladies home.

I could have been given no better demonstration of the cheerful, generous, but practical, national characteristics of the New Zealanders than by the way in which my lovely and wholesome friend parked me in her parent's living room and, before I was been able to start some sort of gradual European-style seduction, she disappeared only to return a few moments later in appropriate attire for the occasion – a small and short nightdress and a pair of fluffy slippers. Once her requirements were met, I was given some jolly thanks and returned to the other side of the front door so that she could get a decent night's sleep.

I wandered aimlessly off in a sort of walking trance through her Auckland suburb. Unfortunately, I paid no attention to direction when the taxi had brought us there. I accidentally staggered into the path of the only car that was about as the dawn came up but, by fortunate coincidence, it contained Grant, Dick and Tub.

We arrived back for breakfast again. Immediately after this I fell into a coma on my bed. I only managed to remove my jacket, trousers and shoes. I was awakened about two hours later by the sensation of my bed capsizing and my body striking the lino. Grant, Dick and Tub seized portions of me and bore me horizontally along to the bar. At the bar door they did a "one, two, three, heave!" and threw me into the middle of a Sunday morning cocktail gathering.

In a home-based mess there would have been an icy silence while one clutched one's shirt-tails about one and rapidly backed out – and one would have received a message that the CO, preceded by the Adjutant, wished to see one first thing the following morning. However, the New Zealand Brigadier area commander and his subordinate Colonels, and their elegant wives, roared at the spectacle and eagerly followed Grant, Dick and Tub out to watch them throw me in the fish pond.

Mercifully, after this my novelty seemed to have temporarily worn off and I was left to squelch back to my room, with my wet shirt and nearly transparent underpants, to expire until the Monday morning.

And so the months passed; gun drill in the vast field by the Depot lines, hard troop formation runs in boots and webbing up and round Red Hill, classroom exercises in technical aspects of gunnery, small arms firings on the range, jungle warfare training in the Fiji islands, artillery firing at Waiouri (Why-oo-roo), Friday 'Happy Hours' that seemed to start ever earlier and not end until several hours into Saturday, visits to the Camp cinema and the pale gold Auckland beaches and the pale gold Auckland girls

I quickly grew to love New Zealand – old New Zealand that is. The population when I had first arrived had seemed to be largely composed of sturdy and imperturbable men who all qualified for RSA membership by participation on one, or several, of the seven wars that country had assisted in during this century. On smart occasions they wore baggy suits and broad brimmed trilby hats. They had conventional, but neat wives and were proud of being New Zealand British. The companionability of sparsely populated rural areas spread to the towns and a pleasant conversation or a friendship could be struck up anywhere. Everywhere was safe from street robbery or unprovoked assault. Every male who was physically able, played rugby. Maori and Pakeha (Park-ee-ha, i.e. European) traditions seemed to have entwined to form a very distinctive national character.

Tragically, over the years I was to see quite an erosion, as New Zealand caught up with Europe and North America. It seemed more noticeable to me because my considerable overseas service meant that I saw my new country at infrequent intervals which would make the changes in the people more apparent.

The situation in New Zealand by 1980 was probably much less bad than any where else, but the change had happened fast and one had not expected it in that green and gold paradise of a land.

Surprisingly, I already had a fairly close encounter with the Vietnam war, even before I had left New Zealand. I was the Orderly Officer at Papakura Camp a few weeks before my departure and as often happened a batch of New Zealand Army wounded arrived at RNZAF Whenuapai and were being held overnight in Papakura camp hospital. As was my duty, I met them at the airbase to see if the Nurses and Medics required any additional assistance and to escort the ambulance convoy to Papakura.

They were a typical collection of serious gunshot and mine wounded. There had been some with only one arm, some with only one leg and one with no legs. Once they were all settled in for the night, I strolled back to the mess. I did not forget, of course, to invite the Nursing Sisters to join me for a drink as soon as they could get away.

About an hour later, I was called from the pleasant company in the bar by a telephone call from the duty nurse who asked if I would assist her.

Waiting in her office was a blond, clean-cut young RNZA Gunner in a dapper rifle green tropical walking-out uniform, desert boots and Regimental stable belt. He came neatly to attention as I entered the room and smiled politely. I shook his hand and introduced myself. He apologised for being unable to salute me, as he had somehow lost his beret on the flight. I said that it did not matter and I would ensure that a new hat reached him as soon as the QM's store opened.

"You see, Sir, I don't know what I'm doing here." He said. "I mean there's nothing wrong with me. I'm certainly nothing to do with the rest of the flight. I mean, have you seen them? I should be back with the fellas."

He also apologised for having lost his beret and went agitatedly through the story of its loss, several more times. Again, I said that it did not matter.

"Well, you look fine to me." I said. "But you had better stay here until the Doctor comes round in the morning." I had been getting concerned that someone might have usurped me with the prettiest nursing sister.

However, he became even more insistent that there had been a terrible mix up somewhere and he had gone on again about his hat.

I had been about to come the heavy handed fascist and order him to bed but had finally decided to give the Medical Officer a call – as I knew that he was currently in the mess bar anyway. He was not our usual MO (who was a kindly and efficient RNZAF doctor whom we shared with the local air base), but a Territorial Force (reservist) doctor who was standing in for him. He had been an MO in Korea and with United Nations' forces in the Congo. He was tough and cynical and told super rude anecdotes in the bar.

When he had arrived he had looked intently at the young Gunner for a few seconds.

"Hold out two fists." He had said.

"Now stick out your two forefingers and keep this sheet of paper balanced nice and steady on them."

Despite the Gunner's mask of concentration, his hands had shaken almost immediately and the sheet of paper had fallen. Then he had burst into tears. I had stayed with an arm around his shoulders until two medical orderlies had arrived and had led him away down the dark and bare corridor. My last sight of him had been his poor face contorted with silent and helpless distress.

"Battle fatigue, shell shock, or whatever you like to call it." The Doctor had said. The nurse had found the Gunner's medical card and he had nodded sadly over it.

"In some ways, matey with no legs is luckier than that one." He had murmured before turning his head sharply away.

Finally, one dawn I was part of a beret and highly pressed jungle greens wearing queue that had shuffled slowly through the departure area of the air trooping part of the Auckland RNZAF base.

I glanced furtively around in case Jeanette and, or, Cheryl had come to see me off – which they had both independently expressed the desire to do. Although I was terribly fond of them both, I felt that, for diplomatic reasons, it would be a good idea if they did not meet up. I had, therefore, been discouraging and had suggested to them separately that it would be better to spare ourselves the pain of an airport parting, etc. I also been slightly vague about the exact date and time of my flight and had hinted at dark reasons why such information might need to be imprecise. It therefore, seemed unlikely that there might be any recriminating scenes, but New Zealand girls are a very determined species.

However, there was an odd element of regret, mingled with the basic relief, when I was finally and irrevocably locked into the Hercules aircraft. They had both been as bright and fresh as that Summer. I had hoped that one of them might have waited for me as they had promised. However, I had already been a soldier for over four years and really should have learnt that it is only in fairy stories that fair damsels wait for knights who go on crusades.

My farewells did not go as I would have wished. As I left Jeanette's house three very early mornings previously, I was looking back, giving her a brave and devil-may-care wave as I pulled away down the drive and accidentally drove into the ornamental pond. She had to wake up her angry older brothers (but, fortunately, not her Colonel father) to help me get my car out again. They were all rather distressed as well, as they were rather fond of the goldfish that I had inadvertently run over.

Late the following night, my last sight of Cheryl was as she had departed homewards seething with fury and in a muddied evening gown and a dried-manure caked trailer that was being towed behind a tractor driven by two massive and beaming Maori farmers. I previously drove into a swamp and got my car totally stuck. We were driving back from dinner at La Boheme and had nearly reached her parents' house in the country when, by mutual, but unspoken, agreement, I turned down a tiny rural lane in order that we might have a few final private moments of farewell. I saw what, in the moonlight, looked like an open and flat grassed area and drove onto it. A while later I looked out of the window to note that the external area was level with the door sills. I vainly spun the wheels a few times and then waded around the still sinking car to see what could be done.

Cheryl stayed reasonably tempered for a while and had even gamely tucked the bottom of her skirt under her waist band and, in long stockinged leg and suspendered magnificence, attempted to bounce the car while I tried to drive it out. Thigh deep in liquid mud, dishevelled, but still stately, she was a premonition of paddy-field girls yet to be seen.

The Maoris, on their way from the pub, then chugged into view. They roared good heartedly at the scene and made a thorough but vain effort to get the car out with both the tractor and their colossal physical strength. They were, of course, neighbours of Cheryl's parents and offered her a lift home. Cheryl realised that accounts of, and innendo as to her doings, would have the Mercer tavern public bar guffawing for weeks. It took an Army truck to get my car out.

I spent my last night before my reinforcement flight in the mess bar with Grant, Dick, Tub and Father Frank Scott, the finest military padre I have ever known. He was a fighting soldier in the second world war before he was called and knew men – as well as something of the ways of God. I doubt that he thought much of the selfish and shallow fop that I was.

The great Hercules aircraft had borne us, on our hard canvass seats, across the Tasman Sea. We all crowded our heads into the little porthole style windows to look down on Sydney Harbour Bridge and exclaim in awe. We flew for hour upon hour over the seemingly eternal dry vastness of the Australian central deserts. We landed at Alice Springs for the night and all got drunk to varying degrees. We all had a decent night's rest in our motel-style transit barrack beds or in a dried up ditch, with perhaps an hospitable Aboriginal girl for company and warmth, in cases where the former had not been achievable.

The following day we droned on over many more hours of desert – exchanging paperbacks and sandwiches from our packed lunch boxes and getting bored. Tropical seas appeared below and finally we landed at Changi in Singapore in the clinging damp heat of a tropical evening.

We again drank too much in the various military and local bars and listened to members of the Singapore garrison complain that they, who were acclimatized to, and already resident in Asia should have been going to Vietnam rather than ourselves. We felt that they should have been grateful for their two years of cheap electrical goods, cheap drink, cheap sex and sunbathing and should have shut up.

At three o'clock the next morning, the crash of Ghurka ammunition boots coming to a halt on my stone floor awakened me. The Royal Malay Brewery Tiger and Anchor beer that I drank the following evening attempted to suggest a slight lie-in. However, the Ghurka Rifleman who happened to be the piquet member responsible for getting us up would not depart until his duty was executed and we were all either greenly studying our faces in the shaving mirrors or standing under the cold showers.

The final leg of the journey to Vietnam was by a camouflaged and highly warlike looking RNZAF Bristol Freighter, frequently referred to as many thousands of nuts and bolts flying in close formation. One of the cabin crew stole my paperback while I slept. Cabin crew personnel would, on occasions, attempt to use our returning dead companions' coffins as airfield loading area seating and, although presumably drawing a military salary, seemed to feel free of the necessity for any form of military behaviour. Usually it was necessary for the senior Army officer on any flight to gather them together for a one-sided talk. This would leave them surly and muttering.

Ton San Nuit, the military airfield by Saigon, was under mortar attack as we arrived. I think I only ever passed through it on one occasion when there was not the thud of explosions, people darting about and a pall of oily smoke suspended just above the ground.

We had been checked off on a list and were informed that we were posted to Vietnam for a year. Then we were driven in the back of an open truck and passed row upon row of fighter aircraft set in neat sandbagged compartments until we had arrived at the Caribou that would take us on the last hop to Nui Dat.

A catchy popular tune, sung by a lovely, fruity voiced Australian girl, was been ringing out of our bus driver's transistor as he ferried us to Changi at about four o'clock that morning. It took the first violent action to dash it from my mind and stop me humming it:

"Rocking, rolling, riding . . . all bound for morning town many miles away."

"You've got a rifle with you. Haven't you?" asked the blond sun-tanned cherub-face pilot of the Australian Army Air Corps.

I was gripping it between my knees and my hands were clasped on it, so I answered in the affirmative.

"Its just that if we go down – and live," he went on, "that will be our only hope. My pistol's no use in a ground fight." Yea. I thought I remembered you had one with you when we started out."

There seemed some possibility that we might go down. As we screamed towards the communist bunker complex, I could see the flicker of the tracer rounds      that seemed to be streaming from a number of it's apertures. The enclosed cabin   and the aircraft noise mercifully cut out the sound of the mass fire being directed     at us.

For a very brief moment, I though that crashing on the ground might perhaps be preferable to continued flight. Since we had spotted the fortified bunker system, and my gung-ho companion had decided to take it on with just we two and a very light aircraft, my body had discomforts inflicted upon it as never before.

After radioing the bunker's position to our ground forces, he spun up and away out over the South China Sea. He gunned the incredibly manoeuvrable little long-nosed Pilatus Porter aircraft straight up like a dart and flipped it into the reverse direction at the top of the climb so that we were now streaking back to earth in the style of a German Stuka. My stomach, and other significant organs, had moved to different and incorrect locations about my interior. At the top of the turn, I think everything went into my diaphragm, or even my throat.

I was now being crushed into my seat as the awful spectacle of the enemy fortification rushed towards us. What seemed to be the crossing point of the cross fire was approaching by the milli-second. I tensed for the end, but suddenly we were through it without a hit on anything critical.

The pilot had obviously been originally intended for Emperor Hirohito's air force, as it did not seem possible that we could pull out of this dive.

"OK yer bastuds!" he called and, even above the scream of our dive, I heard the bang and hiss of the departing rockets.

We chased the twin burning tails towards the ground. He bracketed the target, but by too much. One rocket exploded on the rearward slope of the bunker in the jungle's edge, while the other actually went off in the surf nearly two hundred metres in front.

"Bugger." He said.

"That's the trouble. The only sighting device I've got is the centre of the windscreen. It's a bit too approximate. We'll have to go for a steeper dive."

Just as I felt I could have started to count the grains of sand, he returned us skywards with what seemed like a partial back somersault, that compressed me into an area around the base of my spine.

Oh God, I though, he has six missiles in the pods under each wing. One pair have gone, so we have got to go through this five times more – and steeper!

I fear that the ever present memory of the agony of the ensuing five dives makes it difficult to recall much else. However, I do remember feeling hard done by. After all, I had been in Vietnam for only eighteen hours. I was not even time qualified for the campaign medal. Had I not seen all the supposedly authentic war moves? What had happened to the meetings, greeting and jokes with one's companions in the whitewashed out-of-combat-zone lines, the dances with the members of the female services beneath the punka fans in the local hotel and then the gradual move to the front? I seemed to have totally missed out on the 'phoney war' phase.

The rest of the rockets hit the North Vietnamese position fairly accurately. They ripped and tore at its surface and once we seemed to pull up amongst its flying debris. I felt that I should not really be a party to this inflicting of damage on the property of others. Close encounters with the invaders' civilian subjugation programme had yet to bring personal feelings into it all.

What was happening down there? Were we merely inflicting a little cosmetic damage – re-arranging the top soil – or were we killing men with the flying splinters of their own structure or burying them alive under their falling earth roofs? Were there bunker corridors and chambers full of unscarred corpses – as I was to see later after bomb and artillery attack – where overpressure and concussion had collapsed the life force instantly? Certainly our rockets were reputed to have the impact effect of a 105 millimetre artillery shell.

Only just over twenty years earlier, my father and my companion's father had returned from the Second World War and here we were, another generation, still at it in another place, for another reason.

It had all started rather mundanely.

"You're late." My Battery Commander said as I stepped off the Caribou that landed me on Kanga runway at the ANZAC fire base of Nui Dat the preceeding afternoon.

He was an impressive military man whose red hair and piercing blue eyes, as much as his name, betrayed his Scots ancestry. I was to discover that he was quick to lose his temper, but even quicker to regain it. He had been awarded the Military Cross during the Borneo compaign a few years earlier.

"Your Company started their new operation two days ago and Nick is having to stand in for you. I don't have FOs (Forward Observers) to spare you know!"

"I am terribly sorry, Sir," I said glumly.

"I am afraid that these were the flights I was sent on."

"Then, of course, you've had no time for any in-theatre training," he continued.

"Do you know how to call in fire in a jungle?"

"Oh yes, Sir," I said.

My experience of calling in gun fire in the Royal Artillery and in New Zealand was in the traditional style. That is to say, standing on top of a hill on a clear day with the target as an object on the panoramic view below. A day or so before getting on the reinforcement aircraft, it had dawned on me that things might be different when standing on flat ground in thick jungle. Fortunately, my friend Grant, a combat veteran FO, had, with the aid of a blackboard, described to me the method of walking the fire towards you and doing a sort of sound ranging with ears. It seemed simple, as long as one knew the principles of artillery, so I felt that I should be able to do it.

"Well, that's a relief." The BC said – brightening a little.

"The best I can do by way of local familiarization is to get you on a ride on the road recce. They fly round the province at dawn looking for any signs of new digging – mines on the roads, that sort of thing. Take a map and you can get a general idea of the layout. You can join the operation later tomorrow morning. In the meantime, Tom, he indicated the tough and cheerful Battery Captain, will get you sorted out and ready."

Before dawn I had met my perky and brave young Australian companion and a few minutes later we lifted up and out of the base and were skimming over the fast lightening tree tops. Almost immediately I started to wonder what the sensation of suddenly receiving a bullet in the seat of the pants might be like.

"If we keep low, we come onto their positions too quickly for them to open up on us," he said, as though reading my thoughts.

The spellbinding sight of Vietnam starting a new day made me totally forget any personal concerns.

Along the roads had streamed colourful people on their way to work or war. There was every kind of transport. Buffalo carts, scooter-buses, Hondas, bicycles and trucks. Pedestrians carried interesting wares in two large bundles on either end of a carefully balanced bamboo shoulder-pole.

Nearly everyone wore the traditional broad-brimmed conical straw hat. I saw little villages of gem-like Buddhist temples surrounded by neat huts. Mostly, of course, I saw the overwhelming acres of undulating green jungle top.

We had seen no signs of new minelaying.

"I'm supposed to check the beach once in a while." The pilot said.

I haven't been there for a bit. Let's give it a look, aye?"

And off we went – following the line of a beach that could have beaten any millionaire's playground anywhere in the world – had it not fallen into the 'no-man's land' category of real estate.

Suddenly, there it was. Cleverly camouflaged and probably not noticeable to any but our low and slow flight.

"Jeeze! Look at that!" my friend exclaimed.

"The bloody infantry will take it out – if the Nogs make a fight of it – but let's have a go first, aye?"

"Ya-hoo!" he yelled deafeningly as we changed from minimum to maximum speed. He was still whooping a few moments later as he fired us towards the enemy's heart.

I was inadvertently in my first warlike event and was unable to influence its' outcome in any way.

"Well, I need to re-arm," he said finally. "Wasn't it great?" And we spun off in a lurching manner to deceive the vengefully pursuing ground fire. My face was probably the colour of my uniform.

I thought he must be going to make a testing pass over the airstrip, but to my alarm, he suddenly plopped the aircraft down. Then I remembered that we had taken off while I thought he was still taxying. It was the most agile little aircraft I have ever flown in.

"All the best," said my comrade in arms, giving me a firm and sincere handshake.

"You can keep that bloody jungle. Christ, I don't envy you down there."

I tried to be as effusive as one could who considers that he is on the verge of collapse.


"Go!" mouthed the helicopter crewman and then quickly looked back around the ominous darkness that surveyed us from amongst the encircling tree trunks, despite the glaring brightness of the day and the reflection from the dried elephant grass above which we hovered. The side gunner on my side suddenly levelled his fifty calibre machine gun on its mount and traversed along the tree lined border of the jungle clearing with both his gaze and gun barrel.

I was aghast and hesitated. We were still the equivalent of two floors up.

The crewman appeared to speak into the little microphone that curved round in front of his face and we lurched down a bit more. He clapped me on the shoulder again.

Like a parachuteless paratrooper, I launched myself out over the helicopter's skids and dropped down for what seemed an age. Neither the calf-depth bog I sank into nor my bent legged posture prevented the knee jarring landing that the height, and my heavy pack, caused. The pack also, after its negative 'g' wore off, pitched me forward onto my face. However, I did manage to hold my rifle up and out throughout the entire process so that it did not get its sights jarred out of line.

With a dramatic increase in noise the Iroquois shot up to safe altitudes and swept away over the tree tops.

I had been delivered, totally alone, into a hostile area of Vietnam. Somewhere within the surrounding jungle area enemy units of the most skilled and cruel close country fighters in the world would be for certain.

All jungle training seemed to have left me. For a moment I remained numb on all fours where I had landed. I was cooking in the glaring, sweaty heat and I had never known such silent loneliness. The helicopter's clatter would bring unwanted attention my way sooner or later. Suddenly I realised that I had to unstick my boots from the reddish mud and do something. I spun some frantic glances around the tree walls and darted in a crouching position about thirty metres to a taller looking clump of dried grass and dropped into it. I looked around more deliberately this time and actually had my rifle at the ready. Scan from right to left, I reminded myself. It is unnatural to most people and so you notice more. The jungle edge, about 600 metres away in every direction, still looked unoccupied by humans. I started to notice insect noises in the surrounding grass and what might have been bird calls echoed within the jungle.

Worryingly, I had to stop looking around me in order to orientate myself. I got out my map, compass and protractor. Between each movement, I popped my head up again and gave it a quick swivel. It was difficult to concentrate and my hands were clumsy. I could not seem to fold the map to the right part. The compass needle would not settle quickly enough at magnetic North.

At last I found the already marked clearing in which I lay and the Westerley bearing into the jungle to a point some one hundred metres within where the Australian infantry company and its New Zealand forward observer party had said over the radio they would wait for me.

I orientated my map and looked in the direction that my bearing line indicated I must go. The segment of jungle fringe was identical to the rest. It all looked as though unthinkable things lay in wait, beyond the light, within its sinister interior.

I made my way tactically across the clearing trying to look in all directions at once and where I was putting my feet. Most people went to war in the middle of vast armies. I lamented self-pityingly. My innards became leaden as I approached accurate weapon range. Would I get all the way to the trees only to get a point blank shot through the chest? I went to ground a few times and tried to peer as far as I could into the twilight caves.

There is an old and unofficial military principle that states that if one seems to be in danger and cannot think of anything else to do – then charge. I rushed the last seventy metres to the tree line and, after a few paces on the thick pile dead leaf carpet beneath the high dark canopy, I dived to ground again. Masses of flies rose excitedly from the surrounding foliage, but nothing else showed any interest in me.

I listened intently for a bit, then got to my feet, rechecked my bearing and started, as soundlessly as was achievable, to push my way through the chin-high foliage that grew beneath the dark green ceiling. Stunted rubber trees I recognised, but there was quite an additional variety of vegetation. There were things that looked like flowerless rhodedendrum bushes, waterless reeds, hedge-like bushes that were remote from suburban front gardens, oversized ferns and a variety of bamboo – some of which had prickles.

Despite the sunlight speckles that flickered in that shadowy world, a clammy hand of dread held me. This neutral chirping greenery would allow sudden shock, pain and death to creep up to you or allow you to blunder into it. The human imagination, of course, made matters even worse than they actually were. Menace seemed to lurk all around.

I had been going for what had seemed a long way, but which in fact was about fifty metres, when a tree on my right suddenly wished me a "good afternoon" in English and stopped me as though I had been hit by a science fiction paralizing ray gun.

"It's OK, Sir," the voice went on. "Don't panic. We're over here."

A typically British style Sergeant Major, complete with handle-bar moustache, stepped from behind a tree and shook my hand. He then conducted me round the tree and through a line of bushes to where the company of the Royal Australian Regiment were harboured. I was introduced to the youthful company commander, his headquarter's personnel and platoon commanders. Then I saw Nick whom I had last seen in New Zealand several months ago. He would assist me into the world of the Vietnam artillery Forward Observer until I was deemed safe and effective on my own. Nick introduced me to the members of the Royal New Zealand Artillery FO party with whom I would spend most of my tour. Two, including the Bombadier Assistant FO were beamingly cheerful

Maoris and two were European.

Everyone was squatting around sipping tea from metal mugs which seemed an unexpected, but rather reassuring, thing for them to be doing – albeit the machine gun pairs were deployed out and around on the approaches to the position.

I tried to get to grips with the realities of it all while at the same time trying to answer Nick's questions as to what happened to old so-and-so, how was old whatshisname and which dirty lucky bastard was currently serving that gorgeous girl from Takapuna.

After about fifteen minutes the sign for 'saddle up', i.e. pull on your pack and equipment again, was made and we got ready to continue the search for enemy in our ten kilometres by ten kilometres AO (Area of Operations).

The company headquarters waited, while the company commander, holding his signaller's radio handset, checked that his outlying platoons were in the formation he wanted. When this was done we all moved, in sequence, from our all-round-defence deployment and into slow and deliberate file as we moved away. In order that a single burst of gunfire would not bring down several men, we were tactically spaced – which, in that area, averaged out at about five metres from each other.

Apart from artillery fire support when we made contact, I should also have the added responsibility of orientating the company headquarters. The only method of navigating in a jungle is to chart oneself like a ship at sea. One must keep track of exactly what distance and on which bearings one has travelled since the last known point. In addition, therefore, to trying to move like a tactical jungle rifleman, I regularly checked our direction with my compass and constantly counted my paces. After One hundred and forty or one hundred and twenty on open ground, I would make a wax pencil mark on my rifle stock to show that we had come one hundred metres more. As soon as we harboured again, I would count up my pencil marks, draw our bearings and distance on the map and give the company commander an eight figure grid reference for the LOCSTAT (Location Statement) that he would send to battalion headquarters.

Each pace was made with mines, booby-traps and snapping sticks in mind. One constantly scanned the jungle. Every so often individuals would duck down to look along the ground beneath the foliage. Everyone listened. No-one spoke. Only field hand signals were used when communications were necessary. At half hourly intervals we stopped and radioed our LOCSTAT and a SITREP (Situation Report).

Fifty to two hundred metres in front of the front man of company headquarters would be the last man of the point platoon. The rest of the point platoon would extend forward of him in single file for up to one hundred metres or so. Thirty to fifty metres beyond the front man of the point platoon would be the lonely lead scout and his navigator assistant. The lead scout would not be slashing at the jungle with a machete – as is done in war films – but would be quietly snipping our path with secateurs. It was a tense job, as he would almost always be the one who would make first contact. Therefore the point platoon commander would change the lead pair at half hourly intervals. Parallel to company headquarters and about two hundred metres out on each side moved the flank platoons. A different platoon was made point platoon each day.

We usually only travelled from two to four kilometres during a single daylight span, but by last light we knew fairly well every square metre of the kilometre squares we had crossed.

Just over half way through my first jungle afternoon there was a sudden fussillade of single rifle shots from the front. We all darted into our all-round-defence harbour positions, dropped to earth and silently watched and waited. The company commander took the radio handset from his signaller and waited in disciplined anxiety for the report that would come. Only the leader at the event could command the local battlefield situation and that was a point platoon commander in his late teens or early twenties. He must not be chivied.

After a long five minutes the platoon commander's voice crackled out of the handset. The head of an enemy column had been met. Fire had been exchanged between the leading individuals. One communist had fallen and the rest had made a quick tactical withdrawal. Just like that; a man had died on that damp earth, dead leaf and insect infested floor.

But, it was all still out of my sight and still almost too theatrical to be real. Even the noisy, and worst imagination encouraging, first jungle night that I spent wrapped in my poncho under the leafy roof could not altogether get rid of the feeling that this might be some sort of rather realistic training exercise. However, my surprise meeting with the North Vietnamese colonel political officer and his troops a few hours later and the abattoir-like scenes that ensured, soon put a stop to such simpleton feelings.

During the first few weeks of that six week operation, we had at least one contact every day and sometimes several. They cost the enemy about a dozen dead and an unknown quantity of wounded, and ourselves three dead and five wounded. I was unaware that this was a rather higher rate of contacts than usual and was wondering how everyone stood up to a year's worth of this sort of thing.

"Jeez, its been lively lately", one platoon commander said at an orders group half way through the operation. "The bloody noggies must know we've got a pommie bastard with us. There you are yer see! It's like I always told you. No one likes you lot." And he made the wry grin of a kindly, but worn, veteran.

His National Service commitment would run out shortly after his return to Australia and he was looking forward to the celebrations his family had promised him to mark his twenty-first birthday on the Saturday of his homecoming. Before our current operation was over, he was to win a Military Cross for brave command when his platoon was cut off from us and outnumbered. Before his tour was over, he was to lose forever, the use of his right arm because rocket shrapnel would sever nerves and tendons three weeks before he was due to go home.

A company of the Royal New Zealand Infantry Regiment, with a Royal Australian Artillery FO party, was operating on our right flank. On my second day in the jungle, our New Zealand FO party had been deeply saddened by the loss of some personal friends. During an attack, a directional, ball-baring firing, Claymore Mine had been command detonated and had sawn down a New Zealand platoon commander, a sergeant and several riflemen.

As the weeks and then the months passed, I started to become a jungle soldier. Although I was unaware of the fact, I would have gradually lost my alien European smell as the effects of European food and environment dissipated from my body and local produce, earth and foliage imparted themselves to me and made me their own. Gradually, I ceased to be in constant discomfort from the sweaty and tiny insect infested atmosphere. I started to squat on my haunches for long periods, as the Vietnamese did, and be as rested as if I had been sitting on an armchair. I learnt how to do everything, even cocking my weapon, silently, to notice and know the flora and fauna and take alarm if any aspect seemed different from usual. I came to be unperturbed by the frugalities of life. The diet was slim because of the limits of what one could or would wish to carry. I seemed to shorten my belt daily. Hygiene aids were minimal but a reasonable standard could be achieved. I used to have two water bottle tin mugs. One was for drinking out of and the other was my bathroom. It was very important not to use the latter in place of the former. As soon as the company was raised, just before dawn I would half fill my bathroom cup from my water bottle and shave in it. Next I would wash those personal areas more prone to overheating in the lightly soapy water and finally I would rinse out the airtex underpants and the socks I had been wearing in it. I would then put on the underpants and socks I had washed the previous dawn. The wet underpants and socks would be attached to a buckle on my pack and would dry within a few hours once the sun came up. The Australasians used to find my pommie-trained fastidiousness killingly funny. I decided that no doubt they probably wore their underpants and socks until they totally disintegrated or became fused to them. My jungle hat gradually lost the crisp and dashing cavalier shape that I had tried to affect initially and became as faded, subdued and as shapelessly functional as everyone else's.

The days were passed in slow and searching walking, harbouring and waiting while helicopters clattered overhead and short, sharp localised battles. The nights were passed in listening intently, sleeping fitfully, urgently passing on whispered warnings, explosions and flame jets of rifle fire in the pitch black and the occasional concussing crash and blinding yellow flash as friendly or unfriendly projectiles landed.

When the area seemed calm at night, I would listen to the jungle's nocturnal sounds. Deer would cough, large cats would growl and scream, night birds would call, frogs would chirp and a zillian insects would merge their respective sounds into an endless humming buzz. Distinctive amongst all this was the sound of the giant Ghecko tree lizards. They would inflate their throats and then exhale in a series of reverse gulps – creating the eerie two syllable cooing call that they would make to each other. The troops decided they were saying: "f . . . you!" and indeed it was not a bad approximation of that over used phrase. The number of "f . . . yous" a lizard could do at a session apparently indicated its size. An average number was around eight. Pairs of night sentries would identify a lizard each as their own and would make pretend bets as to whose would make the most calls. It was not unusual for a chap to be going excitedly round the position the following morning exclaiming that he had had an "elevener" or whatever. One member of our company actually reckoned that he had had a "sixteener". We all crushed his delighted sense of personal achievement with our cynicism.

There could be human night sounds too. Sometimes if we were only a few miles away from a South Vietnamese village, we could have the comfort of its humanity. We could hear the mixture of western pop and traditional Vietnamese music coming from the transistors in the little shack bars and eating houses and, perhaps, the odd laugh. We might even be able to see a faint warm sky glow or smell the pungent fishy sauces.

But mostly the human night sounds were those of war: single shots or vast eruptions of massed fire as battles went on, the rhythmic thud of heavy machine guns, the shudder of distant explosions and the pop and crackle of burning jungle.

The ANZAC guns on the Phuoc Tug Province fire bases would bang away at their nightly harrassment and interdiction (H and I) missions. The Song-Rai river and its tributaries seemed to channel their sound to us. There was reassurance in their short gruff barks. They called to us that we were not alone and that they would bring help to us across the separating distance.

The girl was just so beautiful. She had a rare totally flawless beauty. She had a perfect bone structure, a willowy figure, delicate hands, wrists and ankles, hypnotically pretty and glowing eyes, a radiant smile, shimmering blue black hair, graceful movements, and the brightest personality. Her elegant white *au-dai* national dress enhanced her aura of serenity and innocence. Surely she must have been a lost princess from the Court of the Emperor Bao-Dai himself. How easily one could have fallen in love. But what *was* she doing in a bar just off the small square of Vung Tau?

My company was having a weekend off after eight full weeks of combat. My friend Ray, a New Zealand military police officer, had invited me for a drink. He was held in high esteem by the *Mamma-Sans'* (female bar owner's) union because of the influence his calling had in high places to declare establishments 'off limits' or 'out of bounds' to troops. Drinks, therefore, were tending to be on the house. Other things might also have been. This epitome of Asian female loveliness had somehow magically materialised by me.

We had chatted easily and happily in French and broken English and Vietnamese. I was drowning in those exquisite almond eyes and was enslaved by the smile, laugh and perfect white teeth of that divine mouth.

A massive half drunk Australian trooper cannoned past our table and spotted her.

"Hey. I'm gonna f . . . you!" he said.

She politely excused herself from me with the grace and discretion of a Mayfair cocktail party hostess and melted into the great Australian's side.

I made no move to stop anything, as I had known all along what she must be, and I am not able to buy myself company. The daily evidence of the insecurities that perpetual war must bring largely explained why things were so.

Unfortunately the short flashes of light were definitely being made by humans flicking torches briefly on and off every so often to orientate themselves. Most were to our front and moving ever further to our left as that seemed to be the direction of the column or whatever it was. However, there was also the odd yellow stab away to our right as tail-end-Charlies had a quick check for obstacles as well. Then, after a bit of careful scanning, one could actually see the dark silhouettes of the men moving within the edge of the tree line about two hundred metres away. There seemed to be masses of them. I thought the situation unfortunate because if the lights were not made by fireflies, or some other natural phenomina, then I knew what I had to do.

The Australian company commander and I were lying just inside the tree line on our side of the moonlit clearing.

"Yea. We can see 'em too," he whispered into the radio to the platoon commander who was in yet another segment of the tree fringe round the clearing. That particular platoon was in fact roughly in the path of the enemy force – if they continued with their present direction. The platoon was currently being commanded by the Platoon Sergeant as their Second Lieutenant had been shot through the back of the head about two weeks earlier when some skilful and determined North Vietnamese had infiltrated his position during a battle. We were waiting for a replacement teenager to be sent from the reinforcement pool at Vung Tau or a commissioning establishment in Australia.

The Sergeant platoon commander had drawn our attention to the column.

"Perhaps they're South Vietnamese troops out hunting monkeys or something," I whispered optimistically. I sensed the company commander's head turn towards me in the darkness and a foul-languaged criticism of my intelligence cross his mind.

"Right, give it a go," he ordered.

The moment of my first call for fire against a positively identified living target had arrived.

I have pre-registered targets to both the North and South of us, I thought. The northern target, with a right and a drop correction should be the one. I pulled my camouflaged poncho completely over myself and studied my map by red torch-light. I cursed. I had marked my targets in red grease pencil on the map and they were nearly invisible in the red light. I decided which one was the Northern and read off my corrections with the scale on my protractor. For surprise and maximum first salvo damage, I would order a gun battery's worth of 'fire for effect' straight off. I would not adjust onto the enemy's position with a single gun and warn them. The ANZAC Gunners knew the terrain and their howitzers well enough to produce first round accuracy – as long as my map work was correct.

The professional routine, that I had wanted to be so slick, was nearly a disaster. I took up the radio handset myself, forgetting my signaller who was much quicker and more efficient at radio fire orders. In my anxiety, I got the sequence of initial orders the wrong way round and an irritable battery commander's voice broke in to ask me:

"Don't you mean . . ." and to correct me.

I had sudden misgivings about the target number I had sent. If I had chosen the wrong one of the two, our own troops to the South would be in

127

danger. I checked desperately and sent the right number.

I spoke too loudly and everyone had to 'shh!' me. At last and without too much delay, I got the essential information to the gun position.

I knew well the activity that would be going on at the gun position. The Gun Position Officer would call:

"Fire Mission Battery!" and the fire mission bell would be rung.

From all sides the cry of "Take Post" would ring out as the Gunners tore from their corrugated iron and sandbagged shelters to the gun pits. They would swing the heavy trails round to bring the barrels roughly onto the bearing ordered by the command post. The Layer on each gun would then lay the gun precisely on the bearing. Ammunition numbers would be fuzeing the waiting rounds and breaking out more. The Gun Sergeants would be bellowing their eagerly anticipated orders in the language used by British Empire Gunners for over three hundred years. The Gun Numbers would report back to their Sergeant in the same quaint sing song style. The rhythm and pitch of the exchange made it seem almost like the chant and response of a religious ceremony.

"Bearing! . . . Elevation! . . . Lay! . ."

"Steady! . . . Set! . . ."

"Load . . . Charge . . . Correct . . ."

"Good ram . . ."

Even though they would not be doing the formal kneeling gun drill, all movements on each gun would be carried out in an identical, military and precise manner. When the gun was ready, the detachment would come to attention facing the direction their barrel pointed – the direction of their enemy.

The straight figures and the squat equipment with its long upward tilted barrel would be still and silent for a moment – blackly silhouetted against a dark blue and red, translucent tropical night sky.

"Fire!" would roar from the Command Post and the stillness would be shattered by the serried crash of the exploding propellant charges, the blinding flash of the flame jets, the metallic ring of the recoils, and the rush of the departing warheads. Before the sound had died away, the Gunners would again be serving their deadly metal mistresses. Breeches would be torn open, scalding and smoking spent cartridge cases would be snatched out and tossed onto a clattering pile with a single movement, bores would be swabbed and the ceremony would instantly start again.

"Time of flight will be thirty two seconds, Sir." I said to the company commander. I had ordered "three rounds fire for effect" (i.e. all six guns of our direct support battery would fire three rounds each).

It all ripped across the ground with a shaking roar. In the split second of the searing yellow light, I had a glimpse of its effect on the groups of men amongst the sparse trees by the jungle's edge. It all seemed to depend on the way the multi-razor-edged shrapnel fragments, that scythed through the area faster than bullets, caught them. Some were tossed jerking into the air as upward angled swarms speared them into the sky and ripped and tore them as they went. Other men, slightly further from a burst got a more horizontal jet that shredded them where they stood. The majority of casualties, however, would probably only be wounded – losing parts of their bodies or having large irregular tears made in them – which is the characteristic of artillery casualties.

The need for silence in the jungle was gone. Delighted whoops and yells burst out from our platoons all round the clearing. Some jumped up and down in the open.

"Hook in! Hook in!" they screamed.

At "three rounds fire for effect" each time, I walked the fire round in a systematic pattern and pulverised the kilometre square.

The company commander requested permission over the radio to chase and harrass the shattered enemy. However, that presumably did not fit in with some overall strategy and he was refused.

"Well you finally got it right, you dozy old bugger!" he roared and punched me on the upper arm.

I tried not to pull away, but I did not want anyone to touch me, or see me, or speak to me, or ever be nice to me – ever again.

Madam Tee, the manageress of the Grand Hotel in Vang Tan was an extremely beautiful, elegant and distinguished lady. It was difficult to tell her age, as Asian ladies have the fortunate ability to look young for most of their lives. Albeit, they tend to have a sudden chute into extreme old womanhood finally. In the midst of war, I found her such a civilised relief. She spoke perfect French and during my breaks from the front, I could sit at her supervisor's table in the main salon and forget much in the therapeutical and calming interludes of our cosmopolitan and cultured conversations.

Her main business was, of course, girls and apparently, if one was considered a sufficiently deserving person, one might even be accommodated by Madam Tee herself. I, however, resisted all offers, as I still remained naively confident that somewhere my crusader's reward of a pure, and unrelievedly devoted, maiden awaited me – as opposed to one that anyone could buy with, in order: dollars, bottles of duty free drink, MPC (American in-theatre 'monopoly' money), chocolates or Vietnamese piastre.

The classiest girls in town were, of course, to be found at the Grand Hotel including Number Thirty (They all had numbers like little boats on a park lake – although I never knew what the overall total was). Her real name was Janine. She was half French and was, apparently, incredibly beautiful. I never actually saw her because, as she was so sought after, she was invariably occupied. She was, it was said, the young widow of a dead Vietnamese officer who now needed an income. Considering the volume of traffic that traversed her, I wonder if her beauty lasted. The sadness of her semi-amateurishness apparently revealed itself in the fact that she actually responded to, and became genuinely fond of, some customers. Any ANZAC servicemen who knew her immediately go into serious romantic mode at the mention of the name 'Number 30'. Part of a whole generation of the ANZAC made love to her and loved her. I am glad that I did not meet her.

Madam Tee had an excellent personal collection of older romantic music tapes and, at my approach, she would hurry to put on one of my favourites. She would insist on buying the first round of drinks and, when it was my turn, I was permitted local prices, as opposed to the outsiders' one thousand per cent inflation. She was widely read, of sophisticated tastes and I would look forward to half an hour or more of uplifting (compared with that to be found in the jungle) conversation in female company and smart surroundings, before strolling back to Peter Badcoe VC camp. This was the name of our between operations leave centre – named after a brave Australian Warrant Officer who had been killed earlier in the war while serving with Vietnamese troops.

One day I happened to mention the French military cemetery in the town. It was a very neat, but sad, white walled area. The rows upon rows of square white gravestones all had a little Tricolour inset at an angle into the top left hand corner. I said how curious it was that all the dead were officers. Between rather attractive and almost girlish giggles, Madam Tee proceeded to tell me the story of the French officers' cemetary at Vun Tau.

During the last days of the French Empire in Indo-China, Madam Tee had been a young waitress at this very hotel, which – unbeknown to the French – was a Nationalist Viet Minh centre. The French officers of the area had decided to hold a formal luncheon on the occasion of a Bastille Day and had considered that the Grand Hotel would be the ideal venue.

A full top-class French meal was prepared by the hotel. The French officers were delighted with the quality of it, the exquisite wines selected to go with it and the charming and pretty waitresses who served it. Finally, to cap a perfect event, the Vietnamese hotel manager had addressed the company and asked them if they would do him the honour of accepting a glass of his special brandy on the occasion of their National Day. All had happily accepted and the heavily drugged drink was passed round.

When the entire table had sunk into unconsciousness, or helplessness, the cute little waitresses including Madam Tee, had been issued with the sharp knives from the kitchen and had efficiently cut all the guests' throats.

I still occasionally dropped into the Grand Hotel for a chat subsequently, but some of the cosyness seemed to have gone out of it all.

The Bushman Scout waved to me every time he caught my eye. His expression was one of scarcely contained excitement. We were being re-deployed on the backs of APCs (armoured personnel carriers) and were being led by a Centurion tank. He had asked me, and I had asked the company commander, for permission for him to ride on the tank. He had been told that he could and this was the cause of his rather childish delight.

We used to travel on the backs of APCs (i.e. sitting on their roofs) because of the choice of being sniped off the top or incinerated inside by an anti-tank mine; the former seemed preferable. It saved us walking, of course, but it was a fairly disagreeable experience. Tanks and APCs have no noticeable suspension and a sort of sea sickness could result. An armoured column made the air thick with blinding and dirtying red dust and one was constantly flagolated by bamboo branches and whipping aerials. I used to get on after I had seen my troops up and would end up with the place that no one wanted. I had to sit on the 50 calibre machine gun ammunition boxes. These would slam together as we lurched and try to bite sensitive portions of myself.

Earlier, as we had approached the village of Xuyen Moc in this way, the leading APC (the one in front of me) drove the edge of its right track over a mine. There had been a bang and some metal plates off the front and a portion of engine had flown into the air and had landed with a clang on the dust road ahead. At the same time, a long segment of severed track had slithered from the front right side. It had seemed to convulse up the road for a moment and had then lain still. It had looked like an expiring serpent.

We had been only momentarily startled by the report and had been relieved to see that no great damage seemed to have been caused to either the crew members – there had been no infantry on the leading APC – or the vehicle. The two crew members had come staggering out of the rear door and had seemed almost amused by their experience. However, we had learned later that they had to be repatriated and were suffering from concussion that was probably irrevocable. We had also thought that with a new track, and a bit of work on the engine, the APC would have been alright. However, it too had been written out of the script as the blow from that powerful directional explosion (a Soviet or Chinese anti-tank mine) would have cracked all its welding and loosened all its rivets. It had now become a fairly compact, and considerable, source of scrap metal.

The other aspect that we had been unaware of was the fact that the cunning enemy had intended the event to be a skillful, unmanned ambush. They had been anticipating the typical highly professional, British-military tradition ANZAC column – who, as soon as the first vehicle was hit, would dart out into an all-round defensive position with finely honed, near reflex, reactions and would hurl themselves down into fire positions on the anti-personnel mines and *pungees* (bamboo spikes hidden in little pits) that they had arranged in the surrounding dry paddy fields.

However, we had been nearly at the end of a rather testing six week operation and, as the area looked clear, we had been disinclined to any intense physical activity. Thus, once we had all verified that our own individual persons had been intact, we had taken the opportunity provided by the welcome break to wander up and down the line and lean on the APCs and chat to our friends.

My friend Bob, a Lieutenant in the Royal New Zealand Armoured Corps who commanded the APC troop, did a splendid job. With his natural film star looks, enhanced by his dashing black beret, cravat and drawn pistol he took charge of events, dashed up and down the column, gave defensive arcs of fire to his machine gunners and organised the removal of the dead APC from our path. We had all been happy to let him get on with it.

Our Ideas had been woken up slightly when a senior NCO of the Royal Australian Engineers or Royal New Zealand Engineers had come and roared:

"Don't you lot realise you're surrounded by anti-personnel mines?"

An interesting phenomenon had then resulted; nearly two hundred dirty green clad persons had seemed to vertically lift off as one from the road and land back on the tops of their APCs from where they had anxiously studied the earth below.

Only a few days to go, everyone in my company had probably been thinking. A short attachment to another battalion for a bit of a search by the Song Rai river West of Xuyen Moc and then a pleasant weekend break in Vung Tau. We might have been slightly less perky if we had known that we were going to encounter D445, a communist regular regiment (a three battalion-sized force and one that would outnumber us by twelve to one), and have to fight a harsh, non-stop two and a half day defensive battle.

'Bushmen Scout' was the unofficial title of Viet Cong or North Vietnamese who had decided to join our side. They taught us the enemy's tactics and showed us to their routes and bunkers. They always seemed especially enthusiastic to "hook in" to their former colleagues.

When we had some with our company and they were not needed up with the point platoon, they would seem to naturally drift to my forward observer party. They were tough, cheerful and resourceful men who seemed to be able to survive indefinitely in the jungle with almost no kit. One could learn a lot from them. They were usually armed with Mark One American carbines, as this rather old fashioned, yet simple, light and effective weapon appealed to them. I enjoyed the friendship of all I met. They were often very interesting characters too.

One of ours had been a barber in Hanoi before being empressed into the North Vietnamese army, so obviously his secondary duty with us was the same as he had had with his communist unit. There was another who I am sure had defected for reasons of pornography. Every few days, when we were back at a fire base, he would come hurrying up to show me his latest collection of photographs of European women – the results of his bartering around allied lines – whose bright blonde hair did not seem to match that on other parts being given maximum display. Yet another used to carry a large, smart and brand new Western made transistor radio about everywhere. He did not switch it on, of course, as he was too professional a jungle soldier and knew that could give our position away. The radio may not have had any batteries in it or perhaps he did not know how to operate it. He just found joy in its company and ensured that it came safely through battle after battle.

An encounter with an ANZAC tank was a big event in all our lives. There were not many of them as they could not often be brought into action. But when they could be useful, they could often be very useful. Jungle is not, of course, tank country. Even they cannot get through the giant rubber trees and the close country makes it easy to creep up on them with an anti-tank weapon. There are many bogs to sink into and the monsoon floods carve the river banks too steep for even their clever caterpillar tracks to climb or safely descend. If they stick to roads or paths, they canalise themselves into easy prey.

However, if they could manage to join us at a hostile fortification, they could often remove the requirement to go through the worrying business of a battle. A tank could charge up and onto the bunker complex roof – through which it would sink. This not only won us the day without loss but also removed the requirement for an enemy burial party. Albeit, with modern battlefield thoroughness, we did dig about subsequently for any useful intelligence information.

On a fire support base they made excellent pill boxes and the gigantic shotgun-style canister rounds their great guns fired were devastating to enemy assaults. They also had ancillary machine guns to thicken the base fire power. Their built-in communications made them good command posts. They provided shelter from rocket or mortar fragmentation, an observation post from their turret top and a shady coffee house for the tank commander and his infantry guests.

The presence of this great invincible looking metal beast thundering, squeaking and clanking before us cheered us all. I quite envied our Bushman Scout perched up there behind the commander's turret. At last we reached our drop off point. As usual, I was not overly sorry that the slightly nauseous lurching ride was over. The Bushman Scout gave me a final exultant grin, jumped off the back and landed with both feet at once on an anti-tank mine.

Usually, a foot soldier can step on an anti-tank mine without initiating it because it is intended for far heavier subjects than him. However, the two footed landing from a height of eight feet was sufficient on this occasion.

I was not looking at the bushman scout at the final moment, as I was clambering down from the APC and was as stunned and startled as everyone by the blow of the explosion.

There was absolutely no sign of the Bushman Scout. As an anti-tank mine is designed to punch through and melt armour plating, it had effectively vapourised him. A search was made of the area for any remains. A small piece of something was found in a nearby bamboo copse, but it seemed to be a rather decomposed looking bit of meat and might not have been him. However, it was put into an empty sandbag and sent back to Vung Tau to be transferred to a secured and weighted coffin which would be taken to his village. His parents, wife and children could then to draw some comfort from the belief that his mortal remains rested in their local cemetary.

A bar full of GIs, I thought. The poor chaps were always in their baggy green uniforms – whereas we were allowed civilian clothes, if we wished, when off duty. How nice to have their jovial and open-hearted company for a change. They must have come across from Bien Hoa – the American defended province to the West of Phuoc Tuy. They were our neighbours. I should make them welcome, I decided. I, therefore, strolled genially in and found myself surrounded by scowls of intense hostility.

Earlier that evening, I had sauntered round the ANZAC 'in-bounds' bars of the central square of Vung Tan. I had visited all of them several times during my four to eight-weekly weekend leaves from the front. They were all nice enough places – but I had decided that a change would be agreeable and had randomly wandered off down a side alley.

134

First I had heard the soul music – cool and melodious. Then I had spotted the open door and the cosy-looking red-lit interior.

I was disconcerted by my reception. Were these not my Commonwealth's allies of four wars? I resolved to force my friendship mercilessly upon them.

"Good evening," I said, and miraculously transformed the bar to smiles.

"May I get anyone a drink?" I went on and had the place beaming.

It was while I was paying for, and distributing, the drinks that I noticed that all the GIs were black.

"Say, are you an Australian?" asked my nearest companion shaking me warmly by the hand.

I explained that I was a New Zealander – albeit I was of English birth.

As the convivial evening progressed, the local situation was outlined for me. This was a 'Black Power' bar. Had I been a United States Army white, as they had at first thought, I should have been beaten to a pulp – or worse. However, as somebody else's white, I was forgiven.

Much later that night, as I tottered back towards the Peter Badcoe VC Base, I became a bit sad. I wondered if communist troops paid attention to any individual cosmetic differences between their enemies. Most likely, I decided the only colour that they saw was the green of an alien uniform – and then they would try to shoot a hole through it.

One night, I heard a Vietnamese voice in the jungle very near to me. The voice was authoritative and was unquestionably an enemy commander giving orders. Suddenly his voice was right alongside – then it was far away. It was eerie and unnerving. Then I heard the engine noise of a Pilateous Porter aircraft and the voice transferred to the sky – and I knew what it was. It was a tape recorded Chieu Hoi or Hoi Chan mission – calling on the NVA and VC to lay down their arms – being broadcast about the Province. The tall trees and the enclosed avenues beneath had been channelling the sound in odd ways.

On Christmas Day an ANZAC commander decided to use the aircraft's broadcasting ability to play Christmas carols to the fighting troops. An infantry company had spent nearly two days getting into an area ambush position in open dry paddy fields. They had inched their way in so that they would not be seen above the earth bunds and either deter the ambushees or encourage mortar attack or assault upon themselves. Throughout Christmas Eve and Christmas Day morning they had lain motionless and waiting. Although their skill had rendered them invisible from the ground, they could, of course, be plainly seen from the air. The delighted pilot had, therefore, dropped down and repeatedly circled low over them booming out his cheery tunes.

"Now's the season to be jolly!" he may well have been extolling – But if the company commander had not managed to radio his unit and get him recalled just when he did, he and his flying broadcasting kit would have been disintegrated in the sky by the massed fire of every member of the frantic company.

The jungle was a great assister of confusion, mainly because it made communications by sight, voice and even radio difficult.

One evening, as usual, I sent in my DF (defensive fire) list as soon as we harboured. These were points on likely enemy axis of attack during the night and the gun position would have them plotted and ready for me to call at a moment's notice. My signaller and I, as usual, then ate our dinner and went to sleep (at about five-thirty p.m.) in our low-slung and mosquito-net covered hammocks. The company commander and his signaller would mind both the artillery and infantry radios until midnight when my signaller and I would be woken up and we would mind the sets until six am. when we would raise the company for the new day.

My signaller and I had become perfectly practised at dropping off for our allotted span. However, on this particular night, the company commander became convinced (at about eight-thirty p.m.) that he heard human movement circling our company headquarters harbour. He, therefore, sent his runner round the perimeter instructing everyone that as soon as he fired a signal shot, all were to pour a magazine worth of automatic fire into the jungle to their front. My signaller and I were happily dreaming in the middle of the positions and were forgotten about.

I am not sure what altitude the muscle spasms of shock took us to as the mind-destroying roar exploded all about us, but it cannot have been bad. We hit the ground outwards facing, with our weapons at the ready and our wide eyes staring intently into the dark.

Once his fears seemed groundless, the company commander again sent his runner around, this time to tell everyone to stand-down. Again we were missed out.

After a couple of hours, I dared to move and crawled incredibly slowly, and as silently as I possibly could, over to the shell-scrape and sand-bagged company HQ where the company commander and the CSM were discussing their favourite Sydney restaurants.

Apparently, the company commander felt a tugging at his trouser bottom and looked down and saw me. He was even more surprised by the way in which I staggered off in a delirium of relief upon being told that nothing was wrong.

Soft and romantic lighting enhances any pretty girl. However, there surely cannot be a more exotic and exciting vision of female loveliness than an Asian girl by a small and gentle table-top or bar lamp. Her blue-black hair will shimmer, her mysterious almond eyes seem to gently shine and her even white teeth sparkle and hold you entranced. Her pale satin skin glows. Of all the beauties of Asia, the Vietnamese girl must be the most beautiful. She has the pale doll-like delicateness and symetrical beauty of the Chinese girl mixed with the more individual and character filled look of the Indo-Chinese.

Several times I nearly abandoned my resolution never to buy myself female company. They just looked so attractive as their slender bodies, in traditional *au dai*, or silk mini-dress, glided gracefully about half-lit rooms.

One weekday morning some troops and I drove into the compound of the ANZAC medical centre at Vung Tau. Our weekend off was over and later that day we should start another six week continuous operation. I had been told by my company commander to pick up some stores for our medics. Amazingly, there were hundreds of girls there. A queue of them started at the surgery doors and extended all the way round the outer perimeter of the compound.

Girls who wish to work in ANZAC patronised bars had to have an ANZAC 'hostess card' and be checked by our Doctors once a week. Possession of a 'hostess card' meant that she had been clear of any undesirable diseases at the time that she had last left the Doctor. Troops were meant to demand to see a current 'hostess card' before entering any further into a transaction. We had coincided with the girls time-slot.

Sadly, the magic of the nights was not evident here. In place of the finery, they wore faded floral peasant pyjamas and little rubber flip-flop foot wear. Hair looked uncared for and listless and little beauty was apparent in the worn young faces that showed too many late nights and physical chores.

However, our arrival produced instant change to the sullen and sulky lines. With immediate collective publicity-mindedness, the multitude began smiling and cat-calling.

"Hey! *Uck-da-loi, Tant-tay-lan, bookoo boom-boom?*"

Almost all wiggled a suggestive index finger. Others rhythmically pounded one palm with the other first. Some made a poking movement with one fore finger through a circle made with a finger and thumb of the other hand. Several pushed their pyjama trousers down to their knees, lifted their tunics and pointed encouragingly. A couple turned their backs before lowering their trousers and, laughing either from over one shoulder or upside down between their legs, parted personal groves to give total display to areas that normally have a natural privacy.

The various accounts of who made the huge starburst holes in the front upper wall of the Ba Ria cinema during the Tet offensive was a bit like Jerome K. Jerome's story of the stuffed fish.

You may remember how in *Three Men in a Boat*, the author and his friends called at a Thames side pub that had a varnished fish in a glass case on the wall. A sequence of village worthies then visited the pub and each one recounted in dramatic detail how he had personally caught it.

No-one disagreed as to why the Ba Ria cinema had to be hit – it was because the NVA/VC was using it as an observation post and mass sniper position – but the true hitter was as elusive as Jerome K. Jerome's fisherman.

"I remember it well," my Bombardier assistant forward observer said as I passed by there for the first time on the back of a Vung Tau leave truck. "I was a command post surveyor then. There were calls for fire from all over the place. Well when we got the grid of the cinema we didn't believe it. We said 'verify' and the FO came back very shirty and said fire was needed immediately. So we gave it a round of converged battery fire. It was spot on."

A few years later back in New Zealand, I was chatting with an infantry Captain in a mess bar and BA Ria cropped up. Just as I was starting to tell him the story of the holes, he laughingly cut me off.

"Oh, so you know all about me doing that then?"
He then went on, "Yea, I was on the anti-tank platoon. We were trying to get to one of our Captains who was serving with the Vietnamese. We were too late, of course, the commie bastards killed him. Anyway that bloody lot on the top of the cinema had us pinned down – so I let 'em have it with the old 106."

Subsequently, a helicopter pilot told me that a rocket firing helicopter made them and a former company commander said they were the 'mouse holes' blow by his street fighting company. I heard that the South Vietnamese made them and even that the communists made them.

It seemed sad that the cinema still stood forlorn, mutilated and unrepaired more than a year after Tet. It must have brought a lot of pleasure to the little hamlet during the few comparatively quiet years between the ending of the French empire in Indo-China and the start of the North Vietnamese invasion.

Jerome K. Jerome and his two companions, of course, finally knocked the glass case off the wall by accident and the fish proved to be a plaster model and, therefore, all stories about it had been false.

Unfortunately, however, it was a visual truth that concentrated explosive power had punched its way several times through the cinema front and that there was blood and plasma spattered across the walls and rubble inside.

Konrad Valkendorff brought much dignity and style to what might otherwise have been a rather vulgar sort of war. He had been conscripted for his national service immediately upon completion of his classics degree at Auckland University and had had a commission pressed upon him. He spoke with a very distinguished English accent although he was New Zealand born and very patriotic about his country. He was blonde, aristocratic and distinguished-looking and although he had the most cutting wit that I have ever heard, he was not unkind. I once glimpsed an army record that listed him as 'Von Valkendorff'. He was my fellow, albeit somewhat more senior in theatre, artillery forward observer. He sometimes spoke to me upon discovering that I had done Latin at school. I did not tell him that I had managed to forget most of it – as part of a deliberate policy.

He remained civilizedly aloof from the pedestrian business of the day to day fighting, even though he brought artillery fire down with quick and cool efficiency. He would ponder academically for weeks over some discussion we had had, on a fire base, on the form of a particular Latin verb. I, of course, struggled throughout these conversations.

"It suddenly came to me," he would say authoritatively when our companies met by chance at helicopter bussing clearings or the outskirts of battles. "I was sure it was irregular."

He would then quote a passage in Latin that illustrated the point before the gaping ANZAC troopers.

The military never overawed him. Periodically, when everyone was back at Nui Dat, the battalion, of which our respective companies were a part), would hold a formal debrief. Each company commander would take a turn at standing in front of the map of Phuoc Tuy and tell the neatly seated battalion of his command's most significant recent doings.

On one occasion, Valkendorff's company commander was saying, " . . . following the contact on the twenty-fourth . . ."

"Pardon!" said Valkendorff loudly – shocking the assembly.

" . . . I said, following the contact on the twenty-fourth . . ." the company commander repeated angrily.

"The twenty-fourth?" Valkendorff said slowly, consulting his diary. "I don't remember a contact on that day."

"The burnt out area – just after we passed the ruined temple . . ." the company commander hissed.

"Oh, yes!" said Valkendorff. "Where we threw the grenade with the clip still on. Now I remember. Sorry. Do continue."

The seething Major had struggled valiantly on, despite the titters.

Baiting our New Zealand Battery Commander was another of his hobbies. As the BC was a very short-fuzed Celt, this was a dangerous pastime – even by Vietnam standards. It was almost as though he was using the BC as the subject of some experiment in human behaviour.

The BC would be giving his officers and perhaps senior NCOs, a briefing or pep-talk – which it was his absolute right and duty to do when he deemed it necessary.

Valkendorff would start interjecting witty asides and comments and would finally draw the BC into a sort of cross-talk comedians' act. The BC would inadvertently be the straight man and Valkendorff would do the Groucho Marx bit. The rest of us would cringe in horror.

Finally, and predictably, the BC would explode and fling him from the tent. Miraculously, however, he seemed to survive and stage come-back after come-back. His proficiency at his job and the BC's understanding, generosity and nobility of spirit brought this about.

However, my memory of Valkendorff at his most superior and detached best was one early evening when he and I were hosting two of our American artillery forward observer colleagues to tins of Australian beer on the Horse Shoe fire base.

The Americans were typically friendly and direct. One was staring at the embroidered name tags on our jungle green shirts. The troops of all allied armies kept smarter shirts for out-of-jungle wear. One had one's name above the right breast pocket and one's army above the left. 'NZ Army'. 'Aust Army' and 'US Army'. The Vietnamese, Cambodians, Laotians, Thais, Phillipinos and Koreans had tags in the hieroglyphics of the written versions of their respective languages.

"Say, I thought you *Noo* Zealanders were the same as Limeies," he said, looking at Valkendorff, "but your name doesn't look right."

"That is very true," Valkendorff said in a professorial lecturing style. "Eighty percent of all New Zealanders of European origin do indeed come from Britain. My own mother is of English extraction. My father's family, however, came from South Germany. In fact," he went on, taking out his wallet, "I have here a photograph of my family Schloss. Unfortunately it has been uninhabited since it was damaged during the War."

"Aw, gee, allied bombers in 1945 I guess, huh?" said the American.

"No," said Valkendorff,

"Turkish cavalry in 1640."

Surprisingly, after the war, he stayed on in the New Zealand Army and became a regular. Eventually he became a Colonel instructor at a staff college to the benefit of a whole new generation of potential senior officers.

Not every type of book is suitable reading, nor is every type of film suitable viewing, when one is in a war. Light-hearted and simple humour was unquestionably the most favoured subject. Especially humour of a slightly silly type that would possibly be infrequently read in peacetime. A collection of J. B. Morton's *Beachcomber* articles was the most popular book with all ranks of one company I served with. It was avidly passed around and its absurdly funny charazatures were chuckled over whenever a few of us were able to get together. A copy of *Three Men in a Boat* that my father sent me was also particularly popular – even with roughs and toughs who would probably not normally have had much time for its gentle and whimsical English author.

When back in the Peter Badcoe VC Camp at Vung Tau, we would nearly laugh ourselves ill over the hammiest 'Carry On' film or an old fashioned Hollywood or British slapstick number.

I suppose that the innocent, optimistic and essentially happy world of such books and films soothed the many and various private thoughts.

Whodunnits, cops and robbers, science fiction, horror, ghosts and histories were alright, spies were passable, sex was frustrating and depressing, as satiation might not be too frequently available – but worst of all were ficticious war stories. Phoney and inaccurate action produced contempt initially and then, quickly, anger in men living the daily reality of war.

At Vung Tau when we were shown films on the latter subject, the moment the martial music struck up and the extras, made up to look like battle-hardened veterans, appeared posing behind the opening credit titles the jeering would start. Every time a tough line or action occurred, a swarm of beer cans would hit the screen.

On one occasion we were watching a real classic from the Hollywood World War Two Impossible Heroics Department. It starred a cosmetically tough looking actor who was in reality a homosexual. The mock battles and teeth gritting finally got so bad that even the beer cans stopped and an exasperated silence descended. At last the hero's big scene came. For a long time his nobly grimacing face filled the screen as he delivered tough and homespun pre-battle advice to his troops. His unshaven chin – despite the ample quantities of water in most countryside shots and the razor that he must have carried in his kit – showed that he had been trained by an army other than the British. He also, of course, in the obscure tradition of these things, had the straps of his steel helmet undone and flapping beside his cheeks.

We were all about to desert the gabardine clad Mars and go back to the bar when we became aware of some real activity at the foot of one of the poles that supported the open-air cinemascope screen. A great beefy

Australian was stacking up old beer crates. When he had made himself a flight of steps he climbed up until he was level with the hero's Titan face. He then pushed his shorts down to his knees and peed into the centre of the vast firm-jawed countenance.

The sight of his back view, the silhouette of his action and the poor hero's distinguished, but streaming, face was too much for us; we howled hysterically – and no-one more so than our company projectionist who fell helplessly shrieking against his apparatus, crashed to earth with it and thus brought the performance to an advisable end.

Romantic films could have problems too. When at last the Adonis-like hero and lacquered girl found themselves alone, professed their pure and profound love and fell into each others arms, the hero would receive a considerable quantity of advice from the audience as to what should be his next course of action. The advice would be couched in simple, unambiguous, terse and few worded terms. Although there would be one basic theme, some of the ancillary possibilities would be remarkably inventive.

Good quality classic films, when one could get to see them, were of course a wonderful temporary escape from the excesses of reality in that part of the world.

It was possible to get too absorbed. One night, the troops of my New Zealand battery were watching a particularly good film when an NVA unit in a distant jungle edge spotted the illuminated rectangle and decided that it would make a good reference point for firing rockets into the audience that they knew must be in front of it. Unfortunately for them, they had a batch of faulty fuzes in the warheads, and the rockets, instead of exploding, merely stuck in the ground beside the Gunners' benches and folding chairs like large darts. Everyone was so entranced with the story that they failed to notice that they were being attacked.

The North Vietnamese finally left in despair and, after their film had finished, the Gunners dispersed unconcernedly to their sleeping areas. It was not until the following dawn that the Battery Captain – while checking the compound for litter – spotted the forest of fins protruding from the earth.

The little boy who tried to sell necklaces of flowers around the drunken soldier and prostitute filled central square of Vung Tau each night may have been about four years old. He would grab a tiny fist-full of knee-level jungle green trouser and silently hold up his pretty garland towards the stopped and surprised soldier. He would have a slightly expectant look on his otherwise cross and accusing little face. When he was refused his pretty baby countenance would pout and frown even more and he would toddle off alone into the packed legs and feet of the raucous young adults.

142

Many who turned him down, because it had become an automatic reflex with street traders, would hurry after him once they saw his dear little homeless and sad figure wandering off to who-knew-where. Perhaps they were painfully reminded of a son or young brother so far away at home. He would be given what was locally a considerable sum for his little flowers and, still without speaking or animation, he would continue on his lonely, uncared for and independent way.

The war killed or displaced so many adults and left so many parentless children. There could be families of six, the head of which was probably an eight-year old. The little ones carried the tiny ones about by piggyback. Ten-year old boys served in both communist and western local armies. Pretty little pale gold-skinned and black-haired doll-faced angels in ragged pyjamas with tiny muddy bare feet lay dead and unburied by roadsides. Deceased babies were put in dustbins.

The communists baited urban ambushes with babies they had mutilated – so that their distress would make our troops forget all caution and military training as they rushed to their aid.

Most did what they could. We, the ANZACs, had several local projects for war, and other, orphans from Phnoc Tuy and elsewhere. However, our main effort was concentrated on an orphanage in Ba Ria – just down the road from our main base at Nui Dat. It was run by Vietnamese Catholic nuns.

Our national servicemen, with building or carpentry trades, would go there whenever they could be spared and would enthusiastically put up new dormitories and classrooms or repair and improve existing ones. Army rations, medical supplies and any remotely useful spare items were given to them. The families at home heard of the orphanage and boxes of toys and other treats arrived.

The communists, naturally, disapproved of our assistance to persons that they considered their's alone to mind so they fired a couple of rockets into a packed dormitory one night. On that occasion, the ANZACs – rough, tough and feared the world over – rather spoilt their image by weeping openly, volubly and uncontrollably as they carried the little broken bodies out.

"Mail for you, Sir," said the CSM's man, giving me a large flattish parcel and an airmail letter. The Iroquois had brought us our weekly resupply of ammunition, water, food, spare clothing and any mail. The latter was looked forward to even more than the fresh bread rolls and real milk and fruit that made such a blissful change from our otherwise uniquely tinned or freeze-dried diet.

I had been several months in theatre and it was about time some mail caught up with me. However, my first mail was not particularly pleasing. The letter was a 'Dear John' from a potential fiancee. Apparently she had had an instant affair with a foreigner whom she had met on a holiday beach

"You were not there when I needed you . . . I didn't know what I was doing . . .", it went on.

I wondered then, as I have wondered many times over my library of 'Dear Johns' accumulated during several wars why so many girls who commit blatant indiscretions always find some external circumstance or person to blame for the event. A helpless trance-like state that suddenly descends upon them or something that someone else has said or done that drives them to it. In fact, of course, they must carry out a series of quite practical actions: they must voluntarily place themselves in circumstances where it can happen, remove at least one basic item of clothing and arrange their bodies in such a way that the actuality can occur.

I lamented over the letter for a while before turning my attention to the parcel. It was a dress shirt. It was a birthday present from my mother that had been forwarded around Singapore, New Zealand and Vietnam for a bit before finally catching up with me. I wondered what to do with it. The helicopter had gone, so I could not get it stored back at the fire base for me. I would never have dreamed of throwing away a present from my dear mother of course, but I really did not have anywhere much to keep it. I grinned as I imagined the ANZACs reaction if I had worn it for dinner in the jungle at night. They already thought that I was a "loo-loo Pom." Finally, I took the shirt out of its Regent Street outfitter's box and rolled it, in its inner cellophane wrapper, into a tube and tucked it under the lid of my pack.

Over the next week, until I could get the shirt returned to Nui Dat, my filial loyalty was severely tested. Almost every day we had a largish contact' Many times I frantically ripped open the top of my pack to get at desperately needed additional technical shooting equipment (range tables, or 'picto' – maps made from aerial photographs).

"That bloody shirt!" I would scream and hurl it into the jungle so that I could grab at the kit below it.

However, when calm descended again I would long for my shirt and the direct connection with my family that it gave me in this frightening place and I would go and search the jungle for it. It would once again be neatly rolled up and returned to my pack.

I finally got to wear it after my second tour to the Vietnam war was over. It was much admired. I still have it, and one could still wear it – if it had not, unfortunately, been a casualty of a little impromptu red wine throwing soireé that I attended in some Officers' Mess or other.

There were so many losers in the Vietnam war. In fact almost everyone was a loser – on both sides. The only winners are the ruling North Vietnamese communist gangsters, and their imperial Soviet masters, who were allowed to have their way. Everyone else ended up betrayed, disgraced, demeaned, defeated, enslaved, poor, crippled or dead.

One would think that whores would come quite well out of a war. They usually seem to – as the vast influx of womenless men gives them a near monopoly of a most sought after commodity. Unfortunately for them, this war was not always good for them either.

Many never really got over the shame and revulsion of it as they were nice girls whose only other option was seeing their little brothers and sisters starve to death. The strong Vietnamese girls sense of propriety must have been greatly offended by the Americans marked obsession for a particular peripheral and unnatural sexual act and the occasional ANZAC ten man infantry or gun sections' ten girl, standing up in a communal room, speed competitions.

A large ethnic minority of half foreigners was accidentally created.

Finally, of course, the communists forced them out of their bright little silk mini shifts and back into black pyjamas and back up to their smooth, golden thighs in rice paddy mud. However, even before that there were many who did not prosper.

It was difficult for the troops to get Vietnamese money and the spending of dollars was prohibited, so girls had to accept MPC from all. Every so often, without warning, the United States command would change the design, making all former patterns valueless. The troops could change old for new – but the local girls, of course, could not. Suddenly their savings were gone and the sacrifice of, perhaps, prized virtue had been in vain.

An MPC change would usually bring about quite a crop of young female suicides.

In retrospect, I suppose the initial scene was just like one of those 1940s movies about Burma: a jungle ambush – the hot and breathless night air is filled with jungle sounds – a thousand different types of chirpings, croakings, growlings, rustlings, etc. The ANZACs' steely eyes pierce the darkness. Ears are keenly tuned for the slightest sound of an approaching enemy footfall, whisper or twig snapping. Soldiers try not to shift as they lie prone on the biting jungle floor. Weapon stocks are pressed into shoulders. Fingers hover near triggers. Suspense.

It was at this point that the Company Commander's signaller decided to reach forward and make an adjustment to his radio set. In addition to keeping a listening watch on this military item, he was also listening to pop music on his personal little plastic transistor, from the American

Forces Vietnam Network ("AFVN serving the American fighting man from the Delta to the DM Zee!")

His transistor was silent to us, of course, because he was using a little ear plug that was on the end of a short thin wire. Unfortunately, he stretched forward beyond the limits of his little wire. Equally unfortunately, the end stuck in his ear was more firmly affixed than the end in the transistor. The latter popped out. This has the effect of restoring the normal loudspeaker facilities of the transistor.

Several dozen near heart attacks occurred as the big rock sound exploded out into the tense night. In the panic that followed, someone accidentally kicked the transistor some way off. We foraged frantically in the dead leaves and foliage while the metallic sound of electric guitars twanged and the rhythm pulsed.

At last the unbelievably noisy little object was located and, with either boot or rifle butt, was given no quarter.

The New Zealand Army was fortunate enough to own a unique weapons system that would invariably enable any one of its military units to be superior to an equally sized military unit of another army. This force was the New Zealand Maori soldiers who supplied about forty per cent of the NZ V Force. The Maoris provide about thirty per cent of the total New Zealand national population. These hefty, muscular, tough, innovative, consistently cheerful and enduring men gave colossal strength to anyone they served.

For nearly fifty years of almost continuous war, the Victorian British knew them as unbelievably brave, chivalrous, gallant, cunning and resolute foes. They faced one of the most modern, powerful and disciplined armies in the world and before massed troops, cavalry and artillery they remained undaunted, unbowed and morally unbeaten.

During the Maori wars, they would return wounded British soldiers, whom they had found left on battlefields, not only made better and well fed but with all their equipment – including their musket and probably some extra powder and shot if the soldier had been a bit short.

It is said that Colonel Despard once asked Chief Honi Hiki, at a post battle truce meeting, why he had left a particular bridge intact on the route of the British advance.

"Why, if I had destroyed the bridge you would not have been able to get here and we could not have had a battle," the surprised Chief had replied.

From the fourteenth to the early nineteenth century when different Maori tribes fought over the beautiful land of New Zealand – or A-Te-Aroha – if two armies met up and one had more men than the other, then the chief with the superior force would order a number of his warriors from the field so that the two sides should be equal.

The Maoris' weapons were the club or short handled cutting or stabbing devices, often edged with New Zealand greenstone jade. A Maori would never hurl a spear or fire an arrow at his foe, for these were the stand off weapons of cowards. He would fight close with, as nearly as possible, just the man. They must have been a terrifying sight with their massive barrel chests, biceps and legs, their top-knots, tattoos and spine-freezing pre-battle chants, screams and war dances.

They had to compromise a little, of course, when faced with the Europeans. They went about this very sensibly and bought rifles from American traders which far outranged the British service pattern musket. They devised wooden pallisades that leaned inwards under the impact of a cannon ball and then sprang back and flung it out again. The design of their entrenchments, that gave a defender near total protection, and a field of fire, were not equalled by the European military engineers until modern times.

When, with the advent of this century, the European New Zealanders managed to get themselves a break – by providing the Maoris with the absorbing distraction of some overseas foreigners to fight – there were problems associated with enlisting them into a British force. That still exists today.

Most rural Maoris, despite TV sets and cars, still live in tribal communities *mirais* and *pars* where primitive communism, or 'first up; best dressed', syndrome is the norm. Thus, a Maori soldier who had temporarily mislaid an item of his kit and had an urgent parade appointment would pick up the nearest item of the same type that he saw in his barrack room.

He would be dismayed and puzzled when he was later charged with theft and would think:

"But 'my cousin' was not using it at the time and I needed it?"

An officer friend and former National Serviceman told me a story of Sergeant Dan Waritini – a warrior of legendary powerful physique and presence. One day Sgt Waritini could not find his belt and borrowed my friend's. Days later, my friend asked for his belt back.

"What's that boy? Someone got your belt?" Sergeant Waritini bellowed. "What me? What're you talking about boy, of course I haven't got your belt."

My friend said that his name was written on the inside of the belt so Sergeant Waritini took the belt off and there, sure enough, was my friend's name.

"What's this, boy!" roared the awesome NCO. "What's your name doing in my belt?"

Sergeant Waritini had been an anti-tank section commander in the Korea war. Just prior to one of the epic battles on the banks of the Imjim, word was received that the British commander was visiting all parts of the Commonwealth line.

Sergeant Waritini's troops, who by coincidence were all Maoris, had been gathering up any items of food neglected by the British Commonwealth and American armies and were indulging in another Maori tradition: eating a lot.

On hearing of the General's imminent approach and fearing that he might not understand that they were merely preventing the sin of waste, the soldiers had swept the foodstuffs quickly out of sight. At the last minute, Sergeant Waritini had noticed that a loaf of bread had been forgotten in the centre of the position. He had snatched it up and, after a quick and vain look for a remaining hiding place, he had opened the breech of their giant rocket launcher and had slammed the loaf of bread inside it. He had completed the movement just in time to call his section to attention and salute as the General came in sight.

Beaming genially, the General had entered their gun pit.

"Ah, so this is your weapon?" he had said – patting the barrel. He had then, to their horror, flicked the protruding handle, opened the breech and revealed the loaf of bread.

"Good heavens!" the General had said in total surprise. "What on earth is this?"

"Instant toast, Sir!" Sergeant Dan Waritini had said – without a flinch.

The Maoris adapted magnificently to British military traditions and added to them their own warrior heritage.

On home garrison duty in New Zealand the lack of challenge could make them lazy – but in a warlike theatre, the fighting blood of the centuries took over to make them indomitable.

It was natural that the most respected ex-enemies of Rommel's Afrika Korps – and the first to be invited to their annual reunions – were former members of the Maori Battalion.

When New Zealand troops were first committed to the Vietnam war, Maori soldiers, when in ambush, had to be specifically ordered to open fire on the enemy – otherwise they would burst out at them with their fists, because, apart from their manly traditions, they were concerned that bullets or mine shrapnel might damage the interesting foreign equipment that they wished to collect. Although a blow from a medicine-ball-like Maori fist was usually sufficient to kill a lighter-framed man, the Maoris were inevitably at risk from the firearms of any enemy not turned instantly to jelly by the devastating sudden appearance of these ferocious giants.

They strengthened all parts and all rank structures of all fighting services. They provided rank and file, NCOs and officers including generals. The New Zealand SAS was, at times, composed almost entirely of Maoris.

My favourite statue is not something classical or historic from Europe – albeit many are very stirring in different ways – but that of the paramount chief Te Awe Awe that stands in the central square of Palmerston North.

After a lifetime of honour and gallant fighting service, Te Awe Awe knew that the best future for his country lay in a union of equality and respect between Maori and European New Zealanders.

He stands there in bronze looking above and beyond the horizon and has the greatest aura of natural nobility that I have ever seen. He stretches tall – but is without vanity. His chieftain's Korowhai (Kiwi feather cloak) is about his powerful shoulders and his woven headband circles his fine brows and the single side feather surmounts his aristocratic head. Yet across those strong and handsome features are the magnificent twirls of a typical British Imperial moustache.

On the sides of the pillar on which he stands are inscribed his final words. One side has his statement:

"I have laid down the foundation of friendship for your consummation."

And on the opposite side are his orders to his warriors that shall follow him:

"I have done my duty. Do yours."

He has been obeyed to the letter in the many foreign conflicts of the near century that has ensued.

"Rounds complete, over," the gun position command post signaller reported to me via my man pack radio.

"Rounds complete, out," I replied and, knowing that the whole gun position would be eagerly listening to our battle, via the voices of my signaller and myself on a radio set loudspeaker, I gave them a very quick report:

"Your rounds have been right on target. There's been a lot of shit flying up and obvious damage. We're going in now for a good look. Good shooting. End of mission, over."

The involvement of indirect fire during the Boer War has meant that, since then Gunners have usually not been able to see their shells land and so effectively are blind. Therefore, an account of what their fire achieved gives them some encouragement to continue their hard work and striving for accuracy.

"End of mission, out," came the instant standard response.

"About twenty seconds of flight time left," I said to the Company Commander.

He radioed this to the platoons so that they would stay down on the ground and protected until the last salvo of artillery fire had exploded on the enemy's fortification, to their front.

Right on time the rather cute little oscillating whistling sound approached over the tree tops. The cuteness ended, however, when they clawed their way across the earthworks that I could just see about two hundred metres ahead in the open sunshine beyond the smashed branches. The Schrapnel pinged and hissed in the foliage above our heads. It was customary for ANZAC artillery FOs, when softening up a bunker system prior to an attack to instruct the guns to fire in the high angle (i.e. giving a more mortar-like and vertical angle of descent) and to set the fuzes to delay. This would mean that, with any luck, the shell would not explode on the surface and merely scatter loose earth about, but would wait until it had dropped through the thick roof. It would then explode inside the underground chambers and paint the walls with the occupants.

As soon as the last echo of thunder had died away, we were on our feet and starting to move. The feared an exhilarating moment had arrived. We must make our assault. Our human frames had to surge forward against the point blank fire of massed single aimed shots, fully automatic Kalashnikovs and larger crew operated machine guns and take the position.

Jungle prevents assaulting troops from spreading out into more life-saving extended lines, whereby the force can advance by fire and movement (i.e. divided into leap frogging sections – so that not everyone is on their feet at the same time) with the individuals spread out to get five or more metres between them. Instead, they have to charge in dangerously packed phalanxes.

Almost from the moment we started to rush towards them, the quickly recovering communists opened up. With their usual speed and skill, a stand-off mortar started to bomb us. I could hear the throaty explosions around and behind me. They also fired their shoulder-launched shrapnel-baring, rockets into our advance. As always, the din was disorientating and overwhelming. I knew that some of us would be hit. I loped forward with the others, rifle at the ready and braced myself for whatever might eventuate.

Then on two sides I heard, or sensed, the combination of thud and sickening squelch that is the sound of a bullet smashing its way through flesh, bone and organs.

"Keep going! Bloody keep going!" I heard the Company Sergeant Major roar, as some appalled national servicemen slowed at the sight of their stricken friends.

I was labouring slightly harder than the others, as I was carrying extra weight. It was customary for troops to shed their heavy packs before an assault. However, with the natural instincts of an 'Old Soldier', even when young, I was determined whenever possible never to be separated from my main source of food, water, bedding and other beloved items. I, therefore, retained my main pack during the attack. I had too often seen chaps go hungry and uncomfortable for long hours, or even days, because an attack had got bogged down and prolonged and they could not get back to their packs.

Also, a great deal of care had gone into the selection of the comestibles in my pack. Most of the field rations we could get were American 'C' rations in little individual dark brown tins and not all of these were particularly appetising (e.g. 'salty hamburger chunks'). However, their tinned sausages in baked beans, rich fruit pudding and fruit salads were excellent – so just prior to leaving the base for a new operation, I had to spend a great deal of effort on searching, bartering and looting for my favourite menus. These treasures were not to be lightly discarded and were well worth the extra physical effort I had to make on infrequent occasions.

A violent blow suddenly catapulted me forward onto the ground. My face was against the damp earth and dead leaves. The world seemed to be lurching and my head to be spinning. I felt nauseous. To my total horror, I was down amongst the fallen. I almost got up, then fell over again.

I could feel no pain but apparently for up to half an hour this is prevented by the numbing effect of the shock of deep wounds. I dared not examine my body. I knew that I should see what I had seen with others: spilled blood-flecked human offal, a protruding piece of jagged bone like a blood covered stick set in a mess of raw steak – where a limb had been smashed off, or great pumps of arterial blood erupting from a gaping gash.

Our troops had made it to the bunker and one could hear the cries of "Grenade!", followed by muffled explosions. In addition to the grenades hand thrown through the apertures, smaller grenades from the M79 (a shotgun-like weapon) would be fired deeper into the interior. After a while there were a series of thunderous and jarring explosions as the field engineers blew in the sides of the bunkers. This would end the lives of most of those enemy who had not surrendered to us or fled.

I could not seem to get up. It seemed as if my back was broken. All firings and explosions had stopped, but there were shouts and cries of various kinds coming from a wide area.

Wayne – one of the platoon commanders – came and knelt down beside me.

"Hey, you'll be OK – don't worry, Mate" he said with uncharacteristic tenderness as he gently helped me move on to my side. He looked concernedly down at me and one of his hands rested on my pack. I doubt that I thought of it at the time, but this would have been a moment to have said something noble and quotable – so that whenever an epic film is made of it all, the interestingly featured actor who portrays me – albeit he will be a little taller and not quite as thickset or inelegant – will have a tear-jerking final line.

Wayne suddenly snatched his hand in disgust from my pack and I saw to my total dismay that it was covered by a sticky redness.

"Bloody tomato sauce!" he exclaimed.

"It's those ruddy baked bean tins you hoard!" and he went off to assist with the genuinely wounded.

A piece of flying metal of some sort, when nearly at the end of its run, had hit me in the centre of my pack. It had gone through the blade of the shovel I kept tied there and had further decelerated as it had passed through the layers of baked beans. All it had been able to do after this was push me onto my face and give me a bruise between the shoulder blades.

My aching back made it slightly difficult to get to my feet. Two signallers pulled me upright. Once I had verified that all in need of help were getting it, I was able to start the sad business of seeing what could be done for my poor tins.

"Which unit are you scruffy lot from?" a voice called out piercingly and made us pause and turn as were about to go through the doorway of the shop of the Peter Badcoe VC leave centre.

The shouter was a New Zealand Infantry Major who, as he was wearing the first little dapper and tailored shorts and shirt uniform that I had seen since observing staff officers in Singapore, I assumed to be an official of the logistic base. It was unusual to see an Infantry Officer working in such a place. The hat badges were normally all Service or Ordnance Corps. Presumably he could be spared from the war.

Without waiting for a reply to his first question, he went on:

"You all know that mixed dress is not permitted, so get back to your lines and sort yourselves out immediately"

I was wearing a white shirt tucked into a pair of army shorts and, amongst the green denims of my five companions, there was distributed a couple of pairs of civilian trousers, a tee shirt and two pairs of plimsolls.

He was correct, of course, but there were some mitigating factors. The

152

rest were all non-commissioned, so I spoke up.

"We are just going into the shop to get properly kitted out with civilian clothes, Sir" I said. "You see, we've lost packs and equipment." I went on. "We were in this week's big contact. We had our civies with us as we were supposed to be having last weekend on R in C, but we were called to assist another battalion just as we were leaving. Unfortunately, the contact went on for some days and a lot of non-essential stuff had to be shed. We were only brought back here today because we needed reinforcing, and . . ."

"Get back to your accommodation right now!" he snapped. "You want to argue the toss with me do you? You can bloody rest assured that I shall be seeing your CO to get you confined to your rooms for tonight – if not the whole weekend!"

I glanced back at the racks of lightweight shirts and trousers that I could see just inside the shop doorway and we made our gloomy and muttering way back to our billets.

Fortunately, the whole company managed to get themselves re-fitted out with the required civilian clothes for our local leave. We all contributed our existing items and managed to fully dress a few of our number who could act as purchasing agents for the rest of us. Thus, as they hurried backwards and forwards with armfuls of clothes for us to try on – they would not run the gauntlet of the Major's keen eye. Equally, fortunately, my friends and I did not get the company confined to camp.

Later that evening while out in Vung Tau with my Provost Officer friend, I heard about the lifestyle of the ruling hierarchy of the Logistics Support Group, including the rearward Infantry Major.

Apparently, in order that the wheels of business with the ANZAC, and any visiting American troops should run smoothly, the *Mamma Sans* union provided each of those in influential positions with a *pied a terre* in town with living-in facilities. Our Major spent the year away from his wife and children, and earning the same campaign medals as the fighters, in a free nightly three-in-a-bed situation – with luxury food and alcoholic drink.

It crossed my mind to let some of my companions, currently being cheated to provide for these things, know about it. However, I decided that the publicity that might follow a few summary informal executions that night would do no good to our side's image.

A couple of years later in New Zealand, while standing in an Officers' Mess bar surrounded by visiting Staff College Course members, I heard someone say:

"Of course the lessons we infantry learned from Vietnam . . ." and there, in the corner, holding forth to a group of his peers, was the non-jungle-visiting Major. As an infantryman with campaign medals, he would naturally be listened to with respect. I knew, of course, that he had spent the war rutting away on little slim yellow girls and so, despite my normal courtesy to the military hierarchy, I stared insolently and insubordinatly at him. I could not help it.

I do not know if he recognised me or not – but at least, after a quick glance in my direction, he turned his back before resuming unembarrassedly:

"Of course the lessons we infantry learned from Vietnam . . ."

The fact that the personnel who never encountered the fighting *"pogos,"* as they were called locally, got the same campaign medals as those at the coal face caused much ill feeling. Indeed, many of those furthest from the fighting, especially if they happened to be in the totally protected headquarters in Saigon, might even get more medals than anyone, as they had the chance to be charming to senior Vietnamese and American Officers. This often earned them quite high level foreign gallantry decorations for uniquely international good relations reasons.

I once attended a formal dinner after the war, where a number of combat officers did not bother to wear the miniature versions of their medals on their mess uniforms because, as the logisticians and administrators had the same, they felt them to be debased. I cannot say that I felt much resentment towards these types – so long as they did not dare to start recounting some office war story to me – but listened in humble awe to my stirring tales. After all, someone has to do their jobs.

The Australian Infantry tried to provide some means of visually differentiating between those who actually fought and those who remained back on bases or in offices. They copied the United States idea of a Combat Infantryman's Badge, a little metal brooch worn above the medal ribbon. This was awarded to all infantrymen; including those left with their stores in the echelon area and not to the artillery forward observer parties, medics and signalers who went shoulder to shoulder with the infantry into battle. It was also not awarded to some of the bravest men in the war; the field engineers who disarmed the nightmare booby traps, cleared minefields and ran forward, ahead of the infantry assault, with an explosive charge on the end of a pole to press against the wall of an enemy fortification.

We all periodically have that worst of nightmares where a terrifying and deadly entity is catching up on us from behind and, no matter how hard we try to run, we can make no progress away from it. The jungle war of Vietnam was the sort of environment where any imagined dread could become a reality.

Our point platoon made contact with a much superior enemy force one afternoon. There was a rapid exchange of fire and a couple of enemy fell. The platoon commander, on realising the size of force he had encountered, sensibly ordered his troops to pull back into the company fold. We might then hope to hold them, with artillery, chopper gunship and airstrike support, until they either broke off their attack or a large force could be sent to intercept them.

The platoon made an orderly withdrawal, using disciplined fire and movement and then with the platoon commander at the rear, and with the NVA in hot pursuit, they ran back towards us along the track they had made earlier. There was a sort of crevasse or fissure that cut the path just short of the company perimeter. It was the sort of feature that could be quickly created and abandoned by monsoon water. It was about seven feet wide, as deep as a room and tapered to a close just inside the jungle on either side.

Each member of the platoon leaped the gap in turn and sped on, except for the last two who waited on the far side for their Second Lieutenant.

"Go. Go!" he shouted as he approached the gap and they hurried on.

The very young officer flew across and landed where thirty heavy armed men had thumped down before. The weakened edge crumbled and sent him feet first down the loose earth slope of the side. He raced frantically to get back at the rim, but there was no traction at all and no other direction in which to go. His devoted troops, certain that he was with them were moving ever further away.

One can only try to imagine the total horror of his final moments. The terrifying and deadly entity approached with the sound of relentless running jungle footfalls. His feet and hands tore vainly at the unresisting fine earth. His rifle was far out of reach. The footfalls must have slowed to a couple of easy and confident final steps. There would have been the stillness of the ceremony of the imminent ending of a life as the Chinese or Russian assault rifle was raised into the aim. In those last few milliseconds before the pointed metal chunk of death smashed into the top of his brain, was he still hoping for a miracle to save him or had he become calm before the inevitable?

When the indecisive battle was ended and we were able to get back to his body, he was half turned round as though his last act had been to try and bravely face his foe.

I thought the troops from the Republic of Korea rather good chaps – albeit slightly heavy going. I had only a brief encounter with them on my first tour, although I was to work quite closely with them on my second.

I got to occasionally passing the time of day with them over the barbed wire that separated our respective recreational beaches at Vung Tau. They were certainly a different type of Asian to the Indo-Chinese. The latter have small wiry frames and delicately handsome features and almond eyes. The Siberian Korean men however, have big frames, bull necks, heavy limbs, bullet heads and impressive piercing fleshy slit eyes. They are strong and fit and are all trained in oriental martial arts, and, like the ANZACs and the Asian armies in the conflict wore neatly tailored and pressed jungle greens with shirts that tucked into their trousers (unlike the American voluminous suit with the maternity smock-like jacket).

There was a Korean Major at Nai Dat who ran a recreation centre for our troops. He was helped by a charm of lovely and smiling, and respectable, broad-faced Korean girl assistants.

One evening in Vung Tau, I resolved that I should go and have a drink with my Korean allies in their area of town – even though it was officially out of bounds to me. The Koreans were paid only a fraction of our salaries – so I headed for the poorer quarter.

I heard a different – but very melodious – type of Asian music coming from a sort of bamboo lean-to and there indeed was a bar full of Koreans. I strode in and, after a moment or two of surprise and suspicion, was given the welcome of a comrade in arms. I was totally unable to prevent the poor Koreans from buying my first drink – but after that I managed to ensure that I bought most.

Conversation was a shade difficult. The two who could speak some English remained very formal – while the rest stood in a semi-circle round us and beamed. However, we found humour in simple things and, oddly, it was an extremely enjoyable evening. Some cheerful, and probably cheap, girls started to drape themselves about us.

Unfortunately, after I had been there for about an hour, the Korean military police turned up. Too late I gathered that this rather basic and crude place was even off limits to the Koreans.

In my time, I have been on the receiving end of raids by military police of many nationalities. On a few occasions, I have only just escaped with my Queen's commission, and person, intact. However, the Korean military police raid was novel by any standards.

The second the jeep screeched to a halt outside the bar, the immaculate white helmeted and white webbed troops sprang off and gave an intimation of their approach to their duties by pouring automatic fire through the upper part of the small and flimsy shack. They then fell upon those inside with their long truncheons and one of the most ferocious and merciless brawls that I have ever witnessed commenced.

I flew off towards the indescribable toilets before I remembered that there was no back way of of there. It was a time, however, for instantly decisive thought and action and so I accelerated still more, lowered my head and charged for the rear toilet wall. I bowled over and over several times, in the filth of the rear alley, with much of the wall still clinging to me. However, I gradually shed the bamboo sticks, straw and most of the refuse as I tore along the back lanes. I slowed as I approached the in-bounds ANZAC area and, trying to look my most gentlemanly and reserved, endeavoured to absorb myself in the larger groups. I spent the rest of the evening darting glances over my shoulders and fervently hoping that to Korean military policemen all Europeans look alike.

Radio and television were a linking thread between Westernized urban life and the often unreal seeming world of jungle war. TV could only be watched on bases, of course, but my little transistor radio with its ear plug was able to keep me in touch with ordinariness while on campaign. The artificially produced pop music and the audience-patronizing drivel of the disk jockeys on AFN's pre-recorded, imported programmes added a reassuring touch of normality. I could tell when a Sunday had arrived, and the weeks were passing, by all the early morning religious services. Sometimes it seemed as though the Sundays were only a few days apart – but then I would go back over the preceeding days to myself – the empty bunker with some female VC clothing and a bottle of Pernod left in it yesterday, the booby trapped item of NVA equipment left enticingly by a path that took someone's hand off the day before – and soon I would realise that yet another week had indeed passed.

Last thing on a Sunday morning there was a record request programme compared by an overly cute-voiced and sugary American girl. She would always round off by saying, "And don't forget now – I love you all a whole bunch." Troops would wryly discuss the things that might be done with her, no doubt, peachy body.

The United States troops, far from home, tended to write in requests for an inordinate amount of extremely slow and sentimental American Country ballads. Their heavily Southern-accented morbidity would finally drive me to a local station. Often at night, I would drift away into sleep to the sound of a warm little female Vietnamese voice singing sweetly to an Asian rhythm.

The AFN television programmes, watched on fire bases, were most enjoyable. It was all rather old, but they had selected well from the decade earlier. I used to love watching repeats of 'Wagon Train', 'The Sid Ceasar Show', 'Sgt Bilko', 'I Love Lucy' and episodes of Buster Crabbe's 'Flash Gordon'. There used to be advertisements between the programmes too. They were not for commercial products, but were messages from the United States military to the troops. However, they were far from dull. *Playboy* magazine style centrefold girls used to feature frequently wearing miniscule camouflage material bikinis, steel helmets perched on their stiff peroxided locks, M16 rifles resting on their curvy hips and cooing things like:

"Don't forget we wanna see you Guys back Stateside – so keep your heads down, lovers!".

One message that was very cleverly done and very necessary – but which tended to raise smiles – went along the lines:

*Authoritative Male American Voice*: "Soldier! Soon your tour of doody in Veet-nahrm will be over! Your country is proud of you."

*Warlike scenes.*

"You will be taking many souvenirs home to your families!"

*Scenes of US Servicemen in Saigon souvenir emporiums, followed by shots of an idyllic American wife and young children.*

"However, there is one souvenir they do not *want!*"

*Close ups of some smiling and welcoming, but naughty looking, little Vietnamese cuties.*

"Make sure that your shot record is up to date."

"How much longer have you got?" I said to the Bombadier who looked as though he had been in the country for a while.

He was squatting in front of his *hoochie* (a small, low and sandbag protected barrack hut) on the fire base and, with the tip of his tongue protruding from a corner of his mouth, was enthusiastically pencilling something in on a large piece of paper he was holding.

"Forty-two and a wakey, Sir!" he answered with a grin.

This meant that he had a month and a half left of his year's tour, plus the day he would only have to wake-up on and leave on.

I moved round to study his standard days-to-do-in-theatre chart. It consisted of a bold and striking line drawing of a standing and straddle legged naked Asian girl of spectacular proportions. There was an overlay superimposed on her that consisted of numbered squares totalling three hundred and sixty-five. Each day one could fill one of these in and see visually how one's tour of duty was decreasing. The high numbers were on her toes, fingers and extremities. As one's tour progressed, one crept slowly inwards.

Number One, i.e. the last day, was, of course, exactly where you would have expected it to have been.

I did not see as much of life on the fire bases, or Fire Support and Patrol Bases – to give them their full title, as most of my fellow Gunners, because I was a Forward Observer. This meant that I must be out walking in the jungle with my infantry colleagues as they sought out and fought the infiltrating NVA columns and bunker strongholds, or fended off attack on themselves. It was a merry-go-round of taking it in turns to attack, or be attacked, depending on who had the element of surprise, the numbers and resources on any particular day in any particular place.

We did not fight the VC (Viet Cong – a South Vietnamese communist revolutionary) because they had been decimated when their North Vietnamese masters had given them the bad advice to generally go out in the open and show their colours in 1968 during the Tet Offensive.

Morally, the killing should have ended then – but the ruling North Vietnamese communist gang leaders were determined to own the rich South and so had had to give up all pretence of supporting a popular uprising and turn to blatant invasion using the North Vietnamese Army (NVA). Even the habit of dressing their troops up in South Vietnamese black peasant clothing was starting to be abandoned and more and more we began meeting up with green uniformed and sun-helmeted, or bare-headed, more honest NVA.

I heard after the war that the Russian guided North Vietnamese rulers had deliberately sold the idea of the Tet Offensive to their Chinese backed colleagues and the VC – knowing that it would fail and total power would evolve to them upon the demise of these annoyingly slightly more altruistic parties.

Although it was probably quite a bit safer on a fire base than out in the jungle, it was not all that safe – as a base makes an obvious collection to be used as a target for stand-off rocket, mortar, sniper or poison gas attack or for assault by infantry.

I did occasionally enjoy a bit of fire base life. On the large ones they had messes, bars, cinema screens, shops, showers and near normal sanitary facilities. However, perhaps life could at times get a little too normal. There was an occasion when some infantry friends and I were brought in from a two and a half day non-stop battle; still shaking and shocked beyond sleep, but ravenous, and a white jacketed mess steward told us snootily that: "lunch went off five minutes ago."

At Nui Dat the Royal New Zealand Regiment of Artillery had excellent locally built Messes. The crests of allied Units covered the walls and above the bar of the Officers' Mess was a copy of a Goldie portrait of a

Maori Chieftain. We used to tell everyone that this was our first Battery Commander and must be bowed to. To our surprised pleasure, the tradition became seriously accepted by all outsiders.

The centre piece of the Sergeants' Mess was a montage of pornographic pictures.

The basic construction material of most buildings was old shell boxes. In the centre of the ceiling of the Officers' Mess was a large colonial *punka* fan. This was terrific for throwing empty beer cans into or trying-to-stop-it-with-your-head competitions. From time to time the Battery's officer strength was depleted by fan hospitalizations.

However, there can never again be beer-can-throwing-into-fans like those in the NAAFI at Nee Soon in Singapore. It was a tri-national NAAFI and the sign outside was decorated with a lion, a kangaroo and a kiwi. The inside was very plain and frugal. It was a long high ceilinged room, lined with windows and with all the long tables set end to end down the centre. I once heard it described as looking like a third class railway carriage going nowhere. However, its drunken and fighting clientele were quite interesting – but, best of all was the seemingly endless line of huge fans that constantly whirred far above the pedestrian racket on the ground level.

A beer can, skillfully launched from down by the door, would be gathered up by the first fan and slung into the second. This would be continued down the line. The can would race from fan to fan, with a musical sequence of *tings* and *tangs*, before finally being slammed into the far wall by the last fan. This would bring much satisfaction to the assembled company.

Some cans, of course, only made it part of the way and would fly out and strike one or several of the guests. However, the can would not have had a totally wasted journey as it would usually be the cause of a free-for-all.

There were other sophisticated features of the RNZA Officers' Mess at Nui Dat. There was a beer can disposal unit in the bar wall. This consisted of a metal tube, of a diameter just larger than a beer can, that was stuck through the wall and downwardly angled towards the outside. Thus, an officer 'posted' his empty can from inside and it rattled off down the tube and fell into a large and noisy bin outside. A Gunner would empty the bin the following day.

The urinals were also rather innovative. Behind the Messes, there was a forty gallon oil drum sunk up to its rim in the ground. Oil had been poured into it and, as it had gradually filled up, the oil had floated on the surface and had sealed in all unpleasantness. It was, of course, unemptiable. By the time I arrived in Vietnam, the thing was rather full. Its unthinkable lower levels must have gone back to the earliest days of the war. Occasionally, an unsteady user would slip and submerge a boot, a leg or his entire person in it. The whole neighbourhood would be immediately aware whenever the oil surface had been briefly breached.

There were also urinals made from inverted steel helmets welded to the top of tubular metal tank round containers. The bottom of the metal tubes were steadied on the ground by concrete surrounds and there were metal plug holes set into the insides of the helmet domes.

The officers' sit-down facility consisted of four porcelain toilet bowls set in a concrete floored hut that had been constructed over a tiny fast flowing stream. Early one morning when a group of Gunner officers were socialising in there as usual, someone dropped a purple coloured smoke grenade in upstream. The grenade, releasing its dyed smoke, was carried into the pipe beneath the row of bare backsides, which were forming airtight seals in their individual seats, out of the other side of the toilet and finally away off the fire base. As each junior officer eventually finished chatting and joking to his neighbours over the partitions and stood up to go, he was startled to discover that he had a colour scheme in common with those ubiquitous apes that never fail to be giving maximum display whenever you take young children to a zoo.

A dull and constantly repeated joke used to go about the fire bases that artillery FOs, when out of the jungle, had a natural instinct to sleep at night in monsoon drains. It was true, I suppose, that when one was on a fire base between operations – and it was not for too long, or one would get given odd Battery administrative jobs, there was a tendency to leave FOs to their own devices and we would swap war stories and also, naturally, feel that we should make up a little for some of the beer drinking that we had missed out on. I also suppose that if an intoxicated and sleepy person fell over in any part of Asia touched by civilization then the monsoon drains were often the lowest geographical level and he would tend to gravitate there.

Actually, the curved sides fitted quite snugly round the shoulders, the decomposing refuse and effluent made a warm soft layer and, if sufficiently anaesthetized, the traversing vermin and other denizens of the night would not disturb the restfulness. However, the stinking dawn with the mosquito bites, cramps and bruises – and, of course, the hangover – are best forgotten.

Sadly, the harmony that apparently existed between the two ANZAC branches in previous wars was not always so complete in Vietnam. In general, of course, the relationship was both workable and friendly. However, there were a few prickly undercurrents that sometimes caused minor mutterings on one, or both, sides.

The fact that New Zealand had no national force as such, but had its military units dispersed about Australian formations and under overall Australian command, was bound to produce a basic resentment amongst the New Zealanders.

The differences in the national characters of the two countries also did not help for, despite the fact that so much of the world are unaware that the nautical milage between the two countries is not so much less than that between Europe and North America and think that the personalities – like most of the surnames – are identical, there is no doubt that two separate styles have evolved over two hundred years.

Because their penal colony origins are unchangeable, the Australians have become invertedly snobbish about them. Successive generations have become ever more determined to pull themselves ever further upwards 'by the bootstraps' and a rich and powerful industrial continent has developed. The next North America perhaps.

New Zealand was originally colonised by more voluntary, and sometimes wealthy, farming immigrants that brought the green and fertile land a steadiness and style more like rural Britain. Thus, the New Zealanders sometimes look upon the Australian as a parody of a North American and the Australians look upon the New Zealander as a parody of a mainland Briton.

Both partners largely fought the war with conscripts. However, the New Zealanders sent only volunteers who were given an extra year's pre-theatre training, so the basic quality was bound to be advantaged. Also, because the New Zealand contribution was smaller – the Australians said it was too small – they could be very selective over the Officers, Warrant Officers and Senior NCOs they sent. For example; my BC in addition to being a Military Cross holder from the Borneo campaign, was also an ex Chief Instructor from the Royal New Zealand School of Artillery. This gave him both a soldierly and technical advantage over the Australian CO of the ANZAC artillery regiment, of which our battery was a part, who had spent much of his career in staff appointments. The RNZA would insist on sending Warrant Officers First Class, as opposed to the more correct rank level of Warrant Officer Second Class, as Battery Sergeant Majors. Some of these had more seniority than some of the Australian Regimental Sergeant Majors. Such things can create awkwardness.

The award of battlefield decorations was largely controlled by the Australians. The New Zealanders felt that not only did they treat British decorations like United States decorations – i.e. scattering them about rather liberally on a quota basis – but they were also favouring their own.

Pettiness did occur. But in the main, by far, professionalism, wartime urgencies, goodwill and personal friendships prevailed.

However, everyone liked the Americans. It was felt that their friendly, generous and brave troops might not have been killed in such numbers had their Vietnam soldiers been – like ours – tailored very specifically for jungle warfare. It was also felt that their policy – that we had to follow too – of fighting a uniquely defensive war made the situation unwinnable from the outset. But one had to admire their general sincerity and undaunted attempts to apply smalltown American moral philosophies to the vicious and merciless environment of an Asian war.

During my time in Vietnam, I only ever heard of one small chip on the otherwise unbroken bridge of gold that linked the North East and South West peoples of the Pacific basin.

Four of our New Zealand Gunners, from the same gun detachment, had managed to get a weekend off in Singapore. Predictably, they were on a bar crawl within minutes of leaving Changi. After a while they entered a bar where the only other occupant was a drunk United States Navy Officer. The American must once have had his girlfriend stolen by an Englishman or have been punched in the ear by one, because as soon as he heard them ordering their drinks he roared:

"Hey! are you guys Limies? I can't stand Limies!"

"We're Kiwis," replied one of the New Zealanders.

"Oh that's OK!" said the officer.

"You *Noo* Zealanders are OK. Its just Limies I can't stand."

The New Zealanders looked at each other and nodded in agreement with the American.

"Yea. Too right, mate. Bloody Poms. Shithouses. Aye?"

The officer bought rounds of drinks profusely and they repeatedly toasted the low qualities of the English. The American was obviously about to subside into unconsciousness so they pressed him to a final drink. At last, he slid to the bar floor and they each seized a corner of him and doubled him round to the nearby Ghurka tatooist.

Here they paid for him to have a huge Union Jack permanently emblazoned across his chest, with 'Rule Britannia' inscribed under it, before putting him in a taxi back to his hotel.

"Movement!" my Company Commander hissed sharply into my ear.

"Get some illumination up just in front."

I was rather glad that he wanted that, as it meant that I could show how clever I was.

Firing any sort of shell or mortar round in Vietnam that base ejected[*]

---

[*] A projectile with a time fuse in its nose that, when it descends to its preset height above the ground, blows its' contents and the base plug out of it's rear end.

was a problem. The most usual types of round that do this are smoke – they provide screens for attack or withdrawal – and illumination. These enable one to have a look at the enemy or a suspect area, at night. Albeit, I did hear that during the Second World War, propaganda leaflets were sent to the enemy in this way and sweets to our own troops.

The problem is not with the three dropping chemical smoke generators or the single burning magnesium illumination cannister that will float down on a little parachute, with luck, to the right area: (should the FOO have estimated the wind speed and direction satisfactorily), or even the base plug that will fall vertically to earth.

It is the empty carrier that is the worry, for it must eventually land and, despite the pretty long odds, may strike one of our own troops. The shock of having its insides blown out of its rear end could also cause it to have an erratic flight path. The other safety factor that the FOO had to plan for was the remote possibility that the shell might malfunction and carry on still full and, with its weight and direction unaltered, it would, of course, travel further than an empty carrier.

The in-theatre orders on the matter for field artillery stated that from the point of intended base-ejection there was to be a safe lane (i.e. an area completely clear of friendly troops) extending one thousand metres forward. The safe lane was also to extend for five hundred metres on either side of the point of intended base-ejection. Thus, the shell would base eject at the bottom centre point of a one thousand metre square box. The carrier could then land with impunity anywhere within the box – which was more than large enough to cover any eventuality. Mortar bombs were a little easier as, with their high trajectory and steep angle of descent, they were allowed a half-sized box. However, as there were friends and foes of all sorts milling about everywhere, fitting a box in, in case a smoke or illumination mission was required, was a severe problem.

The most satisfactory situation was to have an artillery unit on call for smoke or illuminating missions that was located behind your force so that their fire would pass over and forward of you. Thus, the safety box would be in an area that you had not yet reached. However, there could still be problems. If the axis of your advance changed then your supporting battery would probably have to be changed as well. Another friendly unit might need to pass across your front at less than one thousand metres distance. Guns firing from in front or from one of your flanks would probably, of course, make your box impossible to fit into an area free of allies. It was a little daily puzzle for the FOOs to struggle with. Sometimes, smoke or illuminating missions were just not possible. However, if there was a greater risk by the lack of a smoke screen or an illuminating mission than by losing a few men from a large dropping bullet, local commanders would sensibly overrule the safety box.

By the end of that afternoon, I had decided to admit defeat. There was just not a fire unit of any sort in any direction – I had them all marked on my map – that could give me a safe box. However, at nearly last light, as we had passed round a hamlet, I had spotted two slightly shabby M2A2 Howitzers in a small compound. Our night's ambush position was about a kilometre and a half forward of them – so what could be better if we suddenly needed to light up the area to our front?

They were owned by either the South Vietnamese Regional or Popular Forces. These were sort of cheerful, scruffy and not very bright militias that defended their home areas. Via a slightly tortuous route of radio relays through various liaison officers, I had also discovered from my signals instructions that they were contactable. They had been the answer to a prayer.

Now that we needed it, I started the process of passing the data for the fire mission through my intermediaries. Despite the fact that the last link in the chain did not speak very good English and the information had to be repeated a few times, the message got to the guns. However, at this point there did follow a rather overly long delay. The troops no doubt had to be got out of pool halls and corrugated iron made bars where they were eating rice covered in rotten fish sauce, drinking Coca Cola and chatting with girls.

"For Chrissake!" the Company Commander hissed urgently. "I can see movement across this clearing. I can hear noise. Get some bloody light above us."

I frantically tried to calm and reassure him. At last a report of 'shot over' was relayed to me. The fire was on its way.

As I had expected, the part-time peasant gunners technical skills were fairly poor and the bright white magnesium light appeared with a 'pop' far off to the left of where we wanted it. One needs to be bold when making connections with illuminations, I remembered from my training, so I gave a 'right eight hundred' that I estimated would bring it overhead and fractionally forward of us – just right.

We actually heard the bang and ring of the gun firing and a few moments later the oscillating whistling sound could be heard approaching over the jungle.

"Right on," I said to the Company Commander.

"Any second now it should pop."

The sound of the shell's flight seemed to be continuing longer than it should have. It also seemed to be getting louder – as though it were descending. Even before I had finished saying uncertainly, "No problem", I realised what had happened.

My pointless scream of,"Take cover!" and the blast of the high explosive shell a few metres to our front were more or less concurrent. Fortunately we had all been lying around and under a camouflaged armoured personnel carrier that was hidden in the jungle's edge, and this protected us from the force. In the dark, some well intentioned, but simple, type had inadvertently loaded the wrong nature of round into the breech.

As soon as the shrapnel finished pinging off the APC, the Company Commander crawled over to where I cowered and whispered of the many disagreeable things that I, and Gunners in general, either resembled or were constructed of. The illuminating mission was abandoned.

There were also problems associated with calling up artillery fire in the Vietnam war that did not crop up in other wars. The usual war has a front line. Thus, you can draw it on your map and probably also put 'us' on one side of the line and 'them' on the other. The front line may ebb and flow but essentially one knows where the 'goodies' and the 'baddies' are. However, the North Vietnamese invaders infiltrated into South Vietnam along the entire length of the country over its Western border, from the Ho Chi Minh trail in the Cambodian jungle, and we were only permitted by our respective governments to fight a uniquely defensive war and so could never move forward into North Vietnam en masse and contain the flow near its source. The enemy were all over the place. In front, behind, to the flanks – everywhere.

Artillery forward observers in most wars have a semi-circular shooting protractor. They lay the straight edge of the protractor along the front line knowing that fire will only be required in the directions indicated by the compass bearings on the round part that points into the enemy's side. Everyone behind the straight edge will be his comrades.

I, and the other allied FOs, of course, had to have completely circular shooting protractors – and very carefully marked maps, as an inadvertant "own goal" was a constant risk. The situation was further compounded, and often desperately needed results delayed, by the requirement to get air and ground clearances before a shell might leave a gun. The FO's location and the direction and location of his desired target were sent by radio, via several headquarters, to someone in Saigon who had a set of current aircraft flight schedules and a map with all known friendly troops positions marked on it. He would not give you an air clearance if there was the slightest evidence of a military aircraft near you; even though the chances of hitting it were about as probable as you hitting a bird by randomly firing an airgun into the sky with your eyes shut. He would also not give an air clearance if a Pan Am flight was likely to be traversing SE Asia. However, as that would be at about fifty thousand feet, and the highest point on the trajectory that any allied gun would reach was about six thousand feet, this would also surely not have been a problem.

Ground clearances were rather quicker – but waiting for air and ground clearances, so that artillery might fire and halt the assault of a superior enemy force, proved a fatal experience for some.

Her Majesty's Vietnam soldiers came in all guises. There were her standard Australasian ones, of course, and the renegade mainland Britons in the two ANZAC armies. Others also had them to an extent.

"Do you think it will be alright if me cousin comes over on to our gun position for a chat, Sir?"

A teenage New Zealand Gunner, with a strong Manchester accent, asked me one day on the Nui Dat fire base. He probably asked me because I was the nearest officer to his gun detachment.

"I ain't seen 'im fer years" he went on.

"We was just kids then. 'is 175 battery's deployed on the base for a couple of days. I couldn't believe me bloody eyes when 'ee shouted down at me this morning from the back of 'is gun as it went lumberin past. I 'ad no idea 'ee was 'ere."

He then outlined the situation for me. His parents had emigrated to New Zealand with him a few years earlier and he had been called up for National Service. He had volunteered to go overseas and had been sent to Vietnam. His slightly older cousin from the same little Mancunian street, had emigrated to the United States of America recently, had also been called up (or drafted, in local terms), had been sent to Vietnam and now – amazingly – here they were.

The cause was, of course, so deserving that I quickly got on the field telephone and requested of an American Officer that their Gunner be allowed to come over and visit ours for a short while. The officer was the usual jovial and generous hearted representative of his country and immediately agreed.

Less than ten minutes later, a typical GI walked onto our battery position: a baggy jungle green uniform covered in formation badges, a baseball style cap and a beaming smile. Typical that was until he spoke – and there, apart from the odd American expression, was the same Manchester accent of his Kiwi cousin, unchanged by exposure to the North American drawl. I showed them into our officers' briefing shelter and got them some cans of fizzy drink. There they sat for several hours during a burning tropical afternoon. One could see them laughing and rocking back and forth on their ammunition box seats as, in uniforms of other countries and in a remote war, they chatted, gossiped, reminisced and swapped news in an ever thickening dialect, of family and friends in a Coronation Street so far away.

I hurried away from them and made myself busy down on the gun line shortly after their first delighted greetings, as their detailed talk of their particular part of England somehow brought the still tree lined waters of the Mole, by Hampton Court, back a bit too close to me for comfort.

"Go!" I screamed to the signaller, trying to be heard above the brain damaging, pounding racket of the helicopter side gunners' thirty calibre machine guns and the rippling fire of the infantry small arms from within throbbing and screaming machines that, for the moment, twitched agitatedly on the floor of the clearing.

We were in a hot extraction situation. That is to say, we had discovered that we had bitten off more than we could chew and, rather than become a stirring military legend, had decided to survive for a luckier day and get out by the fastest means, i.e. helicopters. The last of the company had scrambled on board wherever they could find space and that left only my Signaller and I as the rear guard and last.

I doubt that he heard my voice. However, as his anxious face that peeped out of the long and broad-bladed grass beneath the fallen branches, had been regularly returning from watching the jungle at our rear to look at me, he obviously saw the movement of my mouth. The Iroquois were rising from the ground in a great noisy swarm like blow flies out of the grass just after dawn.

Despite his heavy pack, he sprang nimbly to his feet and sprinted in a semi-crouching position across the clearing towards the side of the last earth-bound helicopter. I waited the agonising period until he seemed to be about ten metres away and then tore forward myself. I deliberately did not think about the lead that must have been pursuing us.

It is, of course, always a point of honour that the commander is the last to leave a dangerous situation (e.g. Captains of sinking ships). However, it was far more important to us that our company commander had control of the situation at our next location, so he would usually be one of the first to be air lifted out of somewhere. That left the artillery FO, as the effective field second-in-command, the 'noble' bit of seeing everyone else safely off.

The Gunner signaller had dived into the mass of dirty green bodies. The helicopter started to rise.

"Come on, Sir!" roared impatient voices, as if my frantic sprint needed any encouragement.

The floor of the open-sided helicopter was now beyond my reach and soon the skids would be too.

Arms reached down for me and, as I clamped hands and forearms with the nearest, the helicopter shot into the air – then bucked, lurched, spun and with a nauseous movement and made a sudden change of direction to deceive ground fire. It was called a stall turn.

Other hands had grabbed portions of my pack, webbing and available person. Albeit I still hung suspended over the jungle that was dropping into the distance below me. It could have been a moment to discover if one was considered a tolerable officer.

They pulled me up and dragged me into their mass. There was a tiny little ledge of floor left for my behind and so, I was only kept on board by the loyal hands that held onto the webbing straps on the rear of my shoulders. With my knuckles showing white as I gripped the outside edge of the floor on either side of my thighs, we hammered back to Nui Dat.

When the helicopter banked one way, it was as though I was hung over an open trap door far above the earth; when it went the other way, I seemed to be falling backwards off a narrow metal wall high in the sky. It was not a situation that I ever became easy with.

Events like this would also remind me again of how distant are the two professions of peacetime and wartime soldiering. Helicopter emplacement drills before going to the war had been a reasonably agreeable and safe experience.

A body of men, with their Officer at the front, would be waiting by the edge of the landing zone. All would be kneeling on one knee in neat rows. Everyone's jungle hat, cap or beret would be stuffed down the front of his shirt to stop it being sucked into the rotors.

The Officer would be scanning the skies looking for the helicopter – just as the helicopter pilot would be searching the ground for the troops. The helicopter would land facing the troops, and the ground officer would raise a thumbs up in the direction of the pilot's cabin to show that his men were ready. The pilot would then reply with the same gesture – to show that he was ready too. One half of the troops would then sweep round in a semi-circle and scramble aboard the helicopter from one flank, while the other half did the same on the other side.

There would be a helicopter crewman inside who would act rather like an air hostess: ensuring that everyone was comfortable, had fastened their seat belts and that only the prescribed number of persons were in the helicopter. Once he nodded in approval over everything, those nearest would slide the doors shut and off we would go.

The Iroquois in Vietnam had the seats and crewman taken out and the doors were off. The only furniture left in the interior seemed to be a few bits of webbing strap attached to the rear internal wall. We would pile in and pile in. The first inside would grab a webbing strap with one hand and a portion of a mate's equipment with the other. They in turn would cling onto others. The crouching, kneeling or sitting bodies would be pressed together. When his helicopter resembled a pile of bodies with a rotor striking out of the top, the pilot would take off. Incredibly, I never heard of us dropping anyone during a journey.

The arrival back at Nui Dat after a four, six or eight week operation for an 'R in C' (rest in country) long weekend at the Peter Badcoe VC centre, Vung Tau, was an event much looked forward to, and talked about, during the preceding, frugal, dirty and disturbing weeks.

Chaps would brag about how much drink, food and sex they were going to have. Theoretically, of course, it seemed quite reasonable to suppose that strong, tough and healthy young men who had just spent a longish deprived period away would indeed more than do justice to such things. The eventuality, however, could be very different.

When we first rushed from the chopper pad to our lines, a large water tank full of chunks of ice and hundreds of cans of Australian beer would be waiting for us. The trusty company commander, who had deliberately gone on ahead to get things organised for us, according to what had become a tradition, ensured that there were at least six cans per man – bought from company funds.

Still covered in jungle filth, we would usually down the first can in one. Unfortunately, of course, our sparse interiors had become totally unused to a bulk item such as beer and – although the constant tensions and resulting alertness had made us forget our lack of sleep during the operation – the first relaxing touch of alcohol released our tiredness onto us. The second can was a very slow one. Two was usually my limit. My remaining four cans would be left for someone more resolute than I to commandeer and I would go to my narrow and dust covered plastic base-camp mattress and fall into the soundest of sleeps.

One would be woken up later by enthusiastic comrades, would have a shower – from a suspended water-filled bucket with holes in its bottom – and, in a laundered set of jungle greens and a beret or slouch hat, would head for Vung Tau on the back of an open truck.

Later, one would order an inordinate amount of delicious-looking Indo-Chinese food in a restaurant and only be able to eat a fraction of it. The richness and quantity was just all too much. After the meal, one's body, which seemed to have chosen this moment to complain of the excessive exercise, falls and other abuses that it had recently been subjected to, indicated that the noise and meleé of the bars and "knocking shops" was not for you.

Most would end up sound asleep in front of the old British comedy or Western showing at the base open air cinema by half past nine. The subsequent two nights in Vung Tau would probably not be much different. It seemed such a short interlude before feeling temporarily clean, marginally more relaxed and slightly hung over, one was in the clouds of red dust, and on the truck, heading north again.

I was rather annoyed with the infantryman just in front of me. Not only had he somehow contrived it that his body was flung sideways, like a rag doll, but also that his head was messily disintegrating, in a mass of blood and grey matter, as he flew. My reaction, during that split second, was probably caused by the natural tendency to be initially irritated when something unexpected happens. The infantryman could not, of course, have been blamed for anything as he had just been hit in the head by a communist anti-aircraft round being fired in the ground to ground role.

For a moment or two longer, I watched stupified as his body thumped down into the dead leaves and plant stems. I then became suddenly aware that the jungle all around had been shaking with the roar of every kind of weapon for about the last three seconds.

I was standing gaping beside a track with my pack half pulled on. We had just had one of our short LOGSTAT and SITREP sending and quick tea brew up stops and had been about to move on. The Company Sergeant Major's signaller, who moved just behind me had spotted a faint, but recently used track that crossed ours. The Company Commander had recalled the point platoon. They had just filed past us, the Company Headquarters, down the newly discovered path; we had just been 'saddling up' and on the point of following them, when it had all happened.

It is the most disadvantageous tactical situation that can befall a military unit. It is a soldier's worst fear. It is ambush.

We were later to discover that we had been ambushed by North Vietnamese regiment D445, a three battalion group that outnumbered us at least twelve to one. They had initiated it with the anti-aircraft machine gun that fired rounds with exploding warheads. This had ripped through our point platoon and instantly killed and maimed sufficient to remove the platoon from the Company's strength. The enemy also had a support weapons company and soon mortar bombs and rockets were exploding about us and amongst us.

There is little hope when well and truly caught in an ambush, as we were, especially when the ambushers outnumber the ambushees so overwhelmingly. The only chance is instant and unthinking, but co-ordinated, action – a Berzerker charge at the enemy's heart, a desperate bid to take the initiative and hope that the shock may deter him or even turn his prepared attack straight round into yours. However, the odds on your success are not good. It is for this reason that anti-ambush immediate

171

action drills must be one of a military unit's most practised pre-theatre exercises.

Our gallant Company Commander quickly led us in a curving sweep round towards the, at present, unknown-sized enemy's right flank. However, we came under close quarter fire all along our front almost as soon as we started. We about turned to go for the left flank and the same thing soon happened. The full horror now dawned, we were in a "U" shaped ambush.

The Asian communists are the most energetic and innovative of field engineers. They have a number of extremely clever ambush configurations. One example is a sort of spider shape. When a jungle patrol bumps into the end of one of the wiggly legs of entrenchments, the occupants of the body and the other legs rush to reinforce the part being engaged.

We had been lured into the bottom of the "U" by the false track that had been laid for us. The camouflaged entrenchments on the base of the "U" had initiated the attack, while those around the sides had remained silent and hidden. Thus, we had thought that those who had fired on us from the front were all there were. As we had made our right and left flanking attacks respectively, the North vietnamese troops had popped up out of the fortified lines that formed the sides of the "U" and had fired directly into us.

Also, while we floundered around discovering that we were inside a "U", other communist troops crept round and sealed off the open end. We were now trapped inside an "O".

If the terrain had not been jungle, then it is sure that none of us could have lived for more than a few minutes in that killing ground. If it had not been for our available technology in the form of artillery and helicopter gunships then we could not have survived the subsequent repeated and resolute attacks that were made on our defence huddle over the next two and a half days. The jungle will not stop all projectiles, but does at least cause limited vision and prevent some of the aimed fire. The mass of combat power that came from the air fended the enemy off us and went some way towards making up for his superior numbers.

A chronological account of those two and a half days is not possible. They are made up of incidents, scenes and visions.

The North Vietnamese had their backs protected by the wide and steep-sided Song Rai river. They had laid out their position and chosen their moment well.

Lookouts must have seen our column, on the preceding day, file out of the jungle's edge at the top of the long and stoney slope that led down to the river. Invisible to us in the jungle's darkness on the opposite side, they would have watched our extended line come cautiously down the open slope. Then they would have seen the laden troops struggle chest deep across the flow – their weapons, and other damageable bits of kit, held above their heads. As it was nearly last light, they knew that we would harbour as soon as we got into the dense jungle that came down to the water's edge on their side.

The lookouts were, of course, too disciplined to engage us while we were in the open river, despite the tempting target that we must have made. They knew that the fire of a couple of men would only bring down a few of us and would make the rest of us withdraw. A little patience would save us for their main force – and the achievement of a massacre.

That night while we had slept, they had prepared.

Everything had started so inauspiciously for us two days earlier. We had been going to go on 'R in C' to Vung Tau. Then we had had it cancelled – merely postponed for a few days, we had been told – as an Australian battalion, newly arrived in the country, was going on its first operation and would have its confidence boosted by the attachment of a veteran company. This all my company were, except for myself who had not yet even completed half a tour.

We had had to redeploy and make a fast and long forced march – an incautious thing to do in enemy infested jungle – to get to the area where the new battalion was operating. We had been en route when all this had happened. Apart from the leading vehicle of the APC column that had initially given us a lift, being blown up outside Xuyen Moc, things had previously been quiet.

For the earlier part of the battle, I was forward – just behind the point platoon – to see if I could help bring in some artillery fire support. If I craned my neck above my fire position I could see some of our dead distributed around the wretched false track that led towards the enemy. Two of them were signallers, and throughout the entire battle their radio sets kept chatting and crackling. It gave their still forms a sort of uncanny alternative life force.

Suicidally brave North Vietnamese kept individually rushing forward to try and seize a set of our classified signals instructions from the signallers' packs. Our rifleman and machine gunners quickly shot them down. The first one tore at a pack lid. The next one got it open. A few more posthumous heroes later, one got away with them. However, our codes would only be compromised for one day – which was the time it took for the ANZAC headquarters to distribute new ones.

The first outside assistance we received arrived within a few minutes and came in the form of the familiar oscillating whistling sound of the 105 mm shells of our Royal Australian Artillery direct support battery. As we were the biggest battle of the moment, this was quickly followed by all batteries of the ANZAC artillery – which included, of course, the Royal New Zealand Artillery. The little shells would not have caused much harm to the communists in their well constructed entrenchments. However, with any luck, they would be encouraged to stay under cover and discouraged from massing a force to overwhelm us. Each ANZAC howitzer was to fire a round every twenty seconds for long periods. The usual whoops and cheers greeted the shells' arrival.

Soon after the battle had started, the distant and often frustrated ANZAC Brigade headquarters (as Vietnam was the war of the company commander) eagerly took command – rather than leave it to the man on the ground. However, we could take decisions on local detail. The company commander obviously decided his defence layout, could adjust the fire support a little if it was in the wrong place and some of his other suggestions were accepted. Albeit, in general, what we did and what support we got (i.e. the strategy or tactics) was directed from above. It was probable that the company commander would have attempted a break-out. However, it made practical sense to keep us where we were as while we stayed there then the enemy would too. Attrition could then be done to them by our fire support and a large force, including tanks and APCs with heavy machine gun turrets, could be mobilised to encircle the encirclers. All we, the "bait," had to do, therefore, was to try and survive for as long as possible.

Australian Iroquois helicopter gunships were soon mobilised in our support. I had known the Iroquois ever since I had joined the New Zealand Army. It was a fairly sleek-lined tough flying work horse. It had a two-blade rotor that made a distinctive 'whop whop'. I had even heard the gunship version practising on a range near Nui Dat. Its mini-guns made a deep and throaty – almost wind-breaking – roar. However, nothing could have prepared one for having the gunships overhead and giving close support.

They swept in, one after the other as ferocious fire-spitting flying dragons. The volume and intensity of their roar shattered the senses and their flame jets brought death in several forms; 7.62 mm Mini (or Gatling) guns, on pylons extending from their sides, blew out a spiral of bullets at 3,000 rounds a minute. It was said that a single burst could kill every person on an area the size of a football pitch. The evil orange tongues from those furiously spinning barrels flickered out to many metres ahead of the diving gunship. Large trees were stripped to the trunk in a second, small ones disappeared; the earth looked instantly as if it had been finely hoed and any humans it caught were transformed to chewed meat. The ground shuddered with the weight of metal lashing into it. At the same time came the bang and hiss of pairs of rockets being fired from the pods on either side. Through gaps in the tree canopy, we could see them streaking down into the jungle and hear them add their explosive thunder to the rest of the cacophony on the ground. We threw coloured smoke grenades to mark our position and told the gunships, over the radio, where the enemy were in relation to the smoke that floated up and out of the tree canopy.

After each Iroquois had swept over the North Vietnamese positions, the mini-guns would switch off – but the rat-tat of the side gunners would start up. They fired back down past their aircraft's tail, to try and keep the enemy down in their trenches so that they would not pour heavy machine gun fire after the retreating helicopters.

It cost the Iroguois to help us. Three went down and several others had their side gunners killed.

One, by coincidence, thumped down and buckled its skids right beside my parent New Zealand battery's position. One of its pilots and both of its side gunners were dead. The other pilot, and last member of his crew half climbed, half fell out, vomiting uncontrollably. Another one was hit and dashed itself, and its crew, to pieces on the jungle floor and, by chance, I just happened to look up to a gap in the tree tops in time to see the third give a millisecond lurch before exploding into a bright orange ball of burning aviation fuel. Apparently, this is a fairly difficult thing for it to do as its fuel tanks are self sealing. The Achilles heel is the linking pipe between the two tanks and the million to one unlucky chance had happened. A burning tracer round had gone through it and initiated the near-instant sequence that would ignite all the fuel.

Helicopter side gunners, as a community, were often types that one could resent upon first encountering them. They seemed rather casual to their foot soldier passengers and each night they had a meal on a plate, some cans of beer and a cot with the in-theatre pale green sheets and pillow cases on it. They would see the jungle's distant beauty and not encounter its close quarter hostile environment. Occasionally they might have to give a defensive burst, take a pot shot or give infantrymen some pre-attack fire.

However, once one knew of the odds against them surviving their first major battle, respect started to form. Hanging out into the sky in their harnesses, on both sides of the helicopter and with their long protruding machine gun barrels, they made an obvious focal point for enemy ground to air fire. Their flak jackets, which are designed to deflect a bullet fired horizontally, deflected those hitting them from below upwards and under their jawbones.

Helicopters would sometimes return to base apparently unscathed. However, dead side gunners would be discovered strapped in their seats and with the tops of their fibreglass helmets blown open and their grey matter spattered across the ceiling.

Finally, one wondered how they got men to do the job and expose their bodies as targets in the bright open sky.

The small Sioux scout helicopter containing the CO of the battalion, that we had been deployed to assist, was also shot down. It made a slightly hard, but safe, forced landing, and the CO was wounded in one hand.

There were a few very brief unsympathetic murmurings from one or two of our company when this last bit of news was received – as it was, unjustly, felt that without he and his battalion we might not have been in our present state.

"Hey! This is Uniform Sierra One-Six. Can we play too?" boomed out a jovial American voice on my gun net.

I wondered who they could be and started looking up their callsign in my signals instructions. While I was doing this, the voice of an artillery officer on the Brigade Staff crackled out.

"Roger, Uniform Sierra One-Six. Your help would be much appreciated. Do you want co-ordinates? Over."

"No that's OK, buddy," came the reply.

"We been listening in. We gocha. Out."

Cobras! I found them in the list. A man-made flying machine that moved like an aerial shark. I had heard of them and thought that I had glimpsed them from afar. However, they did not normally operate in Phuoc Tuy province – as they were American.

The Iroquois was a transporter converted into an attacker. However, the Cobra was a custom built killer. It was the very latest and could have no other purpose. It was narrow, slim and fast. It manoeuvred more like a winged jet than a helicopter. Its array of weaponry was terrifying. In addition to carrying more mini-guns, chain guns and rocket pods than the Iroquois, it also had a 20 millimetre Vulcan gun in a chin turret. This could pour out warheads as big as a man's thumb at a rate of 6,000 a minute. The 7.62 mini-gun has its many barrels enclosed in a metal cylinder. The Vulcan gun is much bigger and its exposed barrels resemble the banded canes that formed part of the symbol of office for the Fascist officials of ancient Rome.

The Iroquois had attacked in single file. The Cobra regiment came in in lines of six abreast. For both friend and foe on the ground it was as though the world was about to end – just on the noise alone. Two giant timber mill saws suddenly exploded into life right up against both of your ears at once. However, just as overwhelming as the sound was the concussing power and energy that filled the sky and made the ground convulse.

The enemy had put thick earth roofs on their entrenchments against such an eventuality. However, they must have felt as if they were being shaken up in a box.

After what seemed like rather a long period of attack by the various gunships – which in fact may not have been particularly long at all – it was decided that heavy artillery might penetrate further into the North Vietnamese fortifications and be a better deterrant in the circumstances. We were finally believed when we said that the chopper gunships were now, for the most part, merely turning over the topsoil and adding an inordinate quantity of metal to it, albeit they were encouraging the enemy to remain underground.

An airstrike was discussed on the net by some distant architect of our fate. One voice said:

"What say we crisp it*?"

However, as both sides were rather close together on the ground, and even intermingled in some places, it was decided against.

United States 175 mm guns and eight inch howitzers opened up in our support. They lobbed shells that were roughly the diameter of the average waste paper basket and about the length of a man's leg over distances of nearly thirty kilometres.

In contrast with the little high pitched undulating song of the 105 mm rounds, the heavy shells sounded to us like superfast express trains – on their final descent. The ground under our feet jolted with each impact and lethal shrapnel ripped for many hundreds of metres through the branches and leaves.

Thai 55mm guns also started firing in our support and so, when one considers that there was the possibility of Chinese and Eastern European "advisors" with the NVA, our little rifle company had inadvertently provided quite a multi-national occasion.

Oddly enough, incidents that were even slightly humourous, in retrospect, arose during the course of the battle.

One of our very young National Servicemen was reconnoitreing a little forward of his section's area. He entered a small clearing just as an equally young NVA counterpart – probably engaged on a similar task – emerged from the jungle on the other side. Both immediately darted forward to the only cover in the clearing which was a large fallen tree trunk. They both peeped over the top of the tree trunk a few moments later, looked into each others' eyes and ducked down again.

They both then stayed prone and petrified on their respective sides of the large log for some time. Each was concerned that if he attempted to pop up and shoot the other, he might be the slower or less accurate of the

---

* Drop napalm.

two. Finally, apparently, and with the same near perfect sychronisation, they both crawled warily backwards and, as soon as they reached the jungle's cover on their respective edges, sprang up and darted back into the comforting fold of their friends.

There was also heroism too. There was not only that of the incredibly brave North Vietnamese who seemed prepared to lay down their lives in a moment for their rulers, but also that of a number of ANZACs.

The young Australian Second Lieutenant who commanded the decimated point platoon gathered his remnants about him and, despite the weight of machine gun, rifle, rocket and mortar fire, pouring onto his position, made a stoic stand – even though it must have seemed that they were doomed. He was subsequently awarded a Military Cross.

A Military Medal was won by a great, lumbering, oafish and bear-like section machine gunner. The very sight of him was always as a red rag to the CSM's orderly military mind. He had, as usual, been operating under open arrest for some offence or other – pending formal disciplinary action when we returned to Nui Dat.

At one point in the conflict, he unexpectedly made a lone charge at the enemy's heart. Firing his cumbersome machine gun from the hip, in a style later to be emulated by the ficticious 'Rambo', he mowed down the occupants of several NVA trenches, took out a group of neatly tailored and red star cap wearing enemy officers, whom we had heard screaming orders above the din of battle, and jogged unscathed back into our lines.

Dedicated and loyal helicopter pilots constantly descended into the murderous ground battle to gather up our wounded and transport them away to be cared for. It made no difference that we warned them over the radio of the perils and that we were unable to offer any of hope of ground security. In they came, again and again – although their aircraft were riddled with bullet holes and their medics and crew members fell wounded. By a total miracle they suffered no complete losses.

For two and a half days we drew our defensive deployment ever tighter – while sending out section sized patrols to creep forward and see what might be next in store for us. For two and a half days, the several dozen large and small calibre guns that strove to support us each fired a round every twenty seconds. For two and a half days the 'tango alphas' (tanks and APCs) tried to get at the enemy from the rear, found river banks that were too perpendicular to traverse and tried again elsewhere. For two and a half days the relief force inched towards us, despite the increasing casualties their forward elements took. For two and a half days we lay in our fire positions on the damp earth and fought. Occasionally, our heads fell forward and we even got a few moments of exhausted sleep – despite the roaring and shuddering world about us.

At times it seemed as though it was not a battle between mortals that went on, but one between great nebulous monsters of violent deafening sounds, blasts, shockwaves, fire and flying steel, who bellowed, rampaged ripped and stomped through a great area of jungle.

Gradually our technology took effect. The enemy was slowly about turned onto the defensive and finally pushed into a retreat.

Despite its efforts, our armoured force did not manage to block their escape and D445 Regiment began to melt away, in an orderly manner, down the precipitous banks of the Song Rai and along its mud beaches and shallow edges. They left an ever diminishing, and ever more bravely constituted, holding party to give the impression that their position was still occupied.

Our patrols started to report that there seemed to be less and less of the enemy and, finally, that they seemed to be gone. The noise of battle ceased and was replaced by a ringing silence. Some people seemed to be immediately cheerful and relieved, others remained silent and brooding.

I had not really had any personal close shaves and so fell into the former category. Once I had ascertained that there was no further risk to my person if I stood upright, I strolled back towards the centre of the Company Headquarters. I was feeling quite peckish. During the preceding two and a half days, I had had to live off the packets of biscuits and little tins of fruit cake that I had scattered throughout my jungle green uniform's many pockets – in case of emergencies – and a large tin of North Vietnamese condensed milk that I had looted from a previous contact.

For the first time, I had left most of my kit behind and had crawled forward with little more than my shooting map, protractor, compass, rifle and some ammunition.

When I arrived back at the Company Headquarters position – which was now a sunny clearing, as the passing fire had swept away quite a lot of the foliage – Gunner Nikora, the New Zealand artillery signaller, was hosting some infantry colleagues with the contents of my pack.

"I thought you were dead, Sir," he said in a cheerful, though slightly disappointed, manner. The others smiled pleasantly through mouthfuls of my sausages in baked beans and my pineapple slices.

Gunner Nikora was one of the coolest and most efficient battlefield operators I ever encountered, albeit he was a total Dr Jekyll and Mr Hyde in some ways. He would render himself senseless with drink the moment we started a weekend off in Vung Tau. He never saw his bed and was semi-conscious, or unconscious, beside the swimming pool of the Peter Badcoe VC camp for the entire three days. One could fall over him on one's way home at two o'clock in the morning or the afternoon.

I contained my distress over the loss of my favourite tinned food as I had become resigned to the Maori warriors' philosophy of community ownership of military items. However, what absolutely incensed me was the fact that the steaming brew that they sipped appreciatively from their tin mugs was made with my best mail-order London tea bags.

I strode imperiously forward to speak, but was distracted before I could start by a great growing pounding in the sky as a huge flock of transporter Iroguois (nicknamed 'dust-off') approached to airlift out our dead and living. The wounded had been gathered up ('casevaced') as soon as possible after they were hit. The helicopter ensured during the Vietnam war that, for the most part, only those shot dead instantly, or those who could never recover, became fatalities. Wounded were moved to a field hospital – with facilities as good as a municipality – within an average time of twenty minutes. Without 'casevac' by brave 'dust-off', it is worrying to think how many times greater the toll of dead would have been.

As our different elements converged from various parts of the surrounding jungle onto a clearing to be picked up, the full realities of what we had just been through dawned. There were the bagged bodies being laid out in a neat line and in the sunshine I saw clearly the utterly wearied and haggard faces of my companions. I started to feel slightly serious.

The helicopters rose up in sequence from the clearing and the route back to base took them directly over the scene of the battle. Clutching onto each other's webbing straps with one hand and our rifles with the other, all of us in my helicopter shuffled on our knees across our aircraft's floor to get as near as we dared to the edges and peered down.

The North Vietnamese and ourselves had together made a sort of great oval volcano crater in the undulating tree-top landscape. It extended vertically down to the earth some forty feet below the highest branches and marked the eye of the conflict.

The first impression of the crater floor was of a clearing newly made by forestry workers. They had sawn the trees down, in a single and quite clearly defined area but had not got around to trimming them and laying them out neatly. However, a closer inspection quickly removed this image. Instead of being cleanly severed logs, the wood had been wrenched out by the roots, ripped, peeled back, snapped and torn again and again in every way. The normally dead leaf covered jungle floor was raw-looking red earth – cratered and crazily ploughed.

As we flew directly over the clearing – which probably had a diameter of a hundred metres at its widest part – the horror of it all could be seen graphically laid out.

There were great blackened parts and some fires still burning. It was a horrible, deformed, obscene, frightening and disgusting area. If the Angel of Death had an appropriate-looking home above ground, then this was it.

The details of the dead could not really be seen from our height and, anyway, the NVA always carried off their intact dead, if they could, and ours were travelling with our helicopter fleet, either inside or on external stretchers. However, we already knew from our patrols what sights were to be seen on the ground: great stains – where a whole body's worth of blood had soaked into the earth, torn rags of flesh, severed hands, limbs and heads, bits of scalp stuck to branches and a human torso that was like a raised painting on one of the tree trunks.

I was awed and ashamed of the extent to which man could abuse and violate nature.

I looked around at my companions – mostly Australians of whom I was so often condemning because of their frequent nationalistic masculine auto-propaganda: the men of all other nations were 'a load of pooftahs'.

The hands that we had clamped onto each others webbing shoulder straps were not only to stop any of us falling out of the helicopter. It would never have been spoken of, but we needed the physical comfort of each other.

The youthful, burly, foul-mouthed, hard-drinking and bar-brawling Sergeant of the point platoon gently held the pale face of one of his young soldiers against his barrel chest. The teenager had clearly been subjected to a concentration of experiences that would not have been fair on anyone.

I remember that I suddenly found that my chin was on my chest and my fist was against my eye. I was about to become exceptionally 'unofficer-like.'

"Hey! Did you hear about Valkendorff's Signaller?" Nick, with whom I had been reunited, suddenly chirped up. Valkendorff had been an FO with the relief force.

"After the fighting was over, he took his hat off and found that a bullet had gone clean through it. He hadn't noticed it happen! Well anyway – by the positions of the holes, it should have gone through his head – but there isn't a mark on him! Poor old Pyle is terribly worried, of course, and keeps asking people if he's alright."

We all visualised the lumbering and guileless Gunner Pyle concernedly sticking his finger through the entry hole in his jungle green hat and wriggling it, then doing the same with the exit hole and then again anxiously feeling his forehead.

It was too much – with indescribable relief, we all burst out laughing. Then, with the lightness of youth, we started chatting away about the tremendous things that we were going to do in Vung Tau over the next few days. And our noisy swarm of helicopters pounded away towards Nui Dat over the rolling hills and valleys of the fluffy green tree-top jungle canopy.

Our battle was not much of a battle compared to others in history. Neither was it much of a battle by Vietnam standards. It did not even bear comparison with the big ANZAC battles of Lon Tan or Binh Ba. However, it was by no means an insignificant event to those who were present at it.

I understand that at one time it used to be briefly studied by the Australian Staff College – although whether we were held up as an example of how to get things right or wrong I cannot imagine.

It is slightly irritating when old men say how easy Vietnam must have been compared with the 'last war'. When they say 'last war', of course they mean the one that took place between 1939 and 1945. However, as even I, during my fairly short period of working with the military, have attended four wars and there have been others that I missed, I wonder why, therefore, it is always the 'last war' to so many – just because it covered a greater area.

Does it really make a great deal of difference to an individual in combat if others are concurrently fighting in the next valley or county or – in the case of a world war – in other countries and on other continents? It seems to me that the concerns of any person in any war – irrespective of how much of the world's area it covers geographically – are basically the same. That is to say, he must strive to complete his localised mission knowing that he is in mortal danger from any enemy weapons that he is in range of. Most limited wars are often fought in remote and difficult terrain for local and highly emotional reasons and can be very personalised and bloody.

Not all of the ANZAC battles in Phuoc Tuy province were out in the countryside. Some of the Fire Support and Patrol Bases were subjected to ferocious and terrifying mass attack in the traditional Asian communist 'human wave' or 'pile on' style – so familiar to Korea War veterans.

At an Australian base one night they just managed to prevent their garrison falling to a vast and resolute enemy attack. At the worst point in the battle, the NVA broke through the defence work – killed the detachment of a howitzer and occupied the gun pit. When the enemy tried to drag the gun away, the other howitzers had to fire 'fleshette' (or splintex) rounds – so called because they fire thousands of perfectly formed little metal darts in a gigantic shotgun-like blast – into their friends' pit knowing that as well as blasting the NVA away, they might be killing their own wounded. Then, so legend has it, Gunners spontaneously rushed forward and, with their shovels and gun spikes, fought a merciless hand to hand battle. Apparently, there was even a sort of tug-of-war with opposing sides on different ends of the howitzer.

Finally, the Gunners of The Royal Australian Artillery prevailed and got their gun back into the fold of their reduced perimeter.

A New Zealand base also had a long night of unrelenting battle. As was often the case, the attack commenced with suicides (either knowing or unknowing). Some acted as human Bangalore Torpedoes (or barbed wire clearers). They had satchel charges (i.e. a pack full of explosive) on their backs that had a mercury detonator. Thus, as they dived head long into the masses of defensive barbed dannert wire, the phial of mercury changed from the vertical to the horizontal, the liquid metal flowed to make an electrical connection and set off the explosion. If they were not shot down or prematurely blown up as they charged, the sacrifice of their life might well make a gap for their friends to pour through.

Others worked in teams of two. The front man held a ball-bearing firing Claymore mine out in front of him and his companion ran behind him, on the end of the mine's electrical wire, with the battery and its triggering device. If they reached the edge of our defences, the mine would be fired. It might well kill defenders in the forward trenches. However, the back blast would also take off the heads and upper torsos of the operators. Concurrent with this activity, and after it, many humans were hurled at the base and mortar bombs rained down.

Regardless of whether or not they have any religious feelings, most East Asians have a fatalistic outlook. It probably happens because of the direct or indirect influence of Buddhism in their lives. This belief that one should submit to all that happens as inevitable must be very useful to communists once they get hold of a nation. It leads on rather well into their philosophy that the individual is without importance, so long as he or she is your subordinate, of course.

In addition to the fact that everyone, including the hierarchy, man their local defence trenches when a base comes under attack, there is also quite a bit of decentralisation of command. This is, of course, essential as no single person can physically see what is happening along his entire perimeter and accordingly decide what to do about it. The infantry lines divide into sectors with sector commanders. Artillery Gun Sergeants take control, but not command, of their guns for firing local defence types of artillery rounds, over open sights, in their particular gun's local defence arc.

At all times, each gun would have had some 'fleshette' rounds made ready and kept in a special place beside the gun for the emergency of local attack. The 'fleshette' shells can be fused to burst at the barrel's mouth or at any point during a nine hundred metre flight. Thus, if the enemy are on top of you, the former setting is used. However, if you see a FUP (Forming Up Point) at some distance, you can get them with a later setting.

Apparently, when one of the 'fleshette's' little metal darts hits something solid, it is as though you had half knocked a nail in and then bent the protruding end over with your hammer. A New Zealand officer told me that after the battle he saw North Vietnamese nailed to trees – with their rifles nailed to their breast bones.

During that night the Kiwi Gunners fired every fleshette round they had, then they loaded with high explosive, set the fuses to point blank and fired them into the ground just in front – to try and halt the great wall of men that surged constantly at them. Finally, there was not even time to screw the fuses into the shells – so they fired plugged rounds that would not explode like giant bullets through the enemy's ranks.

The New Zealanders' eventual salvation was greatly assisted by an anomaly of fate. One howitzer was actually outside the base's defensive perimeter during the attack. It had been waiting on an external helicopter pad, with its detachment and a pile of ammunition to be redeployed elsewhere.

Once battle started they considered that, in their totally exposed and unprotected position, extermination was probably fairly imminent – but they might as well fill in the waiting period as usefully as possible.

Their location meant that they were on the charging enemy's flank and so had them in enfilade. Their rounds, therefore, did terrible execution as they sawed through the attackers length from the side. Astoundingly, they were paid no heed and came through intact. It was subsequently realised what had happened.

The NVA and VC were fairly well off for brave and enduring functionaries – who were clever at local innovation and had plenty of animal cunning. However, their shortfall was in officers trained and able to take a more general overview of a situation and produce larger scale tactical plans.

They had, therefore, formed an elite group of Reconnaissance Officers who, with a few bodyguards, would creep up to allied installations, have a good look at them and then produce a tactical plan to defeat it, e.g. weak points, the qualities of the defending troops, best axis of main attack, covered approaches, etc. The Reconnaissance Officers were, of course, too valuable to risk losing with the attack, so, while they moved on to reconnoitre something else, their plans, all written out in detail, would be handed to a field commander who knew that he must obey it to the letter. The plans were inevitably quite brilliant and had every chance of success. However, they were not able to make allowance for an unexpected change of local circumstances between the reconnaissance and the attack. Thus, if an attack plan did not say, for example, that there would be a lone and unprotected gun on a flank and explain how, and at what point, it was to be destroyed, then most likely nothing would be done about it.

Finally, the intrepid communist field commander realised that his casualties were at an impractical rate and, as the dawn came up, the enemy melted away.

The kilometre deep cleared zone that surrounded the New Zealand base was so piled with dead that a bulldozer was flown in beneath a helicopter to tidy them up and bury them.

It had been a notable battle of the current twenty-four hour period and General Westmoreland himself came to visit his New Zealanders. It is said that the tall, distinguished and pensive man with the deep-set eyes and green baseball cap looked out upon the butchery and said quietly and sadly to no one in particular:

"Say. What happened here?"

It is also said that a nearby Maori Gunner – who was carrying out routine daily maintenance tasks on his gun – looked up in surprise and replied:

"All these fellas turned up last night – took one look at us and dropped dead! Aye?"

The end of my chances to make a contribution to the further defence of the people of Phuoc Tuy province came like a bolt out of the blue one day.

It was a misty jungle dawn. I walked over to join my Royal Australian Regiment company commander, and noticed that he was listening to his transistor – via its ear plug – and grinning.

"Hey! You're going home!"

It was true. All allied governments were trying to hand the war back to the South Vietnamese and were scaling down their contributions. The New Zealand gun battery – to which I belonged – was one of those chosen. We were to go the next month. The enemy activity was not lessening, so those Units remaining would be even more overworked. However, there were political principles at stake and pacifist voters to be placated apparently.

I was amazed. I had never realised that soldiers actually engaged in combat might be plucked out to be sent to unproductive home peacetime duties. It had never occurred to me that once one was in a war, it might be difficult to remain there.

Perhaps it was only luck that the Duke of Wellington did not suddenly have all his Grenadiers withdrawn from Waterloo because they were needed for public duties in London. Could batallions about to go over the top on the Somme have been in constant risk of being told to about turn, run out of the other side of the trench and go home – as they were to star in the Aldershot tattoo?

It was the damp squib to end them all. And my tour was nowhere near over. I did not want to be different from my companions. However, that was it.

We held a farewell parade and General Big Minh was our guest of honour. I thought he had an untypical Asian personality as he was loud, bluff and hearty. He could almost have been one of us. We also knew that he was not self-seeking and corrupt like so many of his high-ranking countrymen who, by their behaviour helped to undermine the chances of the vision, that so many had for the future of the South, from coming true. His name should also be a byword for loyalty and courage for when, over five and a half years later the North Vietnamese burst into Saigon and most of the ruling set fled overseas; Big Minh was there, almost alone, to face communist harshness and to share the police state of their occupation with his countrymen and women. We culminated the parade by singing for him a sort of all ranks male voice choir version of *Now is the hour when we must say goodbye* in both Maori and English.

Back at RNZAF Whenuapai, a politician was waiting to delay re-unions with loved ones while he made a speech to us. However, his back was towards us and his face was towards the TV cameras.

A few days later, to the stirring strains of the Band of the Royal New Zealand Artillery, in 'lemon-squeezers' and jungle greens, the Battery marched down Queen Street in Auckland, towing their guns, as the municipality had invited us to do. There were a few very noisy and derelict-looking demonstrators. They were highly unpopular with the lunchtime crowds.

One officer observer told me that he saw an Old Soldier fight one of the greatest battles of his life – and lose. The businessman was standing at attention as the guns passed. Unfortunately, however, the shouting group of protesters had formed up just in front of him. Directly before him there leaped up and down the most vociferous and scruffiest of the gang. His bushy beard and mane of hair were filthy and matted and he screamed out obscenities, untruths and impossible accusations.

The grey-suited and regimental-tied figure's struggle to remain a model citizen was, by all accounts, very noble. But, finally, he could take no more and furiously blatted the offending object to the ground with his brolly.

Gunners later told me that they were quite moved by the hysteria of many of the hippy girls. Their desperate emotion seemed to show that they needed the cause, or a cause, more than it needed them. Perhaps they had been misused, rejected and unloved and a cause brought back a purpose and dignity that the false gods of lax lifestyle had taken from them.

It was just as well that the police managed to keep the demonstrators off the guns and just as well that no-one watching the parade knew what the Gunners had sworn amongst themselves to do to demonstrators who did touch their near holy objects.

Following the parade, the Mayor and civic dignitaries of the greatest South Pacific city held a reception with drinks and canapes for all ranks – and dear Betty May was there.

It was said that Betty May had lost someone special to her in the Korea war. She had subsequently lived a single life in her home in Levin and, when her beloved Gunners set sail a decade later to Vietnam, she lavished the love that she had in abundance and the means – of which she had rather less – upon every one of them.

Each of the many hundreds of men who must have been cycled through the Battery, during the eight years that it served the war, received at least one letter. Many also received presents. She sent us collective things – newspaper cuttings from country papers, objects and memorabilia – things that would keep us in touch with our heritage at home, familiar and mundane things that brought comfort, reassurance and orientation in an alien environment.

She was an attractive and far from old lady with a delightful – almost theatrical – gushing style of writing and talking. Although her picture had hung on the Mess wall in Vietnam, no one had actually met her before. All ranks pressed about her anxious to pay her homage. However, it was our roughs, toughs and n'ere-do-wells from broken homes, orphanages and brutalized backgrounds who were the most attentive, courteous and gentlest.

I had missed the moment of history that was the parade and the drink, as my last act before leaving Vietnam had been to catch what may have been cholera, but by prompt attention was reduced to a powerful strain of dysentery. I was the only one from the Battery's strength – at the time of the pull-out – to miss the junketings. I was in Papakura camp hospital getting steadily worse.

Despite the fuss being made of her by those to whom she was devoted, Betty May insisted on being taken away early, on to a round journey of about fifty miles, so that she could visit me. She came into my room for a short while, accompanied by some Battery Officers, Warrant Officers and NCOs, and merely exchanged a few lighthearted remarks. Her simple and singleminded goodness radiated from her, and I have never travelled from the doldrums to cheerfulness so rapidly.

I gave cause for some alarm over the next few days as so much essential life-supporting chemical was rapidly exiting from my body. I can remember waking in pain a few times to be told by whichever nurse was sitting with me that a contact was not about to start – it was only wagons being shunted in the railway yard nearby.

Once I was over the crisis, I quickly got better, and the lively Sisters used to act as my fellow conspiritors and assist me to the camp cinema in the evenings when I was not really supposed to go out.

However, any falling in love was sadly nipped in the bud by a posting order to the remote training camp of Waiouru as soon as I was better.

The Battery lived on, but the personnel who had returned from Vietnam with it began to rapidly disperse. The extended National Servicemen started to be discharged. Many of those wishing to serve on were posted and quite a number found home service too dull and left.

There was one very sad phenomenen during the early months after the Battery's return. Almost everyone bought new cars or motorbikes with the money that they had saved while they were away, and quite a number – with the added assistance of such things as roadside telegraph poles – did for themselves what the NVA had failed to.

However, I never heard of any ANZACs either Australian or New Zealand cracking up after the war in the way that we are told some United States veterans did, because the latter had been bowed down by their experiences and could not live with the guilt of killing or whatever.

Perhaps we were helped by the fact that our military heritage was that of the Redcoat: a mixture of hard discipline, maximum preparation and encouragement of the individual in training and fostered, ferocious blood loyalties to regiment and region that produced the unimpressed and matter-of-fact British soldier who made 'thin red line' stands or advanced, as though on a ceremonial parade, into grapeshot. Like those of the British Crown's former wars, Her Majesty's Vietnam Soldiers just came home and quietly got on with something else.

By the time the ANZACs left Phuoc Tuy Province in 1971, one could have walked unarmed through its jungle with your hands in your pockets – whistling. The NVA would harbour in neighbouring provinces that were policed by other armies. Finally, they seemed disinclined to come face to face with men from open countryside who, because of inherited experience and training discipline, could operate as well in a jungle as those born in them.

During the last years of the ANZAC participation in the war, if the enemy sent in a formed force, there was every chance that we could not only defeat it but annihilate it as well. The first reaction of our Force headquarters upon hearing of such an incursion was, no matter how much they outnumbered us by, to get out some cut off to prevent their remnants from escaping out of the province after we had destroyed the main body. It seems probable that our regular contestants – poor old NVA regiment D445 – saw quite a rapid change round of forces as it must have been reinforced again and again.

The British Commonwealth has been in quite a lot of jungle wars in fairly recent times. We had older men in the ANZAC force who had fought against the Japanese in Burma, Papua New Guinea and the Solomon Islands. There were younger men who had served in the Malaya war of the Ffties and many of our rank and file had served in Borneo in the early Sixties. I heard that one year a New Zealand battalion was posted from the Borneo war to Vietnam with an interval back at home – so jungle experience was fairly current. The presence of such men – as well as the invaluable knowledge that they imparted – gave us the privilege of a confidence that could not be so readily available to some of our allies.

A few months after the last combat ANZACs left Phuoc Tuy, the North Vietnamese made their mass conventional invasion of South Vietnam. The ARVN (Army of the Republic of Vietnam) troops, to whom we had returned the province, could not keep the enemy out. They had brave and determined lower ranking officers and soldiers but, with a few notable exceptions, their higher command was incompetent and corrupt and was not worthy of their devotion and endurance. In the end, they were betrayed and deserted by all – from both within their country and from overseas.

A few months after we left, neat and happy hamlets like Dat Do and Ba Ria had been levelled by the advancing NVA and their people had been either killed or had become refugees. The communists took over our bases and their role changed from the defence of the people to their subjugation.

# PART THREE

## THE GREEN BERET AT VINH GIAT

*"It is easy to wage War against a Democracy"*

Ho Chi Minh

The snow, as always, won in the end. It had got into the welts of my boots and melted with the warmth of my feet in sufficient quantities to soak through. At first it was unpleasantly damp but after a while one's feet started to freeze and freeze.

The desultory banging of the National Serviceman on the many small arms ranges, that extended along the side of the valley in front of me, went on and on. As Company Second-in-Command, there was not really a lot for me to do except oversee that all went well and, with a host of well-trained junior and senior NCOs taking care of the details, the super keen newly commissioned Second Lieutenant platoon commanders darting about and (especially) the Company Sergeant Major present, there was little chance that it would not.

Mostly all I needed to do, on such occasions, was to be seen to be casting an eagle eye over everything, walk with dignity and purpose up and down, encourage, pass the time of day and pick up the odd overlooked detail of musketry training here and there.

The snow was getting heavier. It was a good job that the practice that we were firing was to a maximum range of only one hundred metres or the troops would not have been able to see the targets. As it was, I should have to call a halt soon.

I leaned with my walking stick on what I thought was a small hump on the ground – but which in fact was a snowdrift – to sagely study the meteorological trends. As I was climbing out of the snowdrift, recovering my walking stick and quickly checking around to see if anyone had spotted the incident and was laughing, I saw the Company Commander's Landrover ploughing slowly towards us through the bumper-deep snow.

I was not too worried. All was going satisfactorily and correctly and he was an excellent officer and a good friend. Another Gunner and a Korea Veteran, he would creep up on National Servicemens' trenches during defensive exercises and warn unvigilant-looking troops that the *chows*

190

would get them if they were not careful. The Company Sergeant Major would do the same thing, but warn them that the C.T.s (Communist Terrorists – from the Malaya war) would get them, another of our training NCOs would threaten them with 'Indons' – from the Borneo Campaign and I, of course, would go on about the NVA or 'the Cong'.

The bewildered National Servicemen must have thought that, for some unclear reason, any category of Asian might one day attack them somewhere.

Waiouru was a place hated by single Servicemen. Mainly because of its remote location, nearly all-male single population and resultingly limited social possibilities. However, it was quite popular with married personnel. In their case, the remoteness created an excellent community spirit of exchange wining, dining and parties. All the married quarters were in cosy little clutches and had lovely great open fires to huddle in front of when the very changeable alpine climate took a turn for the worse.

On a clear day, the scenery is breathtaking. Bold and interestingly shaped hills, including some with vertical sided upper plateaux on top – that could have inspired Sir Arthur Conan-Doyle's *Lost World*, gradually rise up about the feet of a lone and mighty volcanic mountain. Even in Summer, the crenated ridge of its peak is covered in glacial snow.

Mount Rhuapehu (roughly pronounced Roo-ah-pay-hoo) dominates the centre of the North Island of New Zealand and can be seen from over a hundred miles away in every direction. It is certainly not a sleeping Titan. It has a great boiling sulphurous lake in its blowhole and it frequently fires this into the sky and then showers volcanic ash in depreciation on the minute and lesser entities that presume to live in its proximity.

Its unimaginably vast blood-stream diagram of tunnels, many miles beneath the earth, of super pressured, molten and moving white heat shake the land. Many streams about it are of boiling water and subterranean steam rises from fissures everywhere.

Twenty miles further North, Rhuapehu has a small but more active subordinate – Mount Ngaruahoe (Noo-rah-ho-ee). It too makes an interesting shape in the sky, even though it is the antithesis of Rhuapehu. Rhuapehu is an absorbing treat of irregularity, whereas Ngaruahoe is a vast, and perfectly even sided, conical chimney.

The population is extremely sparse for many miles around and most of the vegetation is the coarse sturdy grass, that clings together in tussocks, and the pine trees of high altitude landscapes.

The altitude and the mountain make their own localised climate. I have been on Summer exercises in Waiouru when chill winds and freezing rain caused hypothermia cases. At the same time, fifty miles away, holidaymakers were overheating on beaches.

191

Waiouru once produced a white Christmas – which is a rather rare event in the Southern Hemisphere.

I can be happy anywhere. However, the unnatural constraints put upon my young life, the fact that my room in the mess was a tiny bare cell and the large numbers of transitees – from camps adjacent to exciting towns – who usually hijacked the bar and the TV set, did tend to make one feel a little underprivileged.

The full-time population of Waiouru camp was constantly swelled by persons coming for courses (most of the Army's training schools were there) or exercises. The vast rugged and empty terrain, of course, is a perfect training area.

My spare time had to be filled by rugby, cross-country running and hanging around the bar even more than I usually did. I passed the New Zealand SAS Selection Course – but there were no vacancies on the Squadron – and a paratrooper course. I did have a few encounters of the thrilling kind. There was the blonde and statuesque sister of a fellow officer's fiancée, a cheekily smiling young lady officer and a very wholesome girl whom I met in the tiny local town's only restaurant. However, they could hardly be called affairs – incidents more likely. Everyone who could, hurried through Waiouru and my seven-days-a-week training job meant that I could only travel away when on leave and I had already guessed that pursuing brief female friendships after a long lapse would be a very bad idea.

Once every few months I had a long weekend off and would usually spend it in either Auckland, Palmerston North or Wellington. However, these tantalising glimpses of the more normal lifestyle of Western world young people tended to have a depressing, rather than restorative, effect. I would see my contemporaries going out in jolly groups of regular friends to pubs, restaurants and parties and having time for proper courtships. I would tour the pubs and restaurants on my own, briefly pass the time of day with the odd stranger, and almost always if I met a nice girl it would be on the evening I had to go back.

On one occasion, I went with my ex-Vietnam infantry friend Harley to a young upper set party in Auckland. All the bright and beautiful of the University and the City were there. However, our visit turned out to be a mistake and we left very early.

All started well and there were so many extremely lovely and beautifully dressed girls. Walking into the main salon was not unlike coming suddenly upon a window box packed with flowers. The men all seemed friendly.

However, because of a brief and incidental remark by either Harley or myself, it suddenly became known that we had served in Vietnam.

Everyone immediately swarmed purposefully about us. Each one of them was anxious to shout the others down in order to tell us the true situation in Vietnam and the criminal activity that we had been accessories to.

"Of course what the South Vietnamese really want . . ." one pubic beard, witch hairstyle and furiously bobbing adam's apple halitosis sufferer started to state directly into my face.

They all spoke of a war of 'goodies' and 'baddies' – rather like the children's books they had given up about a few years earlier or the feature films they saw depicting the second World War.

There were glorious and selfless liberators, on one side – a sort of 'Liberty Marches On' painting – but with Asian features – versus the Nazis, evil for no better reason than they got sadistic enjoyment from being villians, dressed in allied uniforms.

When I managed to get a word in edgeways, I started to explain that there were the sincere, the self-interested and the misguided on both sides. On one side was an immoral regime that left individuals free to make their own choices in life, while on the other was an invader who had started it all and who wanted to include the former, and their rich and fertile country, in their standard communist totalitarian state.

I said that I felt that it was not unreasonable for non-communists to fight back when attacked and we went to their aid as they would do to anyone that they saw being mugged.

It was as absurd as saying that turn-ups on trousers were an inoffensive fashion or that John Lennon and Yoko Ono produced dreary simpleton dirges.

"Shut up you thick, drunken butcher!" A little slender and long golden haired angel-face in a tiny white dress screamed theatrically – her lovely eyes blazing with real, or feigned, hate.

There were shouts of "Well said, Deb!" and "Yeah!" and some cheers from about the room.

I was deeply wounded, as I knew for certain that Harley and I had only two beers in the basement bar of the South Pacific Hotel (known as 'The Snake Pit and where Polynesian girls sometimes put on super impromptu lewd cabarets) en route and definitely no more than one while we were at the party.

Damp and misty Waiouru could drizzle non-stop for weeks on end, which tended to depress the human spirit.

I enjoyed my job. I enjoyed the company of my fellow trainers, and the National Servicemen, and six months passed – rather slowly.

As the Company Commander's landrover drew to a halt, I mistook the twinkle in the eyes of his chilled pink face for a look of piercing anger. Then, when he said brusquely:

"The CO wants to see you," my heart sank – and I tried to think what I could have been found out about.

"You're going back to Vietnam," he added after a pause and broke into a broad rather-you-than-me type of grin.

My smooth and gentlemanly Waiouru CO outlined the background behind my return to Vietnam for me.

After I passed the New Zealand SAS Selection Course, I was told that there would be no Officer vacancies in the SAS Unit for some time to come. I was mortified that I had not been told this before I had embarked on several weeks of enforced malnutrition, sleeplessness and a thousand other types of discomfort and indignity.

I sounded off to my CO and in a few Officers' Mess bars about it and somehow it reached a high ranking ear. Very considerately, therefore, the postings directorate found me an in-lieu special forces post – the United States Special Forces Battalion at Vinh Giat.

Some friends were very worried for me. They said that Vietnam was dissolving into chaos; one would be out on a limb without the support and protection of a large organisation about one, and the chances of getting killed would be high. However, I was even quite cheered by the news. I was qualified for the campaign medals after my first visit – so it was not for any thoughts of some tangible reward. I still had hope that, by some miracle, the South Vietnamese might even be saved from totalitarian takeover. However, I fear that much of the raised spirits that the news brought was the knowledge that I was going to a place where there was definitely a lively and interesting lifestyle and I should be getting away from damp and frugal Waiouru.

I was given a week's leave and then I was to be off. It all happened so quickly. I could not think what to do with my unexpected pre-embarkation leave. However, an advertisement that I noticed in a newspaper gave me an idea: a three day luxury coach trip round some of the most beautiful and unusual natural scenes in the world that, by fortunate coincidence, were all in the central North Island area – Lake Taupo, the Rotorua thermal area and the Waitomo Caves. This way, I thought, I should have a concentrated dose of my beautiful new country and, to an even greater extent than on my first tour to Vietnam, there would be a few appropriate final visions available to flicker before my dimming eyes if I got shot. Each night would be spent in a luxury hotel.

The entire bar population of the wooden colonial style Waiouru Officers' Mess were reduced to helplessness when I mentioned how I planned to spend part of my leave.

"But only old people go on bus tours!" they roared.

"You want to get yourself a motel in Auckland or Wellington," someone said.

"Crawl round the discos. There's more girls than you could shake a stick at."

"No. You've got ten days – if you count weekends," someone else said.

"You've got time to fly to 'Ossie', Go to Bondi. Jeeze, you could root yourself stupid there."

I realised that if I explained the nobility of intention behind the scenic trip, it would be wasted on them.

A few days later, therefore, I walked, with my small weekend bag, along the road out of camp to wait for my bus beside New Zealand's main North South highway – the 'Desert Road' – which passed by a mile or so away. It is called the 'Desert Road' because the great, wide and often empty road tapers away to infinity in either direction between the rolling, dust covered and sparsely grassed hills of a high altitude, near-lunar landscape.

The company had said that they could make a special stop for me – as they passed by Waiouru anyway. All the other passengers would have got on in Wellington. Considering it had travelled nearly two hundred miles (not an excessive journey by Australasian standards) it was remarkably near to the appointed hour.

The coach had been a magnificent, brand new, shining five star affair. It was air conditioned, had soft music playing and was composed almost entirely of panoramic windows – tinted like sunglasses. Its seats were vast and luxurious club-like armchairs. It was full of incredibly jolly people. The process of my getting on the bus and putting my bag on a rack caused welcoming catcalls, whoops and raucous laughter.

It was true that the bus was packed with pensioners. However, the moment that the bus got sufficiently close for the details of the faces at the windows to be seen, I spotted the three attractive girls.

I later discovered that they were an Australian girl, an American girl and an English Girl. They had all met, become friends and joined forces while touring New Zealand. There would probably have been about forty years difference between the next youngest person on the bus and the four of us.

A holiday atmosphere irrevocably set in to our mobile community. My puns, that had rarely produced much reaction in the past, had the bus universally shrieking – and myself seated amongst the girls.

It would have been difficult to have a better three days. The scenery was beyond description and the company was the happiest. We all staggered from place to place clutching our aching sides and wiping our eyes.

My only regret was that it seemed all too brief – and there were only two night stopovers. However, I reasoned that I should probably tend to meet more English girls, than others, in the future.

By an unkind chance, love decided to intervene during my last week before returning to the war. It was not brought about by my meeting with the girls on the bus – for I soon realised that, although they were happy to sample aspects of local life on their travels, their more profound feelings were safely secured away before they left home.

I arrived at Papakura Officers' Mess still entranced by that wonderous bus trip, slightly hungover, pleasantly wearied and with my sports jacket stained with boysenberry pudding (from when I had been pelted while singing for one of my forfeits in the restaurant) to find a note inviting me to a wedding. It was from Harley.

He was inviting all Officers on Station to his wedding on the Saturday and, hearing at the eleventh hour that I was spending the last few days of my pre-overseas leave in Papakura, he kindly left word that I was most welcome.

I was to fly out on the troop plane on the Tuesday morning – so what better way to pass one of my last days in my community than at an occasion of love and hope for the future?

Someone who was driving up from Waiouru, kindly got my ceremonial uniform, accoutrements and medals out of storage and brought them with him. I borrowed a sword and presented myself at the lovely rural colonial chapel just outside Auckland.

Harley's family had served New Zealand well since the early days of European settlement, and fine looking military men of several generations abounded. The ladies all looked stylish and it was a memorable day.

What we could never have ever thought of – as we cheerfully chatted and mingled on that happy sunny afternoon – was that the shy and pretty bride would be suddenly and cruelly taken from her dashing and devoted husband by illness a few years later, when she accompanied him on a posting to Singapore.

I was to hear the terrible news, some months late, while I was serving in yet another war – in Kashmir. I remember that I was borne down with shame, more than grief, that a precious builder should be taken from the community and passing flotsam – such as I – should live on.

Love had cropped up unexpectedly (when does it ever do otherwise?) in the form of Barbara. For some reason I did not see her at the service – but there she was one of the main decorations of the reception. Her hat, dress, gloves, face and body exuded top quality manufacture. She was one of the bride's best friends. The single Officers, of course, swarmed instantly around her. Apart from knowing that such behaviour is uncool – I had no interest in all that. I had insufficient time for romance (so I thought) and the recent memories of the Rotoura and Waitamo hotels, I decided, were quite sufficient for the time being.

I slowly became aware that she was beside me; the others seemed to disappear and we were talking amicably. She was shortly to graduate as a Doctor of Medicine, had a fiance who was a University employee of some sort and occasionally wrote articles for various journals, but alas – their romance was going through a slightly difficult period.

"Well, of course, he is a great intellectual and you know how moody they can be," she said.

I nodded in sad, but silent, agreement. Those vain, snobbish, cloistered, self-opinionated, wing-bagging regurgitators of second-hand views and half-baked philosophies were invariably emotionally indisciplined drips who weakly and selfishly abandoned themselves to any random feeling.

Intelligent girls never usually tolerated me for long. However, the poor bi-ped mammal is, after all, only an animal and even the most thickly fabricated protective cloud of sophistication and metaphysics can unexpectedly evaporate. Fortunately, even intelligent girls can – in spite of themselves – suddenly be overpowered by the vision of the primitive physical nature of the Soldier's profession and the awareness that his body will probably be lean, hard and energetic.

I could not really have been able to divine what the true vacuum in her life was at that time. However, I was able to hold her attention with the simple and superficially alluring pictures that a transient Army lifestyle had encouraged me to learn how to quickly paint.

I used to wonder how women could give themselves to cilvilian males. I supposed that many would never have the chance to know any better.

I stole her and, from that first moment, she stayed constantly with me until it was time for me to set off to the air trooping centre and not even the too many cynical years that have passed can erase the moving memory of the way she clung to me when I had to go and the things she said, and meant – then.

My last week in New Zealand had seemed to have contained rather a lot, so I was happy to rest and dream on the Hercules flight. I even forwent the convention of getting drunk in Alice Springs and going to sleep on the infrequently used railway line or falling into the dry river bed with the mosquitos and the kindly Aboriginal girls.

In the Mess in Singapore, as usual, I listened with a fraction of an ear for a while to the complaints of the garrison officers and their wives about their hedonic life. It was probably that which prompted me to join the determined fun-seekers of my flight down in Bugis Street for our one night on the island.

It is always very convivial down there – sitting and drinking at the pavement tables with Chinese whores, pimps and transvestites – and that night looked like being especially agreeable, as the crews of a combined British Commonwealth and United States fleet were there from a naval exercise.

However, I think I must have been on a higher quality emotional plane than usual – because my heart was just not been in the brawling – so I excused myself from the gauntlet of the flying food, drink and bottles, and the extremely varied propositions, and caught a taxi back to the Mess.

I also had something of a profound shock that evening. A rather genteel and spinsterish WRVS Welfare Sister, of a certain age – whom we met at dinner in the mess – came hurrying out, as we were getting into our taxi, and asked if she might join us.

It would, of course, have been unthinkable to have refused a lady. However, I was uneasy about our intended destination and quietly suggested a few more respectable alternatives to my companions. But before they had time to answer, the WRVS Sister stated that on no account was anything to be changed for her sake as she was just happy to have an outing.

I imagined that the most dramatic type of event in her life previously would probably have been a waitress dropping a scone in the teashop of her English village and was particularly solicitous of her sensitivities. Vainly, I tried to shield her from as many as possible of the Bugis Street extremes of sight and sound.

I was rather touched by the way that, for our sakes, she bravely pretended to be enjoying herself as the scene about us collapsed into lewd and drunken chaos.

Just as I ensured that one of my companions would take care of our lady guest and was making my excuses, a massive British sailor came lurching through the noisy and jostling throng towards our table. He had been debagged by his friends and wore only a short tee-shirt and his shoes and socks. He leaned on our table and, despite his awesome aspect, endeavoured to master his extreme intoxication and politely said:

"Pardon me – but 'ave any of you lot seen my trousers?"

Because of the lady Welfare Sister, my friends and I were struck dumb with horror and gapingly shook our heads.

However, what startled me to my very marrow were her ensuing squeals of girlish delight over a large object that had flopped onto the table cloth beside her ginsling.

The next dawn, we flew in a camouflaged patterned and warlike-looking Bristol Freighter on to our next night's stop at Penanag in Malaya.

A few of the truly dedicated gluttons for punishsment headed for the local bars. However, the other Officers and I spent the very warm, soft and rustling evening on the verendah of the Officers' Mess bar.

I sipped a few drinks and sat hypnotised by seeing again the South East Asian jungle that began just a few metres from where we sat – on the other side of the wire perimeter fence. The CTs – that the Malays and the British Commonwealth had defeated by 1962 – were apparently active again out there. I thought how odd it would be if I got shot because of the wrong war.

Just after we started our final leg to Saigon's Ton San Hut airport, one of the pilots said that I might go forward and look at the view from the great perspex bubble that forms the nose of the Bristol. The pilots fly the aircraft from a sort of upstairs little chamber on the roof. He also gave me a small photocopy of a map with our day's route marked on it. For many hours I lay on the transparent floor watching the beautiful and awesome lands of South East Asia pass below. It was as if I was flying unaided, and the slow and low flying Bristol meant that details of the scenes below could be clearly seen.

Most of it, of course, was the vast jungle sea – secretive, green and undulating and extending to every horizon. However, enthralling sights would appear – like aquatic life unexpectedly popping up on the surface of an empty-seeming ocean; open cultivated areas – a wide river with a colourfully active, but ancient looking Asian small town on its banks, a great isolated temple reaching up above the jungle and sarong-clad people walking up and down its wide steps – a tiny shanty fishing settlement by a coast and the inshore sea speckled with little boats.

We flew North out of Malaya, across portions of Thailand and Cambodia and finally across a corner of the pale blue and shimmering South China Sea. There were tiny crescent shaped atolls and strange isolated pillars of cloud that seemed to be standing on the water.

I moved my finger along the line on the little map and was able to know fairly well where we were at any time. Soon I knew what must appear next. I stared at the front horizon and almost on cue it appeared – a dark coastline that seemed to bar the way ahead.

Even if I was not forewarned by the map of what it was, I could not mistake it. The very first tiny finger of mangrove covered land that we came over had a row of old water-filled bomb craters along it.

Of course, it was Vietnam.

Efficient New Zealand and United States military administrators got us organised at Ton San Hut the moment we stepped out blinking into the searing heat of hot tarmac and the stink of fuel in a thick still atmosphere.

We all doubled after our particular guide beneath the usual pall of oily smoke, and some background exploding noises, to our various in-country shuttle aircraft. Our whole flight consisted of personnel who were on attachments or special duties and so we were split up. We all shook hands, wished each other luck and made a few loud and brave jokes.

The brigand look of the Asian military men who awaited our arrival at Nga Trang again confirmed what I already suspected – that this tour in Vietnam would be rather different in style from the first. I thought the soldiers looked rather darker, rougher featured and stockier than I remembered Vietnamese to be. I was also rather bemused by their black and green patterned camouflaged uniforms, that I had not seen before, and their plain unbadged berets.

Then I realised that they were not ARVN, but Montagnard mercenaries. The Montagnards (and the Mong and Meo peoples) of Indo-China are gypsy-like races who have developed separately to the main populations. They have migratory patterns along the lines of the high ground; they try to avoid others and do not recognise national frontiers. They lead a simple life of hunting for food in the jungle.

Both the French and the Americans had realised that the Montagnards were both tough and loyal – when they had given their word or their chiefs had given it for them – and made good auxiliaries. These wandering races also seem to have encountered a measure of prejudice and persecution throughout the centuries and do not like any of the regular peoples in South East Asia. Therefore, they will unconcernedly shoot anyone for you.

The group in the bare concrete airport reception area looked bright and alert and had the ease and confidence of great familiarity in the way they held their weapons.

There were a couple of round-eyed 'green berets' in charge of the reception committee – squarely built and clean-cut. One was a United States Sergeant and the other was a New Zealand Officer seconded to United States Special Forces – as I was to be.

Outside the airbase was the Jeep convoy that was to take us the ten miles or so to our base – the old Foreign Legion barracks at Vinh Giat. There were more Montagnards in the backs of the vehicles – all armed to the teeth. In addition to American M16 rifles, many had grenade launchers and several of the Jeeps at the front and rear of the convoy were gun-jeeps. They had powerful 30 calibre machine guns on mountings. The amount of weaponry seemed threatrically excessive – until I remembered that the North Vietnamese had made a conventional invasion of the South, during the months that I had been away, with Soviet supplied tanks, artillery and multi-barrelled rocket launchers. We were technically behind their lines, albeit, they had not yet got round to giving our slightly off-the-beaten-track coastal area of operations the benefit of their full attention.

A few miles along the road, we passed through a Vietnamese village market and I caught the scent of Vietnamese life again. I smiled and smiled with pleasure – I could not help it. For some reason, I was so glad to be back. The odour of Vietnam is similar to other parts of South East Asia – yet completely unique. Rotten fish sauces *(nuoc marm)*, pigs, chickens, fruit, veg and humans are part of it – but it remains indescribable.

I was moved – as well as glad. I realised how fond I was of this attractive, naturally courteous, charming, artistic, wily, enduring and sometimes extraordinarily generous race. This time I was not to be just another anonymous member of a foreign allied force – but a trainer and commander of locals. Giving the benefits of whatever I had learned from the opportunities I had had from the best of European military instruction to help them to help themselves. Perhaps this time I really could be useful to these long abused people.

The field fortifications of Vinh Giat were awesome. Stands of criss-crossed nuisance barbed wire started from about a quarter of a mile out all around, then it gradually built up into fences of single dannert (or concertina coils), double, triple and quadruple dannert configurations. A nightmarish razor wire thickened things up here and there, and there were metal piquets, spikes, pungees, claymores and anti-personnel mines buried just beneath the ground under the vast spikey tangle. The barbed wire stopped up against an inner fifteen foot fence.

Just inside the fence were regularly spaced and heavily sandbagged goon towers. Each one had an outer veil of chicken wire arranged at several meters out from its observation cabin. This was to pre-explode rockets fired at the occupants.

The place bristled with weaponry. In addition to the many different types of personal arms than the defenders would have, there were tarpaulin-covered 50 calibre machine guns at close intervals around the circuit of the compound, a few M2A2 105 millimetre howitzers (with the barrels parallel in the 'open sights' role and a neat stock of 'fleshette' rounds beside them) mortar sections and, to help defend the main gate area, were two Gatling mini-guns set up in the ground to ground role.

The camp itself was about one kilometre in length and half a kilometre wide. The architecture of the old single-storey Foreign Legion lines brought an odd touch of the Mediterranean – with their slatted shutters on either side of each unglazed window and the green pantiles on the roofs.

The camp was internally divided up by still more fortifications – so that as each compound fell to the enemy, the survivors could fight on from the next and so on.

We were all on at least our second tour and we knew that it would not keep Asian communists out if they really wanted to take the place. They would get through any defence that we made by overwhelming it with as many lives as were necessary.

Incredibly, brave, skilled and stealthy sappers would secretly make unnoticeable cuts in our wire, so that whole segments could be quickly pulled out and would remove anti-personnel mines during the days or weeks before an attack. They might even somehow slip a few sections into the base to hide until the right moment came during the attack, to burst out in our midst and cause the maximum of chaos and confusion.

The attack would commence with a heavy barrage from mortars, rockets, heavy machine guns and small arms fire – then the human wave pile on would start. They might well have their human bomb men to the fore to blow gaps where wire entanglements could not be dragged away. Human bodies would fall on our wire and flatten it and human bodies would absorb our fire power and keep it off those that followed. Finally the main body would come in through the gap, like a rapier thrust to the heart, over the highway of their stacked friends.

If the Reconnaissance Officer had calculated well it would be over fairly quickly. They would not wish to settle down to a prolonged siege, as this would give time for our bombers, straffers and gunships to arrive.

Once they had taken the base, every surviving defender (Asian and European) would be butchered – with the exception of any American senior officers or American technical specialists who might, respectively, have a propaganda value as prisoners of war or be useful. Albeit we tried to observe the Geneva Convention on the treatment of prisoners, it was a war of no chivalry and little honour. It was unlikely that they would occupy the base once they had defeated it and destroyed the defenders and their equipment, or had taken it for their own use. Upon being satisfied that we had been irrevocably struck off the Allied order of battle, they would evaporate away back into the jungle.

The only thing that would save us would be if the Reconnaissance Officer had under-estimated our fire power or quality and had not massed sufficient men. Once a certain percentage loss was reached, the field commander would call a halt for practical and not humanitarian, reasons, and the communists would make an orderly withdrawal taking their wounded and as many dead as possible with them. They would adjust their plans and get us for certain the next time.

Individual enemy soldiers seemed to be very considerate of their companions. However, their power hungry leaders, Ho Chi Minh, Le

Duan, Phan Van Dong, Vo Nguyen Giap and others, were ruthlessly determined to be men of destiny and history – at anyone's cost, at any price and by any means. What did it matter if it cost three thousand men to kill a garrison of six hundred? All that mattered from a practical and historical point of view was that a victory had occurred and yet another brick had been kicked out from under the enemy that might one day contribute to his fall. Professional communist activists coldly planned for lifetimes ahead, so individual lives had no significance. They also seemed to have plenty of people.

The Vietcong might have been enthusiastic amateurs and mostly volunteers, who on some occasions were a nuisance to their foreign controllers, but on other occasions could be used and sacrificed – as in the 'Tet' offensive. However, membership of the NVA was not voluntary for North Vietnamese young men and women. Draft dodgers and conscientious objectors in the West may have been imprisoned, fined and harrassed, but in North Vietnam they disappeared without trace.

As we were not too far from the sea, the camp floor was composed mainly of sand instead of the usual Vietnamese red dust – that could be like talcum powder when dry and plaster of paris when wet.

My colleagues-to-be were a particularly interesting group: there were about a dozen New Zealand junior officers and SNCOs, who had arrived on secondment to the United States Special Forces' battalion some months before us; the United States officers and SNCOs of the battalion; Vietnamese officers and soldiers, who had the administrative control of the camp; Montagnard Chiefs (roughly Warrant Officer or SNCO equivalents) and the tribesmen paramilitary commandos; a varying number of battalions-under-training of Cambodians, Force Armeé Nationale Khmer (FANK) forces of the Lon Nol government; a Korean military liaison party and a vast collection of Vietnamese cooks, cleaners, housemaids and general duties civilian personnel. It was all very colourful and confusing.

I also quickly learned that it was the Cambodians that we trained and led, rather then the Vietnamese. However, we did take the Cambodians on operations in Vietnam – which would presumably provide some assistance to the local effort – and, using the NVA and VC as a training aid, would help prepare these battalions for their own branch of the war, next door, against the Khmar Rouge.

Uninformed British Commonwealth military often try to incorrectly compare United States Special Forces ('Green Berets') to the SAS. However, they are not really comparable. The USSF are not designed to fight as a formed Unit. Their 'battalion' is only an administrative grouping. They have (or did have) a two-pillar structure of 'A-teams' and

'Spec-Teams'. The former was a command structure to be welded onto the top of friendly local, but not too well trained, indigenous forces. The latter organisation, which consisted of uniquely dedicated experts in some military field or other, would be on hand to give on-the-job training and improve the quality at the same time.

The lowest rank of 'Green Beret' is Sergeant, albeit there are attached lower ranking logistic and administrative personnel. The Lieutenant Colonel who commanded our base and his Major second-in-command were really sort of area supervisors and managers.

The SF Battalion's several 'A-Teams' were commanded by Captains – with a Lieutenant as his number two (I was one of these), a couple of Warrant Officers and half a dozen Sergeants. Each 'A-Team' also had an allocation of Montagnard local defenders and ARVN drivers. The rank and file were, of course, a Company of short, dark and sturdy FANK troops. Their own officers, warrant officers and NCOs would understudy ours at first, then gradually take over and, at the same pace, we would gradually take a more and more back seat role.

The 'Specs' at Vinh Giat were not in teams for the most part – but in a pool, from which we could draw them as required by our pre-operations training package. The 'Specs' usually seemed to be older SNCOs or Warrant Officers who were absolutely the last word on any aspect of a military specialisation. They were walking and talking text books. They could not only regurgitate every line of United States pamphlets on their subject, but had studied other nations' philosophies on it as well. For example: there was an Ambush 'king', a field engineering (digging) 'king', a camouflage 'king' and 'kings' for every type of support weapon and infantry minor tactic.

Each FANK regiment would spend about three months with the SF battalion at Vinh Giat progressing gradually from training to operations, and would finally move to their role back at home as an experienced (perhaps veteran) fighting force.

There were also 'Green Berets' who were neither on an 'A-Team' nor a specialist as the camp had to have an adjutant, quartermaster, transport officer, doctor, catering officer and other usual departments to keep us going.

The base personnel and the 'Specs' lived in a European compound at one end of camp – and we, the 'A-Team' members lived (with our charges) in the Asian compound. It did not really matter where one lived as everyone on the base was co-operative and friendly. The segregation was for catering, not racialist, reasons. One kitchen turned out hamburgers with French fries, while the other turned out cooked whole fish in pungent sauces and boiled rice by the ton.

The Special Forces personnel, and their lifestyle, were also rather interesting. Most had volunteered to return for tour after tour. Some had first served in Vietnam in the late 1950s – before the commitment of regular allied troops, when there were only Special Forces advisors there.

In almost all the cases of the long servers, their wives, fiancées and steady girlfriends had left them during their first tour and, after a lonely leave, they had asked to go back to where they knew that they had dependable friends. Finally, a United States base in Vietnam became 'home' and the United States itself just became somewhere to go to on leave between tours. A few did not even go home between tours. America, it seemed, had let them down badly long ago, while Vietnam wanted them – or at least, needed their skills. They felt useful there and as though they belonged. A number had Vietnamese wives and children, whom they kept in 'safe' villages and commuted to as often as they could.

The Officers' Mess (or, in United States terms, Officers' Club) had been built and decorated in the late 1950s – just over ten years earlier. The music system had nothing but melodic and jolly pre-Sixties tunes and all the huge framed, and autographed, glossy photographs round the wall were of gorgeous curvy and coy fifties *Playboy* nude girls. I thought it was absolutely splendid – as in most matters of popular taste, I got to about 1957, foresaw that nothing but deterioration lay ahead, and stayed.

Our American CO was an energetic and positive commander who was determined that only the very best that we could give was good enough for our worthy calling. Sadly, I heard later that his purity of purpose, honesty and outspokenness with some of the American civilian political persons in Saigon (who did not walk the same straight path that he did) over the greater support that they could give our programme, cost him further advancement. If this is so, then the United States has been disadvantaged, as he was a fine leader, in the classic mould. He was also a big, cheerful, witty, natural gentleman who inspired confidence just by appearing.

My first night back in Vietnam, I lay in my little cot which was in a little hut up against the Northern most part of the perimeter fence and smelt the Vietnamese night and listened to its sounds. It seemed odd, but somehow good to be back. The jungle insect and wildlife sounds were not too loud as great 'killing grounds' had been cleared all round us. However, I could hear the familiar human sounds in the distance – a boom, followed by the roar of automatic fire and the popping of single shots as ambushes were sprung by one side or the other – and men died. Yes. Here I was again.

I was consoled over the fact that my little hut, of wooden pillars and fly-screen walls would be the first thing to goif an attack came from the North, by the fact that the base's Buddist temple was my next door neighbour. It had the ancient Buddhist swastika symbol (that the Nazi's copied in reverse) on its tower and I felt that it gave a holy, and unquestionably more secure, aspect to my little corner.

The second night I rolled quickly out of bed around two o'clock and scuttled into my defence fighting trench outside, in common with everyone else, as mortar bombs crumped down across the camp and their shrapnel pinged, whined and whirred about the place. Cambodians love to sleep out beneath the stars, and our only casualties were from amongst those sleeping thus. Mercifully, everyone in a building or a trench was unscathed.

The following day I discovered that my first quiet night had been the exception and the mortaring on the second was more the rule.

"You see, until they can get a force down here to take us out, they like to remind us that they are still around," someone said encouragingly.

In many ways I found life more agreeable and civilized than on my first tour. Instead of having to spend most of the time constantly on the move through the sweaty, dirty, itching, biting and bar-less jungle – where there were no soft beds – I lived in a pleasant camp with fresh sea breezes blowing. I commuted to the war. We would set up a day long ambush or go on a day's patrol, giving our Cambodians real experience with simultaneous instruction, and the enemy had the decency not to turn up – initially. Occasionally, we would have a week's worth of operation; it almost seemed like a peacetime exercise – when there was no enemy to spoil it. However, mostly, once the day's instruction was done, I would saunter down from my end of the base, cross the Asian camp, pass the time of day in French here and there, cross the European camp and have the odd English exchange before going into the Officers' Club for my hamburger and French fries and American beer. Later, I would wander back to my cosy little shed and narrow cot and cheerily greet all the Montagnard sentries in the goon towers as I passed. The base's working day started at four-thirty so I was usually asleep by nine o'clock in the evening.

The base, and the surrounding area, abounded with pretty girls. They worked on the base as typists, clerks, barmaids, waitresses, cooks and cleaners and in the local area as salesgirls in shops and markets. They were not directly purchasable – but neither were they unavailable.

Our base was in an area where European featured troops were not regularly seen – and so we were novel and interesting. Also, as we were foreign soldiers, we could inspire a sort of "groupie" style of following in that place.

In countries where security is taken for granted, impressionable girls, when looking for a superior-seeming man, will desire pop-stars and actors and other male entertainers because they appear on their TV screens, or their technician-improved songs are pumped out, and so they seem special, glamourous and desirable for those reasons alone. They have no other yardstick or special need. However, in a land of perpetual war, it is the man-at-arms who is clung to – and particularly the foreign man-at-arms – because he seems to have some power or influence over the chaos and to provide the possibility of some security.

There cannot be a nicer smile than the Asian girl's, for when she wants to smile she gives it fully and it lifts your heart like a sudden bright sunburst. I was dark, lean, squarely built and of reasonable aspect – and was smiled at in scruffy markets and from open front shops. I was smiled at by barmaids, waitresses and girls passing on Hondas. I got full frontal smiles, sideways smiles and shy smiles. They were some of the most exquisite girls I have ever seen, and girls were allowed to stay with you on the base at weekends – after a brief vetting. If I spoke to, and charmed one for a short period and then invited her to spend the next weekend with me at Vinh Giat – she would apparently react like a Western girl who had just been told that she had won a beauty competition or a national lottery.

However, I was serving the *Vogue* front-cover, and newly awakened tigress of passion Barbara – and could not have been distracted by anyone. I had already written to her several times and had received a beautiful reply of alternating desolation at my absence and heated endearments. My life, I decided, would be one of single-mindedness in both my duty and my love.

I had been worrying about my mother's birthday throughout the operation. It was not that I had forgotten it. It was just that I had remembered it rather late for a card to get there in time from a remote area of Vietnam.

I confided my worries to my United States Sergeant and, without a moment's hesitation or distraction from watching the jungle ahead, he suggested that I send a telegram from the Army field post office on the base. It was such an obvious answer that I really should have thought of it on my own. So, as soon as we got back, I hurried along and sent it.

The attached postal operative who ran the place said that it might take a few days as it would probably have to go by a fairly roundabout route – maybe finally via the military office of the United States Embassy in London – but as there were three days to go, it might make it in time.

Following my father's retirement from work in London, my parents had gone to live full time in what had been our Sussex holiday village. On her birthday, my mother had been unable to wait for my father to get up first and bring a cup of tea, as usual, and had hurried down the stairs with almost girlish excitement to see what the postman had brought.

My father came leaping down the stairs the moment he heard the thud of my mother's fainting body hitting the hall carpet. She had my telegram, half opened, in her limp hand.

Both my parents had been through the anguishing experience during the World Wars of receiving terse military telegrams announcing that someone was dead. The moment that my mother saw that it was from a military address it had all been too much.

With trembling hands, my father had opened the telegram the rest of the way and had read the text:

"Happy Birthday Mother Dear."

I had probably been fortunate to have grown up during the last years when, to ensure that children had some chance of becoming likeable adults, thoughtless behaviour was followed by immediate and memorable retribution. Predictably, the left hand side of my bullet head had been a much used impact area for the right palms of parents, teachers, school prefects and village policemen.

My father later told me quite definitely that if, by an impossible chance, I had popped in through the front door at that moment my left ear would have been ringing as well as it had ever done during the two earlier decades.

It all seemed rather fun during the first week: dawn reveille, breakfast, a short burst of PT for the troops, a march or truck ride up the road and a little way inland (the Cambodians had a melodic, rhythmic marching song – 'Moi pee', 'one two' was the chorus), instruction and practise at fieldwork, a picnic, back to base (smiling and waving girls encountered en route), shower, change into smart rifle-green dacrons and desert boots, eat a hamburger and French fries, drink some beers, walk back to the cosy little hut/shed, and maybe the odd mortar round would land during the night to justify the term "war." This visit to Vietnam was rather better than my first I decided. I should definitely cope with a year, or whatever, of this without getting stressed.

On a Friday, my sixth day in the country, I was giving some instructions to one group of troops, while my Sergeant was moving some others on up the track. We would be following them almost immediately.

There was a muffled bang. It was similar to, and no louder than, a bottle bursting in the middle of a bonfire. I looked up and the Sergeant was urgently – but without panic – beckoning me to me.

I doubled up to them and there was a Cambodian with a slightly worried but otherwise normal expression being supported upright between two friends. I followed everyone's silent glances downwards. The end of his right leg was a protruding tibia or fibula surrounded by bright red raw meat and flaps of flesh. A steady line of blood ran onto the ground. A medic tore up and began rapidly applying a tourniquet.

An anti-personnel mine had just blown his foot and boot completely away. It was so horrendously unnatural – and the fun vanished.

I came to be referred to by the Americans as "that limey officer who speaks 'indidge." 'Indidge' was short for indigenous – meaning that I could communicate with locals in a language other than English and without an interpreter. They all seemed most flatteringly impressed, albeit I am not sure if all knew exactly what the vehicle of communication was.

It was, in fact, French. As all the countries in the region were old French colonies, the French language, like English in India, had become fairly universally adopted to get over the problems of too many different languages and local dialects within a single land area.

I was quite glad not to need the Cambodian civilian interpreters too much. They were, without exception, a personally charming lot. However, I never felt sure that they always bothered to convey all the essential details of technical instruction.

Instructing an illiterate whose civilian employment is probably peasant labourer or coolie is not, of course, the same thing as instructing troops from Westernised backgrounds. The latter have encountered machinery and gadgetry and have had the chance to inadvertently observe a few scientific principles at work. Thus, when instructing them on a weapon or a piece of military equipment one is able to assume that, once they realise the category of its motivation and purpose, they will start to move in unison with the instructor. However, this is not so with a man who effectively comes from a pre-industrial age. A 'Do-as-I-do-and-never-mind-why-it-works' training policy is probably the one once possible.

A Combat group of infantry, artillery and supporting services from the Republic of Korea (ROK) were our neighbours by about four miles and some of our principal allies in the area. Their troops were very strongly built, fit, smart and rigidly disciplined. Their organisation and training policies were based on United States army doctrines and publications. The Koreans, however, obeyed these excellent policies to the letter. Anyone over thirty-five in their armed forces had served in the vast and cruel conventional war that had savaged their country half a generation earlier.

Because I spoke 'indidge' my CO said that I was to be his liaison officer with the Koreans. I thought that it might be upsetting if I said that Korean was a language slightly related to Japanese and did not remotely resemble anything spoken locally, or anything that I spoke, so I went out wondering what I was going to do. Salvation came in the form of an

English speaking Korean Major (Major Parkes) who used to drop in at Vinh Giat from time to time to practice his English and have a few American beers. He also seemed to enjoy hamburgers with French fries.

He insisted that everyone in his camp would be delighted to see me anytime. I was always to ask for him and he would interpret and give me any other help.

About a week later, I decided that my first liaison visit must be due. I also had a small matter to discuss with them.

I arrived at the gates of their camp, which was a textbook illustration of a field base of maximum fortification, with my Vietnamese driver and Montagnard bodyguard.

Two sentries put rifles to either side of my head. I showed the Corporal in charge my multi-lingual ID card. He went to a field telephone, cranked the handle and obviously told a superior that there was a USSF Officer (he could not necessarily know that I was seconded) at the gate and what should he do. The superior then obviously said: "Well, let him in, fathead" or words to that effect.

He screamed an order at the two sentries whose attitude immediately changed from official hostility to official courtesy. In perfect unison, they performed a few seconds ceremony of welcome. They twirled their rifles in a set sequence to the accompaniment of a harmonious phrase of chant. Perhaps it was a tradition that had started with palace guards twirling great swords or spears at the court of a ruler of long ago.

Some massive knife rests wrapped in coil upon coil of barbed wire were drawn back, the great spiked gates were opened and we zig-zagged our way into the outer compound. There we passed a soldier being mercilessly beaten with bamboo sticks by a circle of others. Every time he fell to the ground, an NCO would scream at him to get up and stand at attention – which he valiantly tried to do – and the beating went on. I had already heard that the Koreans had arbitrary corporal punishment and, on occasions, arbitrary capital punishment.

The inner compound was dominated by a locally made – but none-the-less magnificent Korean style pagoda. It was the combat group's headquarters and, as I pulled up, the beaming and polite Major Parkes came springing down the steps and warmly shook my hand.

"You are at just the right time", he said. "That is good. The Colonel is expecting you."

I had already heard a bit about the Korean full Colonel who commanded their base. His military career had started in the Japanese army in Manchuria during the 1930s and had continued on with them through the Second World War. When that had ended, he had found ready employment in the armed forces of his own warring country.

Predictably, he enjoyed the reputation of a tough and effective soldier and commander.

I had frequently seen how outwardly smart and martial in aspect the Koreans were, so when I was shown into the Colonel's office I entered as though I had been marched in by a British Guard's Sergeant. I had, of course, learned to do it so well on my countless sessions on Company Commander's Orders at Mons Officer Cadet School. I felt as if all that had happened about a hundred years earlier. It was, in fact, only five and a half years earlier.

I think my formality and sense of ceremony met with the approval of the group in the room. I seemed to sense it behind the inscrutable countenances.

After I had crashed to a halt ('driving the heel of the boot through the square') and snapped a firm-muscled salute up and then down, I studied the group from my narrowed 'at-attention' eyes.

The seated Colonel was behind his desk and was flanked by a standing collection of about three very impressive-looking slightly younger officers. No doubt they were: a second-in-command, an Adjutant and some other executive officer. The Colonel had a white close crop, and the other newly shaven bomb-heads were varying degrees of grey and black. Any one of them, I decided, could have auditioned for the part of "Oddjob" in the James Bond film.

After studying me for a few seconds, the Colonel suddenly gave a short violent order to Major Parkes.

"The Colonel says you are most welcome and how may he assist you?" Major Parkes said as his version of it.

I said that I brought greetings from my Colonel and, as the defence layout of his camp was as perfect an example of such things as one could get, might I bring a group of Cambodian officers up for a look, as a picture speaks a thousand words and it would be most instructive for them.

The group studied me for quite some time before the Colonel made a longish series of aggressive barks and grunts at Major Parkes.

Also without expression, Major Parkes said:

"The Colonel would not normally grant this. However, as you are such a good looking New Zealand Officer, it is OK".

I stood there dumbstruck. "Good looking!" It was certainly not a term that I was used to having applied to me. Various worries started to cross my mind.

The Colonel gave Major Parkes a quick snap.

"It is a joke," he explained.

As soon as the Colonel and his aides realised that I had got the last bit, they alarmingly, and totally unexpectedly, burst into laughter. There was an instant transformation from silent deadpan to noise and facial movement. The bull necks, barrel chests and massive forearms remained motionless. However, the conical heads bobbed, teeth were pleasantly bared and eyes almost disappeared. I joined in with diplomatic gusto.

The Colonel stopped laughing at one point to check his watch – then started again – and even indicated that a little more volume was required from us. Finally, he cut us all off with an arm movement not unlike that of a great conductor bringing the last chord of the symphony to an abrupt end. They all stared expectantly at me.

I racked my brains furiously, but could only come up with the lame:

"I thank the Colonel for his kindness. However, I hope that, when the Cambodian officers see how far they have to go to achieve the military standards of the Colonel's command, they do not despair and feel that their cause is lost."

I waited until all the heads swivelled back to me after Major Parkes had finished his translation and added:

"It is a joke."

The second Major Parkes finished speaking, the Colonel switched us all on again and then off again a while later. I noticed that I was allocated considerably less laughter than the Colonel.

Our pleasant little officer to officer exchange was now clearly at an end, so I took a crashing step backwards, repeated my parade ground salute, about turned with another pagoda-shaker and quick marched out.

Major Parkes hurried after me and furiously shook my hand in a particularly friendly farewell. He must have become able to spot infinitesimally small fluctuations in the Colonel's total impassivity, because he said:

"The Colonel is very pleased with you. You are always welcome here. You will have no trouble."

I re-crossed the punishment compound where a variety of medieval corrective training was taking place. The Koreans were renowned as some of the most effective troops in the war and were not at all the sort of people one would want 'trouble' with.

"Look at this!" I said in annoyance to Captain Jean (albeit he liked to be called 'John") Marrett, our A-Team commander.

During the week that we had been away on an operation, the monsoon rains had filled my little shed, or *Hoochie*, up with water. The rain did not come through the sandbagged tin roof. However, as it fell with such force and intensity, it was either blown or had bounced in through a gap between the roof and the top of the walls. The water had then run down the walls and, rather like the swelling timbers of a newly launched boat, the plywood floor and walls had pressed together to form a water-tight seal. My shed stood on four short stilts – ironically to protect it from outside flooding – so I was now the possessor of a sort of roofed over water-filled trough. The rains of the past week had brought the level up to the top of my cot legs, so my bedding was still dry as was my spare jungle clothing, ammunition, books and Barbara's framed photograph. They were on the shelf. However, my spare pair of boots were underwater.

I had climbed up the two outer steps and then down into the well of the dark interior before I had realised that it was full of water. It was when I had noticed that I was wading about knee-deep that I had called John over to share my indignation.

"Do you know," I said, as I splashed about, "what I really need is a hole in the floor exactly where I'm standing. You see there's a dip here and the water could just drain away as it arrived."

I pondered the hydrokinetics for a few moments more then I said:

"No. Two holes would be better, as one would let the air in as the other lets the water out and a flow would be maintained. I'll go to the carpentry shop right away to borrow a drill . . ."

John, who had been standing in the doorway, above the water, had drawn his issue 45 automatic and was pointing it at me. He had been a Corporal in the French Army at the battle of Dien Bien Phu about seventeen years earlier during the first Indo-China War. It crossed my mind that he might finally, and dangerously, have cracked.

He fired twice in rapid succession at the floor between my feet. The two water spouts whoosed up in front of me and the noise in the tiny space was ear-drum shattering.

"Hey! You were right!" he said happily, in his French-American accent, as we heard the water torrenting onto the sand underneath my shed and the level started to go down immediately – like a plug-pulled bath.

"If only we could solve all problems so easily Eh?" he went on thoughtfully. Then, after shaking his head philosophically for a few moments longer, he left me to my shocked dampness.


"Say! I've got a book on that very subject!" Barry, the Special Forces Lieutenant, with the Silver Star, said excitedly.

I was spending a long weekend back on the base and had been invited down to the European camp junior officers little mess on the Saturday evening. There were chaps entwined with Vietnamese girls on sofas in the main sitting-room, with a largely unwatched sexy movie going on in the background. The rooms were really cubicles as there were no proper doors within the basic building. I was standing with Barry in the home-made, but most convivial, little bar. I had been holding forth about something or other.

"Come here. I'll show you," he said, beckoning me into the partitioned off bit that was his bedroom.

I followed him in, still making a point, but was instantly struck dumb, stopped in my tracks and sent giddy by an aspect of his room.

The very first anatomy-lesson girlie magazines had just started to appear on open sale in United States' and European newsagents. They were mostly of poor quality photography and the crude nude poses were designed to give maximum female genital display. These magazines were also flooding Vietnam.

Every fraction of Barry's walls and ceiling was covered by a female part. The number of photographs that he must have cut up would have been astronomical, considering that the detail that he wanted was, in the picture, only a few millimetres across.

The effect, when you were not expecting it, was totally unbalancing.

Talking about how tough your special forces selection course had been always has prominence in the conversation when the special forces of different nationalities meet. This was certainly the case amongst the society at Vinh Giat.

The Americans were always out to impress: "Gee, there was this guy in the bunk next to mine who used to cry himself to sleep each night". However, the New Zealanders tended to reminisce on the incidentally humourous incidents that arose unexpectedly out of hardship and otherwise unpromising circumstances. We probably also had the Anglo-Saxon's, of those days, instinct for modesty of phrase over personal achievement and, no doubt, were also aware of the greater effectiveness of understatement and innuendo.

I understand that women have been gifted with the curious ability of almost total forgetfulness of the often terrible pain of childbirth once it is all over. Fortunately, a similar thing happened to me following my New Zealand SAS selection course. Horrific memories do randomly flash, and reflash, into my mind at infrequent intervals: a group of us covering many miles across a thigh-deep swamp for a cold and rainy day and a night, and carrying a telegraph pole at the same time, indescribably icy water submersions, terrifying cliff-climbing, endless full combat-kit runs with a rucksack full of wet sand and house bricks, being the quarry on an escape and evasion exercise across near impossible terrains with dozens of experienced troops in pursuit and – worst of all – being subjected to real torturing style interrogation.

However, my most vivid memory of that reasonably short, though impressive, period of my life is not of something that happened to me, but of someone I met and the tale he told. Indeed, the event haunts me still.

I had been jogging throughout a rainy night across a windswept blasted heath of gorse and tussock on the escape and evasion phase. As the dawn came up, the heath gave way to an endless pine forest. After I went a few hundred metres into the forest, I realised that I needed to find a reasonably sheltered pile of pine needles and try to get some rest. As I looked around for a spot that might be hidden from my pursuers, I was startled beyond description to suddenly see a figure watching me with mildly amused interest from a few metres away.

"So its you they're after!" he said grinning. "Jeeze, they've got helicopters and all back there."

He was a tall, thin and fit-looking old man. He had neat New Zealand country clothes, an old khaki Mounted Rifles' hat and a long bag over one shoulder that looked as if it contained a hunting gun.

Sensing an ally, I said, "I've got to get to a safe location about ten miles beyond the forest. I've got another day and a half."

"Hey, yer wet through", he replied. "D'yer want ter come to me cabin and dry out a little?"

I thanked him profusely, but said that I had better not as it was against the rules of the exercise.

"Well", he continued, "I reckon if you don't get dried out, yer bloody toes could be turning up at the ends before the day's out. You've got to get dry or give up," he said authoritatively and finally.

Giving up would mean another session of interrogation so, from several points of view, the drying out idea seemed very attractive.

"Just a quick dry and then yer can be on yer way", he said as we stepped off through the trackless wood that he obviously knew totally and had an infallible sense of direction in.

His cabin was in a small compound by a track. A forestry authority pick-up was parked there and there were sheds that appeared to be stores and workshops.

He gave me an old set of clean and dry overalls to put on while he dried my combat uniform, underclothes, socks and boots out by his stove. He also produced the most fabulous tasting mug of tea and thick sandwich in world history. The second I finished these, I fell asleep in the battered and semi-collapsed old armchair. I heard odd snatches of him working away in and around his sheds.

About mid-morning, I woke up and put on my dried out clothing and he joined me for another exquisite mug of tea, and a doorstep sandwich, and we chatted.

He had been a forester, in this forest, all his life. He had reached retirement age a few years before, but as he was still fit and did not want to hang around with nothing to do, his state employers were only too pleased to have him work on as long as he wished, in a state of semi-retirement. He was held in high esteem and could work as he wanted. He had a married son, also in forestry, who lived in the tiny nearby town, but he did not want to be any trouble and anyway he preferred his cabin. He had lived like that for years before he was married and he had not had Alice, his wife long. After she died, he brought the boy up in their house, but as soon as the boy had grown up and got married the father had given him the house and moved back into the forest. Jim's eldest grand-daughter wanted to get married now.

Jim was too old for overseas service in the Second World War, so was in the Home Guard. However, he served in the first World War and was at the Gallipoli raid – and it was from the mention of that event that his intriguing tale began. He had never told it to anyone before. Perhaps he told it to me because I was a soldier, but perhaps, more importantly, because I was a stranger. He was a naturally private man, yet he bared himself, after over fifty years, without embarrassment and without loss of dignity. I have always hoped that I helped the good man by sharing his concern.

His Unit finally captured some Turkish entrenchments after some murderous bayonet fighting – as the fanatically brave Turks fought ferociously to defend their holy Muslim homeland. Amongst the contents of a trench the unit found an elegant box containing a magnificent German-made snipers' rifle.

"Who shall have this?" the Company Commander said, holding it aloft.

There had been an almost immediate response of, "Give it to Jim", as it was common knowledge that the forest-dwelling youth could "shoot the privates off a blow-fly at two hundred metres with an old Martini-Henry".

Over the next few months, he shot down countless Turks. He was a hunter descended from hunters and knew how to move unobserved into undetectable fire positions – and his aim was deadly.

The Turkish soldiers were stalwart peasants, and particularly stoic in defence, but in general, they did not have their awareness stimulated by much education and often inadvertently gave their positions away by thoughtless movement. My friend bowled them like skittles.

On the day before the Gallipoli operation was abandoned, Jim scanned no-man's-land and saw a Turkish soldier moving about unconcernedly. He was particularly noticeable because he was a very large man.

As my friend took aim, the Turk bent over an object on the ground that my friend could not see. The large backside pointing towards him made an unmissable target. The bullet travelled through the length of the Turk's torso – it could even have exited from his head. The Turk was flung stone dead to the ground.

That night, my friend had, for the first time, the dream that was to recur at intervals throughout his life:

He walks along vast corridors of a great and beautiful Eastern palace. After what seems an age, he comes to magnificent doors that open before him. A colossal chamber lays beyond and is lined on either side by many ranks of Turkish soldiers. He seems compelled to walk forward down the aisle they form towards a great enthroned and noble-looking potentate at the far end.

He dares not look directly at the face – as somehow he knows that it is The Prophet Mohammed himself and that he is within Allah's great celestial domain.

An all-powerful voice seems to speak and to ask him if he knows who all these soldiers are. He dares not answer, so the voice goes on:

"These are the Turkish soldiers that you have killed . . . however, I forgive you for all of these . . . my sons . . . but look on this."

A piece of mirror is held up in front of him. In it he sees again his rifle sight picture of the large backside of the bending Turkish soldier.

"For this one I do not forgive you!" booms the voice.

"For with a moment longer of observation, you could have seen that he was tending a wounded New Zealand soldier!"
And he would awake.

I have never really believed in the supernatural. However, I know that my friend, a totally practical man, believed what he told me with a desperate sincerity.

Perhaps it was just caused by a troubled conscience for the quantity of human life that he took. However, as terrible things happen minute by minute in every war, why should he be singled out for the wrath of a deity?

He said that he started to have the dream again recently, exactly the same as always in every detail, after an interval of many years. I have always hoped that when he left this world he was not propelled into an oriental purgatory. All soldiers who do their duty, as ethically and as honourably as the knowledge available to them at the time allows, surely deserve a final forgiveness.

Both before and between my Vietnam tours, I met some of the last New Zealand soldiers of another age. There used to be Boer war soldiers to drink with in Returned Services Association bars and many first World

War men. Sadly, by the time I returned finally from over five years in Asia (the Indo-China and the Kashmir wars), they had nearly all gone. However, there were some unforgettable people. There was rough, tough, brave, jovial, and decorated, Sister Gough who was still drinking beer each day, in the Otahuhu RSA, with the local boys that she had patched up on the Western front fifty years earlier, until the day she died. I also heard another New Zealand Soldier's tale that I found rather touching.

Although I had missed the historical parade through Auckland, I did manage, between recovering from illness and being posted, to participate in another parade and weekend of festivities, at the little seaside town of Raglan. The small community had provided a number of its sons for our Unit's ranks and had adopted us, i.e. sent highly valued home made cakes etc. Thus, when we were pulled out, they had insisted that we came to them for some hospitality. Indeed, the quality and quantity of the country fare was, at times, quite overwhelming. There was, of course, food, drink, friendly and generous men and uncomplicated, and simply motivated, country girls who can give the best of all to make their soldiers know that they have come safely home.

For a while, the slow swirls of human current, that moved around the little colonial main street between the pub and the RSA, shuffled me into a corner of the back bar and up against a particularly noble-looking elderly Maori gentleman. He wore an immaculately maintained and presented – but incredibly ancient – best suit, that was obviously reserved for only the most significant of family and civic occasions. He stood drinking alone in silent and dignified self-sufficiency.

Slowly, a courteous conversation started between us and his story unfolded.

He had been born, and had always worked, on his Maori Community's farm. One day in 1914, he had ridden into town to buy some supplies and following a short roll on a drum, an army officer had climbed onto the front verandah of the very pub that we were currently in and had called upon all the young men present to gather round.

The officer had then told them the alarming news that the King's realm was threatened by someone or the other, and their help was urgently needed.

The young Maori was, of course, very tribal minded and a call to defend his overall paramount chief, against whatever it was, would have his instant and instinctive response.

There and then, he and a group of other Maori and European young men marched with the soldiers to Hamilton – about forty miles away – where the railway line started. After the wonderous experience of travelling on a train, he received the standard infantry basic training at a depot in

Auckland and was then put on a troop ship.

He served for almost the full period of the first World War. He was in both the Gallipoli and Western Front threatres and participated in most major battles. Luckily, he survived and, when it was over, he returned by troopship to Auckland, by train to Hamilton and then walked back to Raglan and had not moved away from the farm and town area ever since.

I gained the impression that to that day, he had been wondering what on earth it had all been about – but was far too polite to ask.

I strode purposefully, but watchfully, through the overgrown plantation and felt like a true warrior. Strangely and, no doubt, pervertedly, I rather enjoyed the tenseness and sense of danger of being at the head of a jungle column. Life was lived on a knife edge – it was frightening and exhilarating.

As an officer, I did not, of course, get the chance often – as command is usually placed in the centre of a tactically deployed unit where it can best orchestrate events. However, our particular batch of Cambodians were at such an early stage of training that few would know anti-ambush immediate action drills – so it was better that I acted as lead scout myself.

I might either spot danger in advance and have enough time to scream instructions for some sort of effective deployment or be the first to die and not have to witness any ensuing debacle.

There was hot open sky above us and we walked through chin-high grasses with spaced banana palms about us. I held a long thin stem lightly between the forefinger and thumb of my left hand so that it hung down in front of me. If there was a mine trip-wire about, it might tap against it and save us. I held my rifle with my right hand and arm – as I had been taught – in the ready position. The butt was against my shoulder, so that I could whip it up for a snap shot. My glance darted quickly from where I was putting my feet to across the top of the grass ahead.

A young rubber tree was most conveniently in my path. It would mask my approach from any enemy just beyond. When I reached it, I would signal everyone to crouch down in the all-round-defence position while I – still keeping the tree between myself and the way ahead – would slowly pull myself a little way up it, peep round it and scan across the top of the sea of long grass.

It was only a few paces away.

"Stop!" the Sergeant behind me said quietly, but sharply, breaking the jungle warfare rule of silence and hand signals only. He also grabbed me painfully by the flesh of the rear upper part of my right arm and stopped me in my tracks.

I turned in annoyance. He let go of my arm and, with the same hand, patted me gently on the shoulder, indicating that I should keep totally still. He was not looking at me, but had his gaze fixed on the trunk of the tree where it disappeared into the grass. He moved carefully level with me, gave me his rifle to hold and very cautiously parted the grass stems just in front of me.

There were two four foot long bamboo pungee sticks screwed firmly into the trunk. They were at slightly different heights and at slightly different angles – so that they stood the best chance of impaling anyone approaching from our direction, one I would have missed. However, my chest was less than a foot from the poisoned razor tip of the other.

With hindsight, it was all so obvious. Allied troops would most likely penetrate the jungle from the direction of the nearest road – as we had done. The distinctive tree offered psychological as well as, possible, real security and would draw people to it – as I had been.

The type of bamboo sticks used had almost the strength of steel rods and, if cut correctly, would have a point as fine and as unbendable as a lance. Even though they were static and not on any sort of spring-loaded device, the momentum of my heavy body walking onto one would have sent it into me like a meat skewer through a partridge.

Booby traps often came in families, so we searched the rest of the area very, very carefully and thoroughly. Fortunately there seemed to be nothing else. It had just been an exceptionately simple and clever opportunist idea that would have worked – but for the four-years-in-country sharpened observation and instinct of a Special Forces Sergeant.

We pulled them out of the tree and I examined the poisonous green mould on the tips. From my first tour, I knew that this was the constantly available and effective blood poisoner: human excretia. Insult would have been added to injury!

In the early days of the war, pungee traps had been very simple. The standard favourite was a sort of mini animal trap: a little camouflaged pit with pungees standing up from the bottom. An allied soldier would step through the camouflage lid and would observe blooded points sticking up between his laces.

The allies reacted by producing boots with impenetrable soles of steel plates or man-made fibres. The VC/NVA counter-reacted with ever more sophisticated and varied pungee combinations. The little pit remained, but when the allied soldier's fully protected foot went through the camouflage covering he would step onto a pleasantly pungee-free floor. Unfortunately, however, the action of going through the cover would snap shut a pair of wooden jaws and the pungees would be driven into his calf from both sides. In addition, there were springy branches or gravity operated swinging devices that could be armed and left with some form of simple wedge and wire tripping or triggering device, so that the allied soldier could kill or maim himself unsupervised.

I met an Australian armoured squadron commander who had become so enraged by the nastiness of the one-sided pungee war, which had claimed several of his men, that he had decided to reply in kind.

He had felt that learning the art of correct bamboo cutting might be too time consuming and so he had got hold of a large quantity of eight inch nails. With these, he and his troops had made what looked like small squares from an Indian fakir's sawn up bed. Then, with various local materials, they had worked out some spring-loaded firing and initiating devices and had organised some lures to draw the enemy to them.

At dawn, after a small fire fight, he had felt that the balance of justice had gone a little way towards being righted, when he found dead communists attached to his nails by their faces.

I sat on what must have been about the tenth cubicle-less lavatory in from the door. The row continued well on past me for another dozen or more. I hummed snatches of martial, patriotic and classical airs under my breath – as I, for some reason, often do when on my own.

This vast communal sit-down facility in my Asian part of the camp had worried me from the outset.

I have always felt that there is just the one human function that, from several points of view, is probably best done alone. The long narrow building and its layout, was part of the camp's French heritage.

When in camp, therefore, I would choose my moments very carefully. The peak early morning and early evening periods were, of course, to be avoided at all cost so I used to slip away during the mid-morning break between my infantry minor tactics classes. I always had it to myself then.

It was so nice to be on one's own for a while in this crowded camp. I used to spend a longish initial period mulling over the past, the present and the (hoped for) future. Shafts of bright sunlight came through the shutter slits and patterned the concrete floor – but, in general, it was shady and restful in there. The troops scrubbed the place out a couple of times a day – so it was all very hygenic. I was probably humming the best known bars of 'Land of Hope and Glory', 'God Defend New Zealand' or something stirring and cheering – when a startlingly pretty Vietnamese girl walked in.

As a result of a private education and the examples of my home, I started, of course, to instinctively stand up – as a lady had entered the room. However, it suddenly dawned on me that this might be the one occasion to forego the formality – so I sat down again.

She smiled shyly but radiantly.

"*Chow ong, Chung Wee* (Hello, Lieutenant)," she said.

"*Chow Co* (Hello Miss)," I replied automatically – despite my total confusion.

I recognised her – who could miss her? She was a sort of general office clerk who worked in this end of camp. She was one of the host of local girls who held down various nine to five jobs about the place.

Of course the camp had no ladies powder-room, so all facilities had to be unisex.

She chatted happily away in Vietnamese as she hauled her cotton mini-dress above her waist, pushed down her tiny undergarment and sat down on the seat next to mine.

I did not understand every word of her polite and friendly Vietnamese small talk – but I got her drift and replied as best I could. She carried on socialising in the pretty trill of her tonal language for quite a while after she had finished and when some anecdote about one of her relatives or friends got all too funny for words, she rolled her head in silent lively laughter, buried her face in her hands and pushed me softly – the way Vietnamese girls do.

I totally forgot the extraordinary nature of our circumstances until she stood up and looked around for the roll. It was on the other side of me, so I passed it over and, unthinkingly, tore off a suitable length for her as I did so.

I thought that perhaps my service had better end there, although I did briefly wonder if there was any local convention of still further courtesies for such occasions. I was temporarily beyond greater surprise or embarrassment.

She daintily completed everything, while still gossiping animatedly, adjusted her clothing and left me with a smile and a wave over her shoulder as she went through the door. Once again I resisted my training to stand up as a lady left the room.

I remained there musing on the contrasts of Asia: Vietnamese girls will not hold the hand or arm of a husband or lover in public and consider it immodest to be photographed. Japanese girls, always so covered and correct, will unconcernedly strip off, apparently, and jump into a communal bath. Normally ice-cool, nose-in-the-air, rich and beautiful Chinese daughters in Singapore will get the chauffeur to stop the Mercedes and casually ask you, over the automatic window, if you fancied going dancing at the Ming Court that night and generally having a good time – because, as you are a transient foreigner, her reputation is safe with you.

No matter how long I lived in Asia and no matter how fond I was of the place, it was just not possible, with my British upbringing, that I should ever unravel the enigma that it all was.

At first I though that he must be a friendly local, as he seemed to be smiling. Then I wondered what he was doing in this out of the way place; then I saw that his weapon did not have a black plastic stock, but one of brown polished wood.

In a milli-second my heart leaped into my mouth.

"Contact front!" I shouted and snatched my American M16 rifle up into the aim. I was ready this time. The range was about one hundred and fifty metres. Before the echo of my words had died away, the swarm of Cambodians behind me – instead of adopting a covered fire position – yelled and charged in their usual, primitive and stupidly brave way. Distracted, I screamed at them to get down as the NVA soldier, his face grim and his teeth bared, fired a long harsh burst from his AK47. I heard a thump and a cry as someone was hit. Then there were two cracks in quick succession as the cool, gun-loving and dead shot Sgt Wagner got a couple of rounds away from one of his many privately owned and powerful, hand-guns.

The enemy soldier had just turned to run into deeper cover, and I saw a portion of his shirt twitch in the upper right area of his back. He was plucked sideways, as though by a pair of giant tweezers, and nearly thrown to the ground as the first of Sgt Wagner's bullets hit him. I did not see where the second shot struck.

Surprisingly, the NVA soldier recovered his balance, kept on running and instantly disappeared into the thick foliage. However, he was definitely shot through the right lung and would probably expire in his own time. Also, Sgt Wagner was single-mindedly devoted to his trade, and I was never sure that he had been briefed on the passage in the Geneva Convention that refers to dum-dum bullets.

The Cambodians started randomly emptying whole magazines into the area where he was last seen. After about twenty seconds, I called a halt to that and, having seen that Sgt Wagner and our medic were with our fallen man, I called to two of the more mature and tough-looking Cambodians to follow me. In a crouching run we doubled forward through the available cover towards the jungle's edge. A Montagnard – they never minded a fight – also insisted on joining me as, surprisingly, did a Cambodian officer. However, as the officer seemed to have no idea of tactical movement and was wearing a tight, tailored uniform, he quickly got out of breath and fell behind our advance, I doubted that he would be of any use, or even survive a contact, but it remained a gallant gesture.

The communist soldier had fired on us just after we had crossed a railway line that ran along the floor of a fairly open valley. We had been advancing towards the rising ground of the far side and he had been at the base of the slope. The hillside was covered in thick dark green bushes and

I had spotted his head and shoulders as he had observed us over the top of one of the lowest and smallest.

I left the Montagnard and the officer to their own devices and sent a Cambodian soldier out to thirty metres on each of my flanks with instructions that we would sweep round and converge, more or less together, on the enemy's last known location.

They carried out their orders exactly and, trying to put the thought of suddenly receiving a point-blank burst of automatic fire out of my mind, we arrived at the sand-floored, dead-leaf and root-covered spot where the enemy had stood. We advanced a little further, then crouched down and looked intently into the darkening twilight of the thickening jungle.

Just by my right shoulder was a red leaf. There were more patches of blood across the ground as he was obviously losing blood in a steady flow. It was certainly an easy trail to follow.

We doubled back to Sgt Wagner. Our downed man was unquestionably dead. He had been shot through, or near, the heart.

I quickly outlined my plan to Sgt Wagner. I would take a section of some of the most experienced men with me and go after the enemy soldier. He was to harbour in the jungle's edge with the rest of our force of about twenty. I would keep him abreast of events, or summon assistance if necessary, on the radio.

He studied the rising tiers of jungle, then the sky and then looked slowly in all other directions in his expressionless way.

"Why sure, Sir," he said slowly, nodding in agreement.

"If that's what you really want to do, but I figure that way leads off the peninsular and we've been hearing that they're building up and building up out there. If that 'mother' makes it back to his buddies, there could be a whole goddam army here real soon. But if that's what you really want to do, Sir."

I knew only too well of his knowledge and experience of the country in general and this area in particular, and his common sense and practical ability. It would be dark soon.

"Sure is some of the best ambush country I ever saw," he mused gently, as though it was of no consequence.

"But like I say, Sir, if that's what you really want to do, I'll go get the 'bodes' and the 'yards' sorted."

He smiled in a friendly, but respectful way and turned to go.

I wondered briefly if it was worth trying to pretend that I had changed my mind unaided.

"You're right," I said.

"There's nothing more that we can do here now. Get everyone turned round and we'll head back to the base."

He smiled companionably and our column trailed back across the late afternoon valley. The palm trees along the skyline behind us were already becoming silhouettes.

Our dead companion was carried back, rolled up in his waterproof poncho and slung under a big bamboo pole that the troops cut.

After the other post action formalities were completed at Vinh Giat, and after examination by our eccentric Jewish US SF Army doctor, sick or wounded would often get circumcised as well as healed, the dead Cambodian soldier was laid out on the forecourt of our Buddist temple. His poncho was pushed up around him to form a trough.

There was a little spontaneous ceremony by his comrades: prayer, a short chant and flowers were tossed onto his body. Then the Adjutant and his team came forward with petrol cans, soaked him in it and filled his poncho up, so that he was lying in a pool of it.

We all stood in silence while a lighted rag was lobbed onto him and the flames roared up with ever increasing intensity, noise and heat.

The business of burning dead young Buddist soldiers seemed to happen all too frequently. In addition to those killed by enemy action, there was a steady flow of deaths through natural causes. The poorer Cambodians did not have the benefit of regular medical treatment as they grew up and were often taken by illnesses from which they might have been saved if treated a few years earlier, or even illnesses that general innoculation has eradicated in the West.

I was always saddened beyond measure to see a fellow human reduced to a shrivelled dark grey outline of his former self that collapsed into ashes when raked over – except, perhaps, for a few of the larger segments of vertebrae.

The Cambodians were a people of a very distinctive character. They were darker and more animated than the Vietnamese. They also had a more subtle and more frequent sense of humour and a greater range of facial types. All were slightly eccentric in one way or another. However, there were a couple of very significant things that were common to every one of them and were the controlling influences of their lives. The first was their devout Buddist faith and the second was their enjoyment and reverence for their heritage as one of the most culture-loving races in the world. They had lovely and distinctive styles of painting, sculpture, architecture, poetry, music and dancing.

Even the toughest veterans unashamedly cried open angry tears on the day that we heard of the capture of the ancient and fabulous jungle city of Ankor Wat (one of the Wonders of the World) and the news that communist troops were chipping the Buddist figures from the temple friezes to take as souvenirs.

225

Also, they all had a particular love of bathing. Cautious tactical deployment was always forgotten when an advance came upon a river. In they would rush to noisily splash and gambol.

They were demonstratively affectionate once you were accepted as a friend. At first, I was deeply concerned when my fellow officers took my hand as we walked across the compound to lunch, leaned against me, put an arm round me or rested a hand on my knee, if I was sitting, while we chatted. However, I quickly realized that this was no more than an innocent local habit and did not represent any serious tendency or intention.

The United States Army personnel were rendered totally immobile with embarrassment by it.

As the United States Special Forces had effectively sub-let me to the Khymer Army, I had the privilege of being permitted to wear their officers' uniform. I used to do this – particularly when on operations – not only to show solidarity but also to try and avoid being singled out by the enemy for the first shot. The fact that I was naturally not too overly European-looking from a distance was also very convenient.

We were quite a dandified lot. We had well-fitted and individually tailored sets of dark plain jungle greens and French style berets – pulled down on the opposite side of the head to those of the British and the Americans – that have a couple of black ribbons fluttering jauntily from the back. The central part of our metal beret-badge depicted an Ankor Wat temple. I avoided the highly coloured silk cravats, frequently pink and yellow, of most of my companions and went instead for either the traditional New Zealand black silk cravat or a very dark green one – worn in the current London fashion, like a Scout's neckerchief, with a black leather toggle holding it together.

The Khymer Officers – with a few very impressive exceptions – were unfortunately not very well trained or practical in soldierly command. I formed the impression that the most desired qualifications for Officer selection seemed to be: to speak French, albeit speaking English was a secondary option and, ideally, to have a degree in classical French Literature from the Sorbonne in Paris. Those officers who had been commissioned from military academies, or after experience of combat in the ranks, like my tough and natural leader friend Captain Kim Son, seemed to be in a lesser league for promotions and appointments.

However, Cambodia was one of the world's leaders in the creative arts rather than in military studies.

Sadly, we heard that thirty to fifty per cent of the Cambodian soldiers who trained with us were killed within a few months of leaving Vinh Giat and returning to the war in their own country. Ill prepared military leadership was reckoned to be the cause. There was, however, no lack of courage on the part of the Cambodian officers as they invariably stayed to die with the troops they led to disaster. One of our battalions died to a man as they fought to hold the communist advance down one of the main highways.

Prime Minister Lon Nol – who, like so many of his countrymen, was tired of the ducking and weaving of the country's ruler, Prince Norodom Sihanouk, to please absolutely everyone and stay in power – had taken charge of Cambodia in the name of democracy and the Western Allies.

I believe that Prince Sihanouk has been more kindly treated by history than he deserves

His political attitude was more flexible than The Vicar of Bray's religion as he bobbed between royalism, democracy and communism to try and either gain aid from the West or the communists and sidestep every internal and external threat to his personal position. He, of course, says that he behaved as he did for completely unselfish reasons and it was all done for the people of Cambodia as his rule was the best and the most stable and unifying form of government that they had had or could have.

However it should be remembered that, after Lon Nol took over, he joined with the Communist Chinese who were the paymasters and suppliers of the Kymer Rouge. These moronic murderers (realistically portrayed in 'The Killing Fields') were the most vile of all the communist forces in South East Asia, which includes the Viet Cong, the Pathet Lao and the North Vietnamese.

It has always been incomprehensible to me that a country that could produce people as honest and humane as those I met at Vinh Giat could also produce the Kymer Rouge and, the Alcibiades of our times, Norodom Sihanouk.

Buddism is, of course, a most noble, cultured and respected global religion. However, its influence in a modern military world could be a mixed blessing.

Each one of our Cambodian soldiers, no matter how poor his background, wore a little gold statue of the Lord Budda on a piece of string round his neck. They believed that this made them inviolate to all weapons. Thus, they tended to doubt the need to learn life saving modern military minor tactics and made carelessly brave and confident frontal charges when under fire. Often to make absolutely certain that they were fully bullet proofed, soldiers would hold their Buddha figure in their mouths during the attack.

Unfortunately, of course, a number were shot down. However, this was always attributed to the deceased individual's imperfect devotion.

I noticed that the kitchen hand, who ladled us out our lunchtime portions of boiled rice, always left a thin layer at the bottom of the dustbin. As the quantities of fresh food that we got – when we were in terrain that could be reached by truck – were not exactly excessive, I asked him why he did that.

Captain Kim Son, who was beside me, explained that this was Buddah's portion. I also noticed that each individual left a little of his meagre ration at the bottom of his mess tin for Buddha. Then the mess tins were washed in the nearest river and the dustbin washed in the kitchen back at Vinh Giat, Buddha's portion, of course disappeared. It was, none-the-less, a most admirably disciplined and self-denying way of tangibly showing faith.

However, as all expendable commodities were treated in this way, I used to fervently hope that one day we should not come off second best in a fire fight for the want of the Lord Buddha's reserve of bullets.

A touring troupe from the Cambodian National Dancers put on a show for us. They are orphan girls who have been gathered up and raised in a sort of national boarding school and dance academy in preparation for their life as dedicated traditional Cambodian dancers.

They were as something from another world. They were an ultimate of delicate and exquisite grace and beauty. The physical bodies of their world seemed to be without the constraints of either the usual design of human joints or the law of gravity. They rippled, floated and twirled without a fraction of effort and bent and coiled like little serpents. Their entire bodies danced from their perfect tiny feet and bangle laden ankles to their haughtily charming heads with the temple tower shaped headdresses. Even their toes, fingers, necks and eyes merged into the rhythm of the dance.

All our nationalities sat totally bewitched. If a communist army had burst in on us, with guns blazing, they might have had difficulty in snapping us out of our hypnotic entrancements.

A Kymer Army female platoon also used to visit our base from time to time. They were commanded by an attractive Sergeant whom everyone called 'Nancy.' They wore very neat jungle green military skirts and blouses but very spectacular, skimpy and frilly undergarments – apparently. They all had proper army ID cards and in the box headed 'military trade' – instead of 'infantryman', or whatever, the word 'entertainer' was typed in. However, I cannot say that I ever remember any of them singing or dancing or producing rabbits out of hats.

Barbara's 'Dear John' letter, when it arrived, was not altogether unexpected. It was, as is routine, preceded by a long period without communication. She had in fact only written to me once anyway, and that had arrived during my first few weeks at Vinh Giat.

Of course, one kids oneself at first that one's inaccessible warlike environment would, naturally, cause long delays with the post. However, sooner or later – depending on how much of a veteran recipient of 'Dear John' one is – the fairly sure realisation dawns. The actual 'Dear John' then merely becomes a formality to confirm the situation.

One can almost always tell a 'Dear John' by the envelope. It looks hurriedly written and there are careless mistakes with your name and address. Indeed, no special care has been taken over it – because you are not loved any more. Inside, the pages, if there is more than one, are in the wrong order. Before it gets to the point, odd stories will be repeated that were recounted in the last letter. There will be a few lines of hollow sounding regret and then by some previously unimagined set of circumstances, the blame for the beloved giving themself to another will often be put onto your distant and anguished self.

Barbara started off by recounting the doings of various friends of hers that I did not know and ended up with the casual:

". . . by the way, Murray came round the other night. He was so upset and begged me to come back. I realised that we have this great mental thing and so the engagement is all on again . . ."

I have always found that the evidence that the paragon is just another pathetic thing who slides into the easiest line of proximity, has the merciful effect of transforming my feelings into almost instant contempt and then quickly into indifference. I have, therefore, never suffered for too long.

'Dear Johns' do hit some chaps very hard while they are in a war. Back in the ANZAC province of Phuoc Tuy, soldiers used to expose their unhappiness to the daylight – by pinning their 'Dear John' onto the latrines door. Their mates would then read it, laugh at the coy phrases the girls used to describe what they had done, buy the victims a load of beer and tell them what a lucky escape they had had "not to be saddled with a slag like that."

Every single member of a New Zealand Company actually wrote personally to one weakling childhood sweetheart who had particularly devastated a teenage comrade of theirs. In many colloquial forms, phrases and expressions, they strongly conveyed their views on what sort of woman she was to do that sort of thing with another while the man who loved her bravely faced the foe. Apparently, they achieved a suicide attempt which, at the time, was considered a not unreasonable result.

I realised that I had been saved from serious commitment to the sort of person who could give herself to a physical and emotional weakling – and even felt quite cheered by the sense of relief. Neither could I feel remotely antagonistic towards the breast-beating Murray – as he was getting the sort of girl who could give herself instantly to an oafish soldier – for non-cerebral reasons. I lamented, unspecifically, for a while on the state of womanhood in general. However, there I was, emotionally free again and looking forward to my next romantic adventure.

I could, therefore, afford to be generous-spirited. I wrote a letter to Barbara of my unchanged feelings of affection and friendship, wished Murray and herself every happiness, thanked her profusely for the temporary facility of herself, expressed how privileged I felt to have been able to broaden the details of her experience in some areas and, as she would probably have problems over that with Murray, they should feel free to write any time.

After I returned from taking my letter to the mail-room in the European camp, I wondered why my shed looked so tatty and alien to all reasonable civilization, why I was not a peace-time party chatterer having "meaningful relationships" and why was Vietnam so hot, grimy, sticky and hopeless?

"Stand to!"

It was becoming a familiar shout during the night. In fact, if a number of keen or quick-reacting people did not immediately rush out of their hoochies shouting it after the first four mortar bangs and if someone did not always give my shed wall a great thump as they passed, I might have slept through many of the attacks – as I used to do on the Surrey Commons training area a few years earlier.

The NVA mortar man did not seem to know how to bracket a target and would use the ammunition-wasting method of walking the fire onto the camp. Their first rounds were usually far enough out for the sound of the exploding bomb not to be loud enough to wake me up. By the time they had inched the bursts up to our wire and onto the edge of the camp, their ammunition usually seemed to have run out and they would stop.

The observer was obviously always on the high ground to the West and so the fire would usually just clip that side of camp. I lived on the North Eastern side. It really was becoming an inconveniencing bore. It was getting into the same league as the Mons demo platoon's rifle-cockings and 'blitish johnny' shouts.

I did 'stand to', of course, as I had an example to set to the Cambodians. I started fairly quickly to pull on a United States Army green tee-shirt, a pair of camouflage-pattern trousers and my boots.

The observer must have made a bold left correction for a change as there was suddenly a deafening crump, followed by vicious pins and whines, in my end of camp. More followed. I urgently tugged on my boots.

Then came the heart stopping sound. The deep-throated and powerful

230

thump– thump–thump of one of our 50 calibres starting up on the North West side. It could mean only one thing – an assault upon us had started.

In a matter of seconds I swore, touched the little First World War French girl's crucifix that had been given to a New Zealand soldier and passed to me by his grand-daughter (whose beloved I once was), grabbed my rifle, stuffed my ammunition pouches with bullets, buckled on my webbing and, with laces flapping, rushed out to ensure that the Cambodians and Montagnards in my sector were in their defensive positions.

The worst aspect was other people's shouting of instructions and sense of urgency in several languages. It was bewildering and it distracted one from methodically going through a mental check list of anti-attack immediate actions.

The explosive flashes were blindingly bright and 50 calibre after 50 calibre was opening up. I could see the tracer streaming away into the dark hillside to the West. I wenched my head quickly back to my own front. That was where my responsibility lay. At the moment, there seemed to be no action in, or beyond, our mass of wire. I went quickly up and down the floor of our trench, placing my hand reassuringly on shoulders and saying: "OK?", cheerfully. Fortunately it was dark enough to hide my ashen face.

Sgt Wagner and the other American and New Zealand green berets were there. Amongst the slightly built Asians they looked big, solid and reassuring.

Suddenly there was a lot of shouting along the perimeter doing the shooting and it all stopped. The mortar bomb explosions had also stopped. The night air was charged with an expectant silence. We waited and watched.

Over three hours later we were still waiting and watching. There had been no reply when I had called our sector commander on the field telephone. Could the command post staff have been wiped out by a direct hit?

"It will be dawn soon," Captain 'John' said.

"Then I send a runner. I send him now – it will cause confusion. Some nervous young Cambodian from another sector will shoot him."

About half an hour later, just as the darkness had taken on its first touch of grey, Barry – the A-Team second-in-command from the next compound – came wandering up from a flank wearing a pair of boxer shorts and rubber thong footwear. He had a towel draped over one shoulder and was holding a soap dish. The officer showers were in our area.

"Say you guys are keen," he said, sitting amiably on one of our sand-bag parapets.

"I guess we should have got up early too and re-checked our defence deployment in daylight as soon as possible. You can't practise too much huh? I mean it didn't last long last night – but there was definitely some 'mother' out there. Probably having a look at us. As soon as we were stood down, I managed to get a couple more hours sleep. How about you guys?"

"Gee, you're isolated here – you're up a real little dead end. Say you could get taken out at night and we wouldn't know you were gone!"

He smiled guilelessly at our stony faces.

"Yea. The North's pouring 'em in," he said with a nonchalant laugh and moved to continue to the shower.

"They'll come for us soon."

The young man's eyes flicked back at us, as he turned away, and belied his cool walk.


"When are you going to let me marry your daughter?"

The very keen, but not very tough or bright Cambodian Second Lieutenant said in French to Major Kum Deng, the most senior of the Unit's Cambodian liaison group. Our company was scattered around a ruined temple eating lunch. Their better educated officers often spoke French amongst each other.

"When you become a Captain. Maybe," Major Kum Deng replied with a smile.

"Have you seen his daughter?" the Second Lieutenant said to me.

"May he see the photograph, Mon Commandant?"

Major Kum Deng smiled again, but with paternal pride, and produced a small photograph from his wallet and handed it to me. The portrait was of one of the most beautiful teenage girls that I have ever seen – from Asia or anywhere else. I could only see her face, hair and shoulders, of course, but these details were exquisite and flawless. She radiated an almost dazzling quality that seemed to shine from the little rectangle of thin cardboard. To be loved by her would be paradise on this earth, I decided. However, she was a long way away in Phnom Penh.

I made laudatory, but respectful, comment and handed the photograph back to Major Kum Deng.

"You are not married," the Major stated, "but you have a fiancée?"

"I did for a while a couple of years ago," I replied, "but she left me for someone else."

Instantly, they both stared intently at me – scandalised.

"But how can she do this?" the Second Lieutenent gasped. "She gave her word. What of her honour?"

"Her family's honour?" Major Kum Deng interjected sharply.

I shrugged and said, "Well, she just did not want to get married to me."

"But of course she will want to marry you. You are an Officer. You have been several times to war," the Second Lieutenant said as though that was the last word on the matter.

I was about to say that most Western girls thought that a man was a fool to voluntarily give up the ability to do as he liked and be a soldier – and an even bigger fool to go to a war. They preferred men who gave them constant company, joined them in popular fashions in opinion, taste, dress and habits, paid them court, kept them physically contented – with or without marriage – and bought them entertainment. However, I realised that in their backward community the warrior defender was considered a champion and nonpareil amongst men and to suggest that any woman would not automatically go for, what they considered to be, the jewel on top of the pile of pebbles – if she had the chance – would be beyond their comprehension.

I therefore took refuge in another mystified shrug. They were lost in concern and thought.

"You give her parents much money!" Major Kum Deng burst out suddenly.

He beamed at me as one who had just hit on the obvious solution to all my problems.

I realised that if I said that Western girls normally did whatever they wanted, could not usually be blatantly bought and only obeyed their parents if it suited them, it would be even more stunning than saying that a warrior defender was not a first prize in the marriage competition.

I merely shook my head in melancholy. It was time to get the troops on the move again. As we walked off, Major Kum Deng put his arm comfortingly about my shoulders.

"Hey, you must not be sad, *mon ami*," he said. "Why any father in Cambodia would be honoured to marry his daughter to you . . ." he suddenly tailed off.

"How much pay you get?" he demanded sharply.

The Second Lieutenant flashed a backwards glance at us.

The jungle thinned out as we approached the top of the conical hill. The six Montagnards were spread out on either side of me and I got the forward Cambodian platoon into extended line behind us as we approached the light. I could clearly see the sunlit crest between the tree trunks. There was a rocky outcrop, or 'tor' on the top.

The moment when the point platoon were too far out of the tree line to make it back if attacked would be a time for holding your breath. A machine gun amongst the rocks could get a quarter or more of our force with a few seconds worth of well planned burst and then be away down the far side.

The natural 'pill box' was like a nipple on a breast and there was no covered approach to it. However, it was ground of tactical importance and we had to get to it.

I halted the company and ordered them into all-round defence within the jungle's protection; this turned out to be a lucky idea. I decided that the tough and wiry mountain men could go and earn their, by local standards, good pay, by creeping up on the tor and checking it out for us.

There was a sudden short and loud sound that was a cross between a whine and a whoosh. It was instantly followed by a sharp crump and a burst of rock dust and chips amongst the boulders of the tor. I felt a tiny, but painful, sting on the point of my right shoulder.

"Down!" I roared at everyone. However, they were already down. Curiously, the sounds and effects of the incident gave me a second or two of nostalgia for my first tour in Phuoc Tuy – as it was a shell from a medium gun that had just passed over and landed.

There was an echoing swish above the valley to our left, which was followed by a crump on the neighbouring hill top on their side. A short while later, the sound effects were repeated on the top of the hill to our right.

An artillery observer was doing one of several things. One possibility was that he was firing a 'mark' (or orientating) mission, i.e. he was walking the jungle and, to check that he was not lost, he had sent what he thought was the grid reference of an obvious in-view feature – to mark it and thus, orientate himself.

Another possibility was that he was firing H and Is (harassment and interdiction) missions, i.e. he was selecting either places that he had previously visited or features on a map that looked likely to have enemy passing by, or loitering at them and had lobbed a round over on the off chance.

A third possibility was that he was establishing DF (defensive fire) targets, i.e. pre-selecting obvious points or directions from which attack might come so that the previously organised gunfire could move quickly, arriving when required.

A final possibility was that someone on the gun position was just testing the accuracy of the gunner's laying and his guns' calibration and having a non-specific practice or even a fun shoot. However, the main point was that a large quantity of high explosive and lethal shrapnel had just dropped unexpectedly out of the sky and gone off near us.

I opened my shirt front, lifted the right hand side of my collar and peered under the green denim material at my wound. It was about as serious as the sort of thing one might have got by scraping oneself against a large rose bush or some prickly bamboo. A minute fragment of shrapnel or chip of rock had just touched me.

However, I felt that there was every chance that the wound could probably be permitted to grow a bit as I told and retold the tale over the years to come in the Saloon bars of my village or in Servicemens' clubs.

I was briefly contemplating the semi-circle of attentive faces and the drinks that would be pressed upon me, when the Teutonic Sgt Wagner appeared noiselessly at my side.

"You're the Gunner, Sir," he said.

"What was that?"

I outlined my thoughts to him and was mortified that he did not deem the tiny patch of blood on my shirt as being worth a comment.

"It wouldn't be the North Vietnamese' Soviet artillery," he said thoughtfully.

"They haven't got it this far South yet . . . I reckon its the ROKs. We seen them firing up here before, ain't we?"

I agreed with him. However, the Koreans should not have been firing in this area today as they had been notified that our operation was taking place. It was part of our routine co-operation. I took the information over to Major Parks each month myself. I also sometimes got the privilege of a few moments in the presence of Ghengis Khan as well.

On this occasion communication seemed to have broken down somewhere along the line. I radioed an account of what had transpired back to Vinh Giat. We then made ourselves comfortable in our 'all-round-defence' attitude for about two hours until we got word, over the radio, that the Koreans had been notified that they had been firing where they should not have and had agreed to stop.

We then set off for the tor with rather more confidence.

Two days later when we got back to Vinh Giat, my Colonel sent for me.

"You get over there!" he said, banging his desk. "You get over there and you tell that Korean Colonel, from me, that it isn't good enough. We've got these procedures and *we* follow them. Tell him he needs to tidy his act up!"

I was aghast at the thought of saying any such thing to the Korean Colonel. However, I was 'indidge' liaison officer and my Colonel had given me an order.

About half an hour later, and immaculately starched and polished, I marched, with my usual ceremony, into the main office in the Korean pagoda. The Colonel was obviously becoming ever more kindly disposed towards me. I had become quite good at spotting microscopic changes in his immobile features. The group of standing heavies behind his chair watched me steadfastly.

I bet he has got his old Samurai sword on a shelf under his desk top, I thought to myself – and wondered, not altogether jokingly, if I should get to the end of my speech before my head left my shoulders.

I braced myself and, via a shaking Major Parkes, delivered my Special Forces Colonel's message. To my intense relief there was no violent reflex action. In fact, at first, there seemed to be no reaction at all. Then, without taking his eyes off me, the Colonel snapped a couple of tones into the air.

Two of the heavies immediately took off at the double. We heard their boots thundering down the pagoda steps outside.

For what seemed an age, the room remained a frozen tableau.

Then there was another furious racket on the steps – except that this time a more numerous quantity of big boots could be heard coming back up.

The two infantry majors crashed back into the office with a worried artillery major between them. I got the gist of the exchange that ensued. The Colonel roared and the artillery major prevaricated. The two massive infantrymen then clattered out again and, after another interlude, reappeared with a hapless artillery Lieutenant.

The Battery Commander had obviously said, "It wasn't me. It was my duty Gun Position Officer."

The Colonel harshly trilled an order and, to my amazement, the artillery Major started to beat the artillery Lieutenant with his bamboo cane. In keeping with what appeared to be the Korean tradition – every time he fell down, everyone screamed at him to stand back up at attention again.

Predictably, he got to a state where he could no longer do this and remained horizontal on the floor. The two infantry Majors carried the limp and red welted form out and the artillery Major was dismissed.

Then, to my total confusion, the Colonel smiled the first smile that I had ever seen him give. It was as if he said, "OK? Anything more I can do for you?"

It was as overawing as if I had unexpectedly come across a living dinosaur in a forgotten valley. I was in the presence of perhaps the last of the old school Asian warlords – as naturally spontaneous with his kindness and generosity as he was with his mercilessness. He was probably by then obsolete even in his own country and was the type of military leader that my Western fellow officers could have no concept of, let alone encounter.

I marched out smartly, but dazedly.

"Have you met Scottie?" said Tony, another of the New Zealand Lieutenants.

I withdrew my head and shoulders from the floor level locker, in which I had been rummaging, and stood up straight. It was late afternoon and there were a number of us in the Officers' kit room, sorting out whatever we might need for the 'morrow. The incredibly youthful-looking Captain had just been posted in.

I took his strong hand shake and bade him welcome. Apart from the merest hint of slightly sharpened New Zealand vowels, he was the epitome of the clean-cut all British hero of classic school-boy yarns.

He had a tall, strong, athletic and elegant figure, finely chiselled masculine good looks, steely yet twinkling-blue eyes, and his smart green beret was sat upon neatly trimmed blond curls. He was Bulldog Drummond, Biggles and Richard Hanney all rolled into one.

He was exactly what I have always wanted to be. Sadly, however, in any melodramatic epic, I could have played the sallow and dark villain opposite his pink and gold hero. Figuratively speaking, I often feel that I keep getting run through the body and fall off high turrets into moats.

He and Tony were obviously old friends and were dying to resume their exchange of personal news. I, therefore, excused myself and bent into my locker again.

"How's marriage?" Tony said enthusiastically.

"Oh great!" Scottie replied even more enthusiastically. "Except for the farting!"

I banged my head on the open metal door of the locker above mine.

Obviously sensing an enquiry in my movements and expression, he went on, "Well there's nothing better than lying in the old sack and really letting strip whenever you need to, is there?

I mean when you're single its not really a problem, because you're only occasionally in bed with a Sheilah and you only have to control yourself for a short while . . . But a bloody wife is with you all the time, isn't she?"

He smiled ruefully round at us and Tony nodded sagely. Still chatting animatedly, they went out to continue introducing Scottie around the camp.

I was left thinking deeply; I decided that it was probably just as well that any girl that I really liked always went off with someone else, as the problems of marriage seemed many and varied. Indeed, there were some that would certainly not readily have occurred to me.

A terribly hurtful memory that I had tried to block from my mind swept back. It had been flatulence that had blighted one of my life's most beautiful moments. However, not anything committed by myself – I hasten to add.

Following my early retirement from public school, I had studied for my 'A' level GCE subjects at a college for young adults in Weybridge. I would catch a train each morning from Esher station.

One day I just missed the usual train. However, my annoyance turned to joy when I saw that the girl whom I silently worshipped had also missed it.

Here was the perfect excuse to strike up a conversation. Partners in adversity. She was a fabulously expensive and fabulously beautiful daughter from Oxshott. She was as lovely as an English willow on a Summer's day. The sun shone across the green of Sandown Park race course and the station hollyhocks waved gently.

Soon I was confessing that I had admired her for some time and – unexpected joy of joys – she admitted that she had noticed me and liked me.

A short time later we were strolling up and down the platform hand in hand, standing close together and intimating at the possibility of a future of each others company.

I drew her into the empty waiting room and we sat on a bench. We were able to talk with ease and were naturally relaxed together. My heart was singing.

Suddenly a very large and distinguished ex-military businessman in an immaculate suit and bowler, and carrying a tightly rolled brolly, strolled into the entrance area between the double doors that were propped open on that warm and fresh early Summer morning. We were out of sight just behind one of the doors.

He exploded into a thunderous sequence that could have rivalled the final cannon part of the 1812 Overture. We froze in embarrassed horror with the first window shaking rasp.

"Ah! That's better!" he said to what he thought was an empty room. Then he spotted us.

"Morning! Sorry!" he said with friendly and cheerful unconcern and sauntered back out onto the platform.

My poetry had deserted me; her attention was lost and the forming rose tinted cloud of romance had been blown away. Our purity was tainted. Her hand fell from mine and she moved up the bench. Desperately I searched for the line that would save the day – but it would not be found.

These days I think that a young couple would find such an event instantly comic and the shared giggles would bring them closer together. We, alas, had been brought up during the last days of an era when such things were not supposed to be even thought of.

We travelled awkwardly to college on the later train and her eyes avoided mine for ever more.

I found the two new-pattern big thirty round M16 magazines that I had been looking for and pressed the bullets into first one and then the other.

Like myself, she would be in her mid twenties by now, I thought. Her beauty was so hypnotic, she must be the wife of a charming, handsome and successful man.

The absurdity of the detail of what happened has never altered my sense of a tragic loss of classical proportions – nor ever lessened the memory of the total magic of about twenty minutes at a sunny little railway station so long ago.

"Blimey!" I exclaimed, unable to stop myself at the sight of the mass of deep scars on the Sergeant's shoulders and back. I then apologised to him for my outburst. He was standing in for my Sgt Wagner who was on R and R. Our force was harboured along the banks of a stream and we had taken our shirts off to have a quick wash.

He said that he did not mind and then said unconcernedly that he had been a prisoner of the enemy for a short while once.

I thought ruefully about the way that we – mostly – obeyed the Geneva Convention with prisoners and the enemy gave it not a thought.

Part of the pre-Vietnam package was what to do if taken prisoner. You were explained your rights under international law, the small amount that you were permitted to say to your captors and how to resist interrogation. We were also shown the training film *Captured* which showed the interrogation methods used by the Russians, who assisted the army of the North, during the Korea war.

However, we were all aware that the series of lessons was something of a gesture – designed only to assist our morale. The only persons the NVA/VC took as live prisoners were: high ranking American officers, for obvious propaganda purposes, American pilots, for parading through the streets of Hanoi to rouse their own people and the world's press and any highly skilled military specialists who could be milked for useful knowledge. Everyone else, including all lesser allies, would be put to death as horribly as the circumstances allowed.

In our hearts, we all knew that the real instruction concerning possible capture should have been: 'If defeat looks imminent, then sell your life dearly – it is all that you have left.'

The main difference in overall character between the Asian wars and others is that, in accordance with the ancient conventions of the Continent, they tend to be wars of no quarter.

During my first tour, one of our Company Sergeant Majors tried to get to some isolated young soldiers during a night battle and fell into enemy hands. He was found at dawn with his throat cut. The same fate also befell a NZ SAS Corporal who stayed to fight a lone rearguard action, so that his friends could escape.

I had already been told that one of our American Captains had been

239

captured and had made a lucky escape.

One member of the communist unit that had dragged him away from the battle field had spoken English and had told him gleefully of what they intended to do to him once they got to him to a place where there was less risk of interruption.

He was dumped in his trussed up state in the stern of a small river boat that motored off towards the communist lines.

The American officer decided that any death was better than the slow horrors that awaited him and managed to slide unnoticed off the low stern. He was tightly bound and the river, he believed, would mercifully drown him.

To his amazement, however, he dropped onto a tiny submerged sandbank. If he sat up, he could just keep his nose above water. He sat for over two days and, just when he knew that he could stay conscious no longer and would slide under, he was spotted by a South Vietnamese patrol moving along one of the river banks.

"They cut you a bit," I said to the horribly scarred Sergeant. "Tried to make you talk, huh?"

"Nope" he said."They didn't want me to talk." He twisted his head to look at one of his shoulders. "The surgeons did wonders with tidying me up. No, when our guys burst in on them I was unconscious from when I got shot and they were a good way through skinning me alive."

"I was acting as side gunner on a chopper then," Sergeant Wagner was saying animatedly to a multi-national group of our officers and NCOs on the rifle range.

"Gee! We were almost past when I see this elephant come out into a clearing right below me. I only had time to get a short burst in – but I saw it sink to its knees on its front legs . . ."

"You what!" I roared – totally involuntarily.

"You wounded it! Asian elephants are an endangered species. It was doing no harm. It will have died slowly and painfully! How would you like it if someone shot you for fun? Like all living things, it was a completely individual miracle of creation."

Sgt Wagner roared with sincere and happy laughter.

"You just wouldn't know how the *Chung Wee* is always joshing me!" he said to the others, shaking his head.

"You know the English humour. How they say the opposite of what they mean all serious like. At first I could'nt figure it out, but now I got used to it. It's real crazy and real funny. It's just like David Niven in that movie with Marlon Brando when he's like a high class con."

He beamed conspiritorially at me. He was one of the coolest, bravest, most professional and dependable Senior NCOs I had ever known – just why did all Texans think that, with a few human exceptions, most objects (both inanimate and animate) have been put into this world solely to provide them with target practice? He was forever giving me near heart attacks as he made sudden lightning draws, with yet another of his personal giant magnums, to blow the head off a distant dozing tree snake.

I smiled back at the big boyish-looking man, who had spent several dedicated years in this war, believing that he could compensate for wavering and mismanaging politicians; I just could not help it.

For some obscure reason, I seemed to have developed a phobia of attractive and interested young ladies. Perhaps I felt that if I remained pure the watching Deity might, for some reason, reward this exercise in self-denial by sparing my life. Or perhaps it was just that it made me feel all smug and superior by being ice-cool and not constantly slavering after girls like the other Europeans.

When girls smiled shyly at me as I jeeped through market places, I would snatch my head round to look away from them. Immediately after I had done that, and I saw the bewildered and hurt look on the young and pretty face, I would curse myself and wonder why I had done it.

Major Parks said that he had told a touring troupe of Korean traditional girl dancers about me and one had asked to be introduced the next time they visited our local Korean camp. I had made some unnecessary and feeble excuse not to go.

A couple of times Pan Am air hostesses had helicoptered in to spend an evening in our Officers' club and, on both occasions, I had stayed up in my end of the camp listening to Cambodian music, chatting and eating dried fish and rice. I really could not explain it.

Yung, however, gave me no chance. She was a receptionist at a little hotel. I had parked my jeep outside it while I went to buy some United States Army tins of sausages in baked beans and fruit salads from the black market. We got mostly Asian style ration packs on the base and the black market was a quick, and cheap way to get things that were not readily available – which was not often the case with the incredibly efficient and bountiful American quartermaster system. You could buy bullets in the black market if you had to.

When I came back to the jeep, she was blocking my path. I could not have got round her to get into the driving seat. She had looked at me from the hotel verandah once or twice. She was staring nervously downwards; then she looked quickly up, flashed a very shy smile and looked down again. She was like an Asian Barbie Doll. She was tall and slender, yet curvy, and had an unusually large bust for an Asian girl. She wore a tasteful little pastel coloured beach-style outfit of a sleeveless top and a pair of tailored Bermuda shorts – that showed her long, smooth and shapely pale tan legs. Her shimmering blue-black hair was in a medium length style that involved an attractive soft sweep across her forehead.

The big almond eyes stopped flicking round the sand about her little pink canvas sneakers and she asked me a quick question in Vietnamese that I did not understand. However, I did hear the name 'Vinh Giat.'

I nodded and smiled.

"I come from Vinh Giat," I said, tapping my chest with a forefinger.

I had obviously got the question right. She smiled a little more confidently, looked directly at me and asked another question, also about Vinh Giat. This time I was completely stumped.

She realised that I had not understood and after a shaky giggle, a quick burying of the face in the hands and a gossamer light millisecond touch of soft fingers on the back of the hand that held my shopping in front of me, she too pointed at herself and then North towards Vinh Giat.

"Vinh Giat? Vinh Giat?" she asked sweetly, like a polite child.

She wanted to go to Vinh Giat. And then I was surprised and moved to see that it was because she wanted to be with me. What an odd mixture of demureness and directness Vietnamese girls were. I passed through the town almost daily when not away on short jungle forays.

Sunshine seemed to break out inside me. I realized that I did want to care, and be cared for, especially in these times.

I smiled and nodded, and her stunningly, pretty and beaming face took much past heartache away. I could not remember when anyone had looked as if they had wanted my company so much.

The next day was Friday and just as the red Asian sunset was at its most breathtaking she stepped out of the old and dusty bus by the camp gate where I was waiting for her. This time she was in a shimmering green *au-dai* and wearing a traditional broad brimmed and flattish conical straw sun hat. A red ribbon tied in a bow under her chin kept it in place. She carefully carried a spare set of cream *au-dai* on a coat hangar and quickly and embarrassedly gave me her toothbrush to mind – as she had no suitable pocket for it.

Yung stayed until Sunday. We ate hamburgers and French fires. We seemed to talk about so much although we did not really have a language in common. We watched the Officers' club evening feature films with snugly linked arms – in the way I used to sit with the peerless Denise in the Richmond *Odeon* and I realised that my fortified shed was in fact quite a delightful, small and simple rural Asian residence. Before, I had been a well intentioned visitor in Vietnam. Yung seemed to give me family membership and, oddly, the country came to seem as much home to me as anywhere I had ever been.

I had forgotten the intensity of monsoon rains until I encountered the monsoon again on this tour. At four-thirty in the afternoon, as usual, the water started. There were just a few pats on the leaves about our ambush position and then it roared down.

The branches and leaves jerked and danced crazily as the heavy water rods drove vertically down to them. The surface of the river at our backs was an evenly boiling mass, as if steel shot were constantly being fired into its every square inch.

It was at times like this that I briefly wished that I wore a steel helmet in the jungle – like the Americans and the Asians – instead of the British Commonwealth jungle hat. The former was at least waterproof. In seconds, the water was through my hat, poncho and jungle greens. A film of water was flowing over the jungle floor beneath our bodies.

The ambush was set so there was nothing to do but lie there. By the time it got dark, our body temperatures would get extremely low, despite the climate. I should be alright for a while, with my European 'blubber.' However, the skin and bone Asians would soon be shivering uncontrollably and hypothermia cases could start. Eventually I should have to abort the operation – but I could probably give it another hour. Just after it got dark, the rain was switched off as quickly as it had been started; the start time of the day's rain was fairly regular. However, the endings were more variable.

I remembered on my first tour how – despite the little awning I used to assemble above my hammock – the water would run down the ropes and bounce in and gradually fill my little bed trough up. The weight would slowly press me down to the jungle floor and the pincers that awaited my canvas covered bottom. If the rubber trees that were supporting my hammock were too slim they would be bending over me by the time either the excrutiating nips or the unpleasant dampness woke me up.

Suddenly in the dark to my front, I saw a bobbing light. I had seen its like before. The NVA and VC often took the risk of using a torch at night to travel more quickly, as the vegetation prevented its light from being seen from too far away. They probably thought that it was a lesser evil than noisily crashing about in total darkness. Because of the many problems with it, we rarely moved at night.

The torch light seemed to be at about one hundred metres from me and moving erratically across our front from right to left. The others must have seen it and I was surprised by the lack of little tense shiftings from around me.

However, they knew the signal for opening fire. It was with the firing of the Claymore or when I let off the first shot. It was a pity that the enemy were not on the track just in front of us. Nevertheless, the firepower that we could pour into the column that obviously must follow the torch holder would probably decimate them. I arrived at the torch light and then moved my point of aim fractionally back to where the man would be. I started to squeeze my trigger.

Then I saw that the light was closer to me than my foresight.

I should certainly not have been the first person in a jungle war to have shot at a dancing little firefly. The eerie little brightly glowing flying insects give the exact illusion of a distant light being flicked about amongst tree trunks at night.

It was during the year that I was at Vinh Giat that the American actress Jane Fonda made her contemptable visit to the North Vietnamese headquarters in Hanoi. Apparently, recorded excerts from the speech that she made for them were played on the AFN news.

I remember one of the New Zealand Corporals, who had listened to the radio, coming up to me in the compound. He was beside himself with rage.

"Do you know!" he said, "Do you know – she went around wearing one of their hats, believed every word they said about how they were nice and, on the wireless she called us all prawns!"

"Pawns," I said.

"Eh?" he replied.

"I expect she said pawns," I went on, "Chess pieces of the least value and, therefore, the most expendable."

"Oh," he said brightening. "Well that's alright then."

The English actress Vanessa Redgrave also felt that she was a romantic revolutionary by attending disorderly events in London that had a Vietnam excuse. She would wear a white "peace" headband about her brows like an albino Apache, would very shrilly sing the popular peace dirges and would make statements to the press such as: "Anyone who does not support the Viet Cong is a fascist."

However, ageing actresses, desperate to make all the world their stage, were merely a few of the West's vain who used a distant existence struggle, of which they had made no detailed study, as the vehicle for their poses. Not that facts were particularly important to the chattering classes on any topical subject then. Fashion dictated the only possible opinions.

"Well, you're artillery. You should know what it is," 'John' Marrett said, grinning. Barry looked worriedly and expectantly at me.

It was late on a Saturday afternoon and – with towels round our waists and carrying sponge bags – we had been walking along beside the perimeter wire to the shower block when we heard the ripple of booms across the other side of our valley.

"Mortars," I said.

"Yea – even I figured that out," said 'John.'

Are they the primaries (the sound of the bomb leaving the mortar) or secondaries (the sound of the round exploding on the ground)? I pondered.

Mortars were not really my speciality. The sound came from the direction of the Korean camp. It could have been them being mortared and we might be next. I decided that most likely it was the Koreans registering a DF, as they often did. However, the explosions did seem to have a bit more of a *crump* – which suggested a secondary, rather than a *bonk* which suggested a primary. . .

"It's the primary," I finally decided. "You see, I can tell by the sound . . ."

I suddenly realised that I was talking to myself. Then I heard the whoosh above me and, with almost a racing dive, I joined the others in semi-naked indignity in the muddy water-filled ditch. The trio of bombs shook our end of the camp.

The irrigation ditch would have contained human excretia, as our sewage system kept fracturing, and every tropical and water-borne virus known to man. I decided that being riddled with shrapnel was a better way to go and slipped and slithered my way out. A communist observer was obviously only registering onto us in daylight – an ominous sign – as, now that he had got the range to the camp, he ceased firing.

Both the Koreans and ourselves could now be hit again any time by that observer – if the same mortar position and technical data were used.

The other two joined me. 'John' gave no-one in particular one of his vacant laughs and, covered from head to foot in pale brown mud and slime, we continued on to our, now urgently needed, showers.

Saturday nights were back to being a few *Budweisers* or *Slitz* with the chaps, after either my hamburger and French fries or fish-heads and rice, as my beautiful, and much loved Yung was gone.

Her parents and younger brothers and sisters lived in the North West, which was thick with Northern invaders. She had received no word for several months nor had she been able to contact them. Almost from the moment I met her, I knew that she was very worried and preoccupied. In unguarded moments, when not distracted by our absorbtion with each other, she looked so touchingly forlorn.

As I was aware of the sense of family duty amongst the Vietnamese, I did not attempt to dissuade her from trying to get to them. All I could do was rather lamely entreat her to be careful. If I thought that I could have obtained some local leave and escorted her, I should have.

I saw her off on the bus that would take her on the first of the several stages of her long journey. My present of the latest pattern tiny transistor radio cheered her for a while.

She stayed with me until the driver and other passengers got politely impatient. European-style passionate farewells were not permitted, of course, so we shook hands and bowed to each other.

In other respects, it was quite a pleasant morning. The monsoon season was ending and although it had not varied much for several days, the weather had not yet got hot and dry. The red Vietnamese dust had changed from its Plaster of Paris to its talcum powder consistency. I watched the bus, and its attendant red cloud, disappear round the furthermost green corner. I could smell its burning diesel fuel for some time after it was gone.

As she could not write in English, I gave her a postcard addressed to me that she was to send when she arrived. She was going to draw an X kiss on it before she sent it.

I have always hoped that its non-arrival was because of either an inefficient postal system or a subsequent disenchantment with myself and not because of an encounter with a cross-fire or murderous military rapists of some nationality or other.

Every beautiful detail of her is still so acute to me, it seems difficult to believe that all we had was a few days.

Most localised jungle military actions start off with a single shot which, almost as if it had been fired through a nest of exploding wasps, sets off a mass of instant and noisy activity even before its echo has died away. Sometimes ambushes start with Claymore mines being fired into the victims, so there is a roar followed by a furious fusillade of automatic fire. However, the single shot initiation, followed by a rapid escalation as everyone – on both sides – joins in, seems to be my most familiar memory of these things. It usually reaches a furious crescendo and then starts to lessen as the side taken at a disadvantage either falls down dead or breaks contact. It finally peters out into a few final desultory bangs.

It all started according to form one night as we were setting up an ambush about five miles from camp on the boggy and scrub covered countryside between the South China Sea and the nearest North South highway.

Off went the first shot as foes met up about a mile to the South of us and away went the build-up of firing and noise. However, on this occasion it

246

carried on building up and building up. Like the expanding rings of water that emanate from the point where the stone was thrown in the pond, so ripple after ripple of musketry started up as more and more were joined in battle ever further from the point of initiation.

However, what alarmed me, on this occasion, was the fact that it was spreading rapidly in my direction.

A group of Special Forces specialists and I had been organising a platoon's worth of virtually untrained Cambodians into an ambush party. We had not known that the coastal flats were going to be so crowded. We had received no intelligence that it would contain anyone other than ourselves and, if we were very lucky, perhaps a few quietly creeping VC or NVA for us to catch in our ambush.

Unfortunately, we seemed to have inadvertently joined a close quarter meleé between two quite large North and South Vietnamese units.

The Warrant Officer in charge of the SNCO specs hurried over to me and in a hoarse whisper above the racket said:

"Sorry, Sir. We godda go!"

Which was perfectly correct as our orders were that specs were not to be involved in battle. Trainers to put the local armies on their feet were too precious a commodity to arbitrarily waste on some bit of short-term, localised, military action. They might be able to indirectly change the future of the region.

They all piled onto the back of the fortified truck that was already starting to pull away. The engine could not be heard above the din of battle. It showed no lights, of course, and it was a black and moonless night. I could just see it lurching away across the countryside. They were obviously going to try and circumnavigate back to the road and then make a run South, along the edge of it, for Vinh Giat.

I prayed that no-one saw them as neither side could know who they were and would probably fire at them.

Some minutes later, there was a brief lessening of the firing and shouts and cries could be heard – and the sound of the truck tearing along the road.

My heart stood still. The truck was completely invisible on this darkest of nights and had a black hillside behind it. However, a few random bursts were fired from several places in the general direction of the engine's sound. I saw the lines of tracer streaking towards the road area.

Finally, during another millisecond's abatement in the noise, I just caught the sound of the truck fading into the distance. It had made it. I later heard that the only casualty from the amazing battlefield tour was an SNCO in the cab who had a bullet graze on the top of his head.

My elation at the good fortune of my friends faded somewhat when I considered the situation of the Cambodians and myself.

I thought about joining the South Vietnamese there and then and fighting alongside them. However, I abandoned that idea when I realised that I did not know where either side was. If I led my gaggle of semi-trained Cambodians crashing about in the dark scrub and tried to get close enough to any group to see who they were – everyone would assume that an approaching force that was not their own was an enemy and they would, not unreasonably, shoot us.

Next I thought of just harbouring where we were and waiting until the waring parties either fought to a stop or left. However, as the battle area kept expanding and contracting and ebbing and flowing, it seemed highly probable that some large force would sooner or later walk over us and exterminate us as they passed.

Just then a jet aircraft passed overhead – obviously called up by the South Vietnamese commander – and dropped a line of parachute flares to illuminate the battlefield. They were directly over us, which fairly firmly indicated what I had already suspected, from the different small arms sounds, that we were behind the North Vietnamese lines. We pressed ourselves into any and every fold in the ground and bit of vegetation and froze. The light produced an earth-shaking roar of an even greater mass of firing.

Removing our persons to a different location seemed like a very good, and even urgent, idea: if I led them to the sea and we tried to skirt the battle by wading round the end. Any more illumination would make us easy targets against the shining water. The route the truck took seemed the lesser of the available evils.

We would go back away from the fight for a little – but not too far because any communist reinforcement would be coming that way – and then curve round to the highway and move down the filthy monsoon ditch that I knew ran along its Eastern side.

I drew the ashen faced Cambodian teenagers about me and explained. I should be lead scout and they were to be in a tight bunch behind me. If we spread out tactically some might get separated from us and if we were caught it was unlikely that anything would save us anyway. If I were killed the acting Sergeant was in charge and they were to keep going. If we were caught fair and square, it was every man for himself to fight his way out, run and get back to base how, and when, he might. The battle seemed to involve automatic rifles fairly exclusively. I could hear few section machine guns. Mortars and artillery had not yet joined in, although the blinding flash and vicious deep crack of hand thrown, and launcher propelled grenades could be heard. I tried to think of it all as just an awful noise and, for the moment, put out of my mind that men were unquestionably falling in great numbers onto the muddy and stoney ground beneath the thickets. The whine and hiss of speeding rounds came from the night sky just above us.

There was an impenetrable piece of creeper and prickles behind us – I had deliberately chosen it to guard our backs for the ambush – so we could not immediately move directly away.

I checked that my M16 was ready to fire and beckoned the Cambodians after me. I sacrificed a measure of stealth in order to change our location fairly quickly, before local conditions altered for the worse.

The countryside on our left – the side away from the battle – was suddenly dark, open and deserted-looking heath. Ideal for a quick night getaway.

A hand-fired flare went up over the part of the action nearest to us. To have dived to the ground would have given us away – so we stood stock still where we were.

There was a glimpse of about three North Vietnamese amongst some stems some fifty metres on our right. They had their backs to us. One wore a jungle topee.

Three rapid aimed shots would get the lot. However, just as I raised my rifle the flare burnt out, so I poured my entire thirty round magazine into their area. The Cambodians had not realised that I was going to open fire and were struck rigid with shock. I had also not realised that I was going to open fire and was in almost the same state.

"*Allez!*" I screamed and we took off across the heath, in any order, like a rabble of gazelles. There was no persuing burst.

The heroes of British schoolboy books did not, of course, shoot people in the back. Perhaps I should have called out:

"You despicable cads! Your end has come!" so that they would turn round and I could have shot them in the chest.

If I had hit anyone, then I had eradicated all possibility of achieving my ambition of being the type of lead character that Geoffrey Farnol or Rider Haggard might have written about. The headmaster who had succeeded the vain mental sadist of my schooldays would never hold my life up as shining star to a spellbound school Chapel. However, it was probable that my friendships with girls and early beer drinking had already irrevocably removed me from that league anyway.

Then again, it is highly likely that to-day's public school boys prefer listening to synthetic pop noises and other modern youthful habits and do not have a great deal of time or interest left for the old-style ripping yarns.

All of this crossed my mind in a flash as we flew across the mud, pebbles and small clumps of bush. Running away, or making a tactical withdrawal, was also, of course, not the way to get into heroic legend either.

I reloaded on the run and slowed my group down as we approached the road. It would have been most advisable to have crawled along the ditch. However, it was so disgusting that I could not bare the thought of it, so we walked along it and crouched gingerly down if danger seemed near.

The battle was still confining itself to the few square kilometres between the road and the sea and, incredibly, no one came up onto the road – even though it was on a sort of causeway and overlooked the swamp, heath and scrub coastal flats.

At last I could see the lights of the Vinh Giat watchtowers in the distance and the lethal exchanges of fire were getting further and further round behind us. A track from the beach crossed the road ahead and our ditch became a large concrete pipe in order to pass under it.

I thought briefly about nipping up onto the road, but it was raised and open at the crossroads and would have been foolhardy. I, therefore, braced myself, got down on my hands and knees on the unthinkable floor of the drain and started to crawl forward.

I heard the click of a safety catch going off and, after a moment of horror struck staring and squinting at the open pipe mouth a few metres ahead, I saw that a prone figure was aiming a rifle straight at my face.

The explosion and the end must come any second and then I saw the silhouette of the figure's American pattern steel helmet.

"*Tan Tay Lan* – number one," I whispered hoarsely. Then I said: "GI! OK! OK!" All proper Vietnamese phrases had deserted me.

The rifleman did not move. However, my call had attracted others from behind him. I repeated my lines and added: "Yellow River!" It was a popular song of the moment with all non-communist allies.

A soldier, who was probably the NCO in charge of this portion of South Vietnamese rear guard, squelched up behind the still aiming sentry.

"OK, OK," he said quietly to all of us and gently lifted the aiming man's rifle from his hands.

My life had been spared again because my sudden appearance along the open sewer had been as terrifying to the Vietnamese sentry as the sight of him had been to me. He had totally seized up with fear.

We all chatted happily in whispers in relief. The sentry gradually came to and grinned around sheepishly. I put a grateful arm around his thin shoulders and realised that he was about fourteen. One could probably have spun his outsize-looking steel helmet round on his head.

He looked over the rim of the ditch at the Dante's Inferno of orange flashes, jets of flame, constant gunfire and powerful ripping explosive noise. "Number ten," he said solemnly and rather unnecessarily.

As we could assist our South Vietnamese friends with flank protection, I arranged the Cambodians in fire positions along both sides of the ditch. The South Vietnamese were giving a good account of themselves. Their Unit consisted of local boys, had combat experience, had been together for some time and knew the area.

Shortly after the Cambodians and I attached ourselves to the Vietnamese, the Koreans charged in as a relief force.

There were few troops in the war who could equal these Prussians of modern Asia. They systematically exterminated the North Vietnamese force.

I visualised the old Colonel down there, advancing unconcernedly through the thick of it, veteran of so many battles during nearly forty years in all parts of Asia – it was his *natural* environment. His voice would be as the word of God to his burly and disciplined Siberians. On the American base, we used to joke that he must have brought his old, but finely serviced, sword with him to this war. I wondered if he really did have one buckled to his side and was flicking it from its scabbard every so often to cut a wretched communist Soldier from the path of his advance with a lightening twirl and slash.

By the dawn, the Koreans had turned the event into a sport. They were laughing and whooping as they flushed each terrified communist out of the thickets and jokingly argued over whose turn it was to bowl the frantically running man. They let some get quite a long run in. They watched as though disinterested until he was a really difficult target – before one of them suddenly whipped his rifle up into the aim and a sharp crack flopped the distant figure onto his face.

Once the five ton trucks, that had come up with the light to clear the battlefield, started to return, loaded first with the wounded and then the dead. My group and I shook hands with the ARVN piquet, climbed out of the ditch and, in single file, started back along the edge of the road towards Vinh Giat.

The battle had not seemed to have had any strategic objective, I thought. Presumably no one was prepared to fight and die over ownership of the quite revolting bit of swamp and scrub. However, it had not been my fight, so it would be silly of me to have got too depressed by it all. The aim of both sides had obviously been to remove as many of their enemies as possible from the overall war – and a chance confrontation near the beach had provided an occasion.

Military traffic of all kinds was building up on the road and, by coincidence, I looked back just in time to see the old Korean Colonel coming up the road in his jeep.

I got the muddy Cambodians into a line facing inwards and called them

251

to attention. I saluted, whipping my left hand across my chest to strike my vertically held rifle with a crash. The Colonel tapped his driver to indicate that he was to slow down. Perched up on the rear of his jeep were two teenage Asian Mr Universe contestant bodyguards. Impassively and steadfastly – their rifles at the ready – they watched the country on their respective sides.

The Colonel stopped level with me and, as I stood at British Army attention at the roadside, he reached out to gently pat the side of my face before moving on. His small smile was like a sudden beam of Winter sunshine. I knew then that here was a warrior chieftain upon whose word even I, idle comfort seeker though I am, would have risked my life in a moment.

He must have mistakenly thought that I had played a significant part in his battle. Sadly, circumstances did not permit us to meet again.

Perhaps it was because I was not too tall, blond, pink, large featured and my eyes were not blue or too round that Asian girls took an interest in me. I was probably European enough to be novel, yet short and dark enough not to be too alien. However, for whatever reason, obvious possibilities kept flatteringly cropping up. Girls in shops, offices and hotels in Nga Trang, Qui Non or wherever seemed suddenly to be at my side and unembarrassedly chatting away as if we were old friends — to the exclusion of my more Nordic companions. This sort of thing had not happened, and was not to happen to me on any of the other three continents.

Sometimes I felt that if I found a new loving friend, then it might help to ease the longing for Yung. In the end, however, I affected not to notice the openings where I might have made an invitation and politely left matters unconcluded. I probably felt that too much pain came with these beautiful, and eventually elusive, Asian butterflies and there was worry enough around.

Yung had, of course, suddenly and irrefutably appeared. Lan, however, just sort of grew on me. Almost without my being conscious of a progression, Lan was with me more and more, when I was in camp and off duty, until she was there all the time.

Yung was an uncontrivedly sexy and spectacular Vietnamese beauty. Lan was a reserved and classic Vietnamese beauty. However, both were breathtakingly striking and utterly unforgettable.

There was no flirtation or courtship with Lan – just a growing need for each others' largely untalking company or an inability to be comfortable if we were not together.

Some senior relative of Lan's had the contract to run much of the civilianised administrative aspects of our camp, mainly catering and cleaning. Lan used to come onto the base two nights a week as the assistant to the Officers' Club projectionist (her cousin). The wonderous United States system used to ensure that, at the front we got the very latest Hollywood movies that were concurrently having their world premieres in New York London, Paris and Rome etc.

She would scurry about with efficiency, skill and natural grace. She would set up the equipment, open up flat round tins and feed film through a complicated sequence of spools. The projectionist would be trying to decipher the English labels on the tins of film to ensure that the reels went on in the right order and generally watching over the setting up. When Lan had everything ready for her cousin, she would switch off the lights, slip off her little flat shoes and squat with long folded legs on the seat of a chair. The projectionist would then grandly step forward and switch on.

She never smiled, although everyone watched her. My eyes would often stray to the solemn pretty girl in the flickering light but she always looked impassively at the screen. Several Wednesday and Saturday evenings passed. Then one evening, as I was once again drawn to take an appreciative glance, she was looking straight at me. This happened a few more times. I started to receive quick and silent half-smiles as I arrived to take a seat. As I would leave for the bar at the end of the show, I would raise my hand in polite farewell and we would smile quickly once again.

One Saturday evening as I was doing that, the pile of film tins started to slip off a chair. I caught them before they hit the floor. She smiled broadly and I continued to assist with a few odd jobs of the tidying up. When I turned to go, she said:

"I won't be long," as though we always left together and, oddly, it seemed to me as if we always had.

She joined me in the Officers' Club and we chatted a little. She had some English as she had studied it at school. It was English English rather than GI English, which seemed a good sign. Later we walked, without either holding hands or linking arms, back home to my little shed.

We stopped and looked at the stars, but were distracted from them by the flashing lights and sounds of a heavy weapons battle in the distance. A rush of screaming whines suggested that a Soviet multi-barrelled rocket launcher was not far away in the West. I saw the moonlight on her eyes as she looked at the stream of streaking lights and felt her sadness. When we walked on we were, metaphorically, closer together.

Both Yung and Lan, like so many grown up and single Vietnamese girls who had to work away from home, while a war was on, had probably had a sequence of army protectors. They were not true prostitutes – as they would not have accepted money. What they did need, however, was a sense of security and comfort in the lonely and frightening world of constant war. I believe too that, with Yung and Lan, being in love was also a mandatory part of it.

The booms and the crackling of distant musketry gradually encroached upon our conversations, and drinking, so we all walked out of the Officers' Club bar, across the small compound in front and looked through our maze of wire towards the sound.

There was a great pillar of orange flame in the night sky about ten kilometres South of us. The gunfire noise came from the vicinity of its base. We decided that it was the United States Air Force camp across the bay. The orange pillar was reflected in the portion of sea that was visible to us.

Everyone speculated anxiously about what was going on.

"They sure have got some fuel on fire," said one of our Captains.

"Could be mortars did it, rockets or an accident," he went on.

"The Air Force Police will be pouring everything they've got into the shadows."

He watched grinning.

"I don't mind taking a few yards, and maybe even some bodes, down to check it out," said the ever dashing and brave Scottie.

"Nope. We don't have either the troops or the communications and its not our business,", a Major replied.

"We are a Special Forces clandestine camp on clandestine operations. There are plenty of conventional troops for this. The ROKs and the ARVN control the province and should react and the Air Force has got all the fighter-bombers, gunships and air cover they could want on the end of a radio. Sure would like to know what's going on though."

A few more junior officers made murmurings of: "We can't just stand here" and "It makes you feel so helpless," etc.

"We'll hear all about it soon enough in the morning," the Major said reassuringly.

"At the moment the commies haven't got a force in the area big enough to overrun them. Say! I might just buy a round!"

With the odd backwards glance, we followed him back into the bar.

Early the following morning, we did indeed hear what had happened at the Air Force base and it was a harrowing story.

We used to rather envy them their life in what was almost a decent sized American town transplanted into Vietnam. Their camp covered a vast acreage and had shops, bars, restaurants, cinemas and a permanent population of girls. Menial tasks were done by locally recruited Vietnamese youths and the Montagnard did all the guard duties. Pop music thundered constantly up into the brightly lit night sky and generators chugged away endlessly to provide electricity to keep the Coke machines iced up and the air conditioning going. Pornographic magazines could be bought without number.

Frozen food was flown direct from the United States. They had steak and apple pie.

A United States airman could do his tour in Vietnam without having to go off the base. He might, of course, hear or see – in the distance – the odd burst of gunfire or exploding mortar bomb or rocket. This would provide excitement without danger. Finally, he could return home with his rows of medals and look back on a satisfactory air force ground tour.

Unfortunately, drugs had taken a hold on the camp. Asia has always produced them in abundance. We had heard of drug-crazed hallucinating men running amok with machine guns and mowing down their friends and irrational, drug-induced arguments between two airmen that ended with deaths, as both went for their weapons, were apparently not infrequent.

Finally, the base commander decided that enough was enough and, apart from the United States Air Force Security Police and their Montagnard auxilaries, all weapons were taken from the airmen and locked in a central armoury.

It was not an unreasonable decision in the circumstances. The unnecessary deaths almost completely stopped and reliable intelligence informed that, as there was not an enemy force in the area large enough to overrun the base, there was no immediate problem with distancing most men from their arms. The base also had ground defence fortifications all round that were even deeper and mightier than those of Vinh Giat.

Unfortunately, however, the North Vietnamese had a comparatively new elite force in their army – the Sapper, or military engineer. Sappers have existed in all armies for hundreds of years, of course. However, the NVA had brought the art to nearly the ultimate state of sophistication. By using the traditional cunning, courage, stealth and manual dexterity of the Vietnamese and combining it with: modern explosives, invention and inspired and daring tactics, they produced a small corps of specialists who could inflict devastation out of all proportion to their numbers.

Agents amongst the resident girlfriends and the labouring force ensured that the intelligence flowing constantly to the North Vietnamese high command was fairly faultless.

When word was received that ninety per cent of the base's weapons were locked in a central armoury it was decided that the moment for attack had come. It was probably realised that a crushing blow was not possible. However, a terrible wound from which full recovery might be difficult, or impossible, was.

To make any impression on the camp with a conventional force, several divisions' worth of troops would have been necessary – so they decided to use two sappers with a supporting rifle section of about ten men.

The fortifications did not worry the sappers – as their lifetimes' study had been in getting under such things unseen. The Montagnard guards also did not worry them as they knew that the Montagnard were nomads and liked movement. The Montagnards fought ferociously when they could dart and run through the jungle. However, they got bored and unobservant when used as static sentries. They also knew that by late at night, much of the camp's population would be either drugged, drunk or engaged with an illegal – but tolerated – resident girlfriend or prostitute.

The attacking communist group set out around mid-evening. The two sappers led. They did not cut the barbed wire because it would have pinged and rattled. They propped it up with short but strong bamboo sticks they carried for this purpose. They also scraped shallow crawl trenches under the wire where appropriate. They avoided or disconnected alarms. They lifted mines by hand – as they had learned to do as children against the Japanese and the French. Many modern mines have an anti-lifting device, so that if you arbitrarily lift them up, they go bang in your face. They would have felt for the anti-lifting devices with their long and delicate Asian fingers beneath the sand, then from their hat-brims they would have taken one of the many large safety-pins that was stored there. This would be used to replace the arming clip that the American minelayer had taken out when he had planted the mine in the ground.

The then inert mine could be either left beside their path or put into a pack to be taken away and used against the allies at a later date.

Eventually, they came through, or under, the fixed wire fence and into the camp. Then, they strolled inwards to the armoury. They may even have had a little map, drawn by one of the resident agents, of how to find it. Anyone seeing the group – once they were inside the base – would not have been unduly alarmed. After all, there were armed Asians in various patterns of military clothing wandering about. The Montagnard love to have an international mix of dress, e.g. green berets, New Zealand shirts, Australian boots, Thai trousers, etc and many national and formation patches sewn all over them.

Neither was it odd to see allies carrying communist weapons. They may have been rather inaccurate over great distance. However, they had the virtues of being robust, simple, reliable and fired a good heavy slug. They were particularly good for repulsing close quarter attack from a static defence position and anyone who picked an AK47 up from a battlefield usually retained it for this purpose.

Once they found the central armoury, they proceeded as quickly, and as unobtrusively as possible, to dig themselves shell scrapes (shallow firing trenches – that one had to lie down in to gain cover) all around it.

The sappers probably left the rifleman to get on with this simple chore while they went off and found a source of inflammable material. There they planted their satchel charges (soldiers' packs filled with explosive and pre-fused). They started the time-set fuses and rejoined the riflemen in the shell scrapes. They were not particularly concerned about the destruction of material. They merely wanted something that would make a noticeable display when it went up and would cause a reaction.

The commodity that they wished to destroy was the one that the Western non-communist nations would anguish over the most – human life.

At the appointed time, the explosives went off. It was sufficiently significant in sound and bright burning after effect to raise even the most semi-conscious or most heavily sexually engaged.

Within minutes, packed masses of unarmed men were surging towards the armoury from all directions – and the NVA cut them down in rows.

The confusion was total. Those at the back of the crowds could not work out what was happening and pressed on until they too were mown down. The command structure was geared to attack from outside the base – not from its centre. It took a long time for them to work out what was happening and improvise a reaction.

Some time after it started, airmen in heavier degrees of sleep or drugedness continued to wake up and come hurrying out. They must have been blinded by the bright light of burning, confused by the shattering noise of the mass of fire and the shouts and screams. They must have wondered why they were tripping over so many dead bodies and sooner or later they would have been smashed to the ground by a bullet themselves.

These were not, of course, simple foot-soldier riflemen GIs who were dying, but very expensively trained air force technical specialists.

About fifteen to twenty minutes after it started, the communists ceased firing. Possibly they had fired all their ammunition or, with such an endless quantity of targets, their weapons had overheated and they were getting stoppages.

They left the base and melted away into the night and – as far as is known – without any casualties to their group.

The vast and sophisticated air force camp, with such powerful combat resources, had been devastated. The latest scientific mass killing flying machinery was left alone as it is just so much inanimate junk without human operators of a like quality. The NVA had seen the so obviously weak pillar, had knocked it away with a small quick blow and an impressive, but flawed, structure had fallen.

Over the next few months we saw gallant attempts to resurrect the base. However, its heart must have been irrevocably stricken. First it was fully reinforced, then reduced in size and scope and finally it was stripped of much of its valuable and expensive technology and abandoned.

The locals then looted what remained of the portable contents and the refugees from the NVA invasion, who were constantly streaming South past the base, gradually removed all the wood and corrugated iron sheets to build their temporary roadside shanty towns. Soon new vegetation appeared on its paths and open areas and – apart from a marooned runway and some other tarmac patches – the jungle took it back.

"Well, Sir, d'ya think you'll make some kinda effort to stay alive when I'm gone?" Sergeant Wagner asked smilingly as we moved towards the departure area of Nga Trang airfield. "I mean – I've come to realise that British military philosophy is unchanged since Bunker's Hill – advance in an upright posture towards where the fire is thickest – but it wouldn't do any harm to be a bit sneaky once in a while."

Yet another of his year long tours of duty was over. I was going to miss him personally as well as professionally.

"I don't suppose I'll be able to get back home – or here – before we've pulled out," he went on.

"Maybe I'll see you in Thailand next year if the dominoes keep on falling – huh?"

He thought for a moment.

"No – do you know that Northern Ireland's getting real bad. I reckon that's where we'll go next."

I said that as it was a British internal matter, I thought it unlikely. However, my reservations failed to impress as he believed implicitly that the United States Special Forces were the whole world's Lone Ranger.

However, the most unlikely things can happen in the military. I could not have imagined that in the fairly near future, I should serve in a mountain war in Kashmir, come under fire outside branches of Boots the chemist and Lloyds Bank on a British street or have to join battle with jet fighter-bombers and a modern regular army in Sub-Antarctica.

Sergeant Wagner looked magnificent. He had a male model face, an athlete's physique and a natural ability to look smart. I had not seen him in his razor-creased khaki walking-out uniform before. At a recent Vinh Giat parade (or 'formation'), he had been awarded United States, Vietnamese and Cambodian decorations to add to his rows. He also qualified for paratrooper wings of all these nations.

He wore a pair of spit-polished New Zealand boots that I had got for him. They were all leather and were considered to be smarter with best uniform than the American ones with the canvas uppers. On his head, of course, was his best green beret. His corps badge was backed by the colours of our Khymer training command.

I suddenly noticed that he was wearing British Commonwealth paratrooper wings on his right upper sleeve. He had expressed interest in them a few months earlier when he had seen me with them on my New Zealand rifle green walking-out uniform. I had given him my spare set as a souvenir.

Seeing my expression, he smiled and said, "All official!"

I was mystified.

"The S1 (Adjutant) made me out a certificate and the Colonel signed it, saying that the *Noo* Zealand contingent presented them to me . . . I always wanted these. I'm entitled to lots of Western sets, but these are the best. Gee, the guys at Fort Bragg are gonna be envious!"

He burst out laughing at my, no doubt, very British bemused face. If I had worn a monacle, it would have fallen from my eye.

"Hey! Don't worry, Sir," he went on lightheartedly, "You're in the Special Forces now! All rules are different!"

Because of his jungle cool and years in theatre, one forgot that he was only in his mid twenties. He was still occasionally able to have the high spirits and instant happiness of youth.

He had spent one tour reporting on the VC/NVA columns that had swarmed past, and over, his hides on the Ho Chi Minh trail.

I shook his hand and said that I was going to visit the United States one day and would track him down.

"You'd sure better had," he said.

Then he took a last look at the Vietnamese jungle beyond the edge of the airfield, to which he had donated four years of his young life, smiled shyly and climbed into the aircraft's hold.

The day of our long anticipated great – and final – battle arrived at last.

We had known all along that our Alamo must come. After all, were we not the very height of impudence, still operating on a cul-de-sac coastal area behind the invader's front line. Despite the enemy's keenness to get South as soon as possible, we could not be left indefinitely. We knew that they were closing in. A few days earlier, we had heard that NVA soldiers, with their AK47s slung over their shoulders, were openly riding about on Hondas in Qui Non and Ngu Trang.

A great communist force was sent to take out the allied camps on our peninsula. However, against all likelihood, we were saved by a miracle – or rather, an incredibly brave US SF sergeant, and a few Montagnard assistants, who just happened to be in a critical place at a critical time.

The enemy's plan, apparently, was to crush the two Special Forces camps – our sister camp on the other side of a hill from us and about ten miles West and ourselves – with a rapid and massive, two-phase night thrust. The head of a vast flying column would kill our sister; then the rest of its body would sweep through, and on, to overwhelm us.

The approach was to be silent, without pre-assault bombardment, and the multitude would have swamped the Western camp before they knew what had hit them. We would probably have had some warning from a final desperate radio transmission, but there would have been little time to organise aircraft and artillery support.

The Sergeant, for some reason, was a few miles Westerly of the Western camp, right in the path of the advance. At nearly last light, he caught sight of the mass of men sweeping towards him. He, and his party, were soon in the middle of them, but managed to remain hidden. Relaying from his little hand held radio set through the nearby base's long range transmitter, he got every available scrap of air combat power onto them. Even though he was in the enemy's midst, he skillfully directed the fighter-bombers and the Cobras onto every part of the target.

It went on for the evening and much of the night. We stood-to and watched the yellow flashes and flickering tongues of orange flame as, respectively, the bombs blasted and ripped and the hoarsely screaming Gatlings mangled and tore.

Our base headquarters staff listened in to the Sergeant's transmissions coming from the loudspeaker of the command post radio set. A New Zealand Lieutenant actually recorded it on his tape recorder.

I heard the recording some years later when a copy was played in a New Zealand Officers' Mess bar. It transformed the jovial throng into intent white-faced silence.

The Sergeant's speech is articulate and to-the-point and the obvious terror is under perfect control. Behind the crackling transmissions one can hear the close explosions, the roars of the gunships' long multi-barrel bursts of fire and the shouts and screams of the enemy soldiers as they are battered on the anvil.

Miraculously, the brave Sergeant lived. One hopes that he was decorated as he deserved, as it was not a case of 'much' being owed by 'many' to 'so few'. All was effectively owed to just one.

By midnight the NVA had withdrawn and on the dawn AFVN news we heard that the Paris peace talks had seemingly agreed that there were to be no new major troop movements for now and a programme for the removal of foreign armies from South Vietnamese soil might be announced soon.

We still continued to lose people, of course, but it was from the usual random shots, ambushes, boobytraps and small local skirmishes. Large annihilating blows were "not on." Our relief was tinged with a measure of unease about the way that things, in general, might be going.

We seemed to be gradually running out of people who might be fighting for things like "Mom's apple pie". Or rather, despite our green berets and American uniforms, we seemed by coincidence, to have less and less members who were actually United States born and bred.

My fine friend and fellow A-Team 21C, the offbeat humoured Barry and his dog were still very much around. They were as American as it is possible to be, even though the dog had a Vietnamese name.

Ape (the dog) was a trained guard dog from the United States who had adopted Barry at his last Special Forces camp in Vietnam and had accompanied him to this one. I was never sure what breed of dog Ape was. Despite the fact that he was massively thick-set, black, tough, ugly and ferocious, Ape would roll helplessly onto his back at the approach of a European and would endure our side's Asians – except for the odd growl. North Vietnamese, however, he would kill the moment the chance presented itself.

Apparently, diet and general upbringing give different human groups different odours. Ape was never wrong and had a score of six personal kills. At night he padded softly about beneath the defensive wire tangle and, if he caught a creeping would-be bomb-planter or assassin, he went for the throat – a black and ugly flash.

Sadly, the United States rules for such single-purpose trained dogs was that they could never return home. Ape was obviously not safe to be left behind in a solely Vietnamese world and so Barry's heart was heavy for when his departure time came and as a last act he must shoot this fearless defender – and his loyal and loving friend.

After Sgt Wagner left, our A-Team had taken on a rather imprecise national hue.

There was 'John' Marrett, our commander, who had started his military life as a French paratrooper, had been at the great battle of Dien Bien Phu and had been a prisoner of the Nationalist and Communist Vietnamese for about a year. After his release he had served ten years in another colonial war in Algeria. It was while he had been visiting Paris (after the Algeria war) that he had met off duty American NATO Servicemen in the soldiers' bars. He had got on well with them, had realised that he had been risking his life for a quarter of their pay, had emigrated to the United States and had enlisted.

Unfortunately, the United States had returned him to Vietnam for another six years. He was not yet forty and had been a total of nine years in Indo-China and had taken part in some of the most violent actions.

261

Altogether his combat time totalled nearly twenty years.

He still tried, but there was little more that he could do. We closed ranks round him and protected him against scrutiny from above because we knew that few soldiers have had to earn their pensions harder. It was not fair to expect him to still go into the jungle and live with the constant tension and menace anymore. For two countries, he had done more than enough. However, he was an excellent organiser and planner, spoke up well for us with the Commanding Officer and was a useful and highly respected leader.

He left us occasionally for his private world. However, he was a kind and generous friend to all and had a delightful, dry sense of humour. Just a couple of times, potentially dangerous military situations were thrust upon him at Vinh Giat and he behaved with courage and *élan*, which is the hallmark of a Soldier of France.

Our most senior Warrant Officer was Sergeant Major Reidel – two Iron Crosses (Second Class) – formerly of the Wermacht. He had been a prisoner of war of the Americans and, after the Armistice, he had achieved United States citizenship in exchange for military service. The idea had seemed to offer a better future than life in a smashed up Germany. He had served nearly the full spans of World War Two, Korea and Vietnam.

Our next Warrant Officer down was Federov – ex of the 'Red' Cavalry. He had been a boy soldier in a Cossack regiment, riding with his father and uncles. One day a harassing raid on the Nazi invaders went wrong and his entire regiment were either killed or captured. The adult prisoners were summarily shot and the boys were left to languish in a makeshift prison for some months.

One day, the doors of the great barn, in which they were all kept, were flung open and two magnificent German Cavalry officers walked in. They had fine uniforms, hand-made riding boots and stylish fur caps with death's head badges on them. The German officers had beckoned to the awed boys to follow them out into the yard. There had been lines of beautiful horses there with high class tack and saddlery.

The German officers had said that they were free to walk home or, alternatively, they could have a horse and a uniform like theirs and serve in one of the Cossack regiments that they were forming. It had been emphasised that they would serve against brigands (who called themselves 'partisans') in Eastern Europe and not against the Soviet Union. To offer a Cossack a choice between a horse to ride and anything else is, of course, to offer him no choice at all.

In the closing days of the war, his unit had surrendered to the Americans – with a request that they might not be repatriated. Federov had managed to miss out on the Yalta Agreement, fate of so many of his colleagues and he had got the same deal, and had subsequently served in the same places, as Sergeant Major Reidel.

Our two permanent Sergeants were French Canadians who had served with the United Nations' force in the Congo War. After that war was over, they had decided that life in the Canadian army was a little quiet and had crossed their country's Southern border and had enlisted in the United States Army.

Upon discovering that I spoke French, they would speak to me in no other language. They also used to relay all their communications with the base's command through 'John', or myself, so that they need use the hated usurper English language hardly at all. They were both young, fit, clean-cut, polite, professional and deadly.

The other fairly regular member of our Team was Gomez – a Mexican and our transport Sergeant. If he had grown a Zapata-style moustache, he could have got regular work in Clint Eastwood movies. He was big, strong and stocky, and his thick black hair fell in short bangs across his forehead.

He never seemed disconcerted by the war – just surprised and curious about everything. Once when a mortar bomb landed near to where he squatted against the sandbags – as though against the dry sunny wall of an old Spanish colonial square – and showered him with dust and little stones, he slowly shook his head and, without changing his position, stared disbelievingly up at the hills.

"Say, where do you think they fire that thing from?" he asked me in his sing-song Spanish-style accent. I told him where I estimated the 82mm mortar base-plate was.

His kind broad face and dark almond eyes turned to me with a look of admiration.

"Gee. Fancy you knowing that. I mean, I thought it was pretty good when I got to drive trucks, but the stuff you got here. It is something else, hey?"

Sergeant Gomez was an illegal immigrant to the United States. However, somehow he had managed to join the Army – and was in hopes of full citizenship for putting up with quite a lot of Vietnam.

When the base was under attack, I used to whimsically speculate: if the North Vietnamese were pouring over our barricades on every face and our last stand was closing ranks and closing ranks what, at the very end, we would all truly fight for, supposing it were not merely for simple self-preservation or the general principle of democracy.

'John', I thought, would probably be fighting for a final gesture of honour for his betrayed comrades with whom he had tried to make French decolonisation an orderly affair.

Reidel, I decided, would fight not for his old Feurer but for a more traditional style of German Kaiser and state.

Federov despised communists and Russians so, at the end, he might have fought for an independent and democratic Ukraine, the memory of Bohdan Khemelnitzky or some other great Cossack leader.

There was absolutely no doubt, of course, that the two French Canadians would have fallen with a final defiant shout of: "*Vive Quebec Libre!*" frozen on their lips.

Gomez, by his appearance, should have fought for Pancho Villa or Emilio Zapata. However, in reality he alone of our Team might just have fought for Old Glory and a suburban American Dream that might have been his.

I still believed of course, that I served my Lady Sovereign and her poor mainland British government and people as well as those of Australasia. I was sure that the majority of the citizens of Great Britain would have wanted the invaded South Vietnamese to be helped.

My original countrymen were, of course, unaware of the honour that I did them, and most of the younger generation would have laughed themselves sick if they had been. I loved the South Vietnamese and I might have fought for the continuation of their traditional lifestyle. One or the other of these feelings would perhaps have sprung to the fore at the critical moment.

However, as one of the last Imperial British Soldiers, I should probably – in my final disorientated and confused moments of life – have gone down fighting for Her Majesty Queen Victoria and The Old Empire.

I stood on the edge of the airfield – a short distance out from the jungle – and studied the sky for the umpteenth time. Then I looked again along the runway. I had driven up and down its length about an hour earlier. It had not been used for many months and there were a few small cracks and some places where vegetation was appearing through the tarmac. However, a robust New Zealand Bristol Freighter could land on it without problem.

There were some Montagnards in fire positions just inside the jungle. As soon as I saw the Freighter approaching, I was to radio Vinh Giat and all the other New Zealanders would come over to the abandoned air force base and get on the aircraft. While they did this, my men and I would provide local protection.

Over the next few days, the Americans would also be flown out. There would be no more allied ground troops in the war. The locals would be abandoned and the Second Indo-China War would be over.* It was the end of an era.

Under the terms of the Paris peace agreement, all foreign fighting troops were to leave. This, of course, meant us and not the several hundred thousand NVA regulars harboured up in South Vietnam. All Vietnamese would stay on the territory that they currently held, and an international monitoring force would arrive. It would be a cosy compromise and the war would end.

Anyone who knew the North Vietnamese at all, of course, could have known that they had no intention of keeping their word. The pause in events would get rid of the Free World Forces and give them time to recover and reinforce. They could then press on with invasion when convenient. Communism is a creed in which the end justifies absolutely any means. Impractical things like honour or gentlemanly conduct have no place in it. We on the ground all knew what the Paris peace agreement was.

The naive shock of those distant Western Vietnam ranters, who had not already found another cause and lost all interest when the Northerners swept forward again, would have amused us if we had not been crushed by sadness for our South Vietnamese comrades of so many years.

On my right wrist was a brass bangle. I am not normally a wearer of jewellery. However, this had been given to me by our Montagnard chief. It signifies that the giver will lay down his life, if necessary, for the recipient. As we were going shortly, it was unlikely that he would have the opportunity to carry out his unspoken promise – but it was a kind thought. Charlie, as the chief of our Montagnards was happy to be called, had been a French auxilary at the battle of Dien Bien Phu. He and 'John' had been in different parts of the great battlefield and in different subsequent POW compounds and had not met.

I fervently hoped that Charlie and his men, and their families, from the makeshift village near Vinh Giat, would get back to their remote hills – with as much useful Western bounty as possible – and would be left alone by the communist occupiers.

A faint drone, a speck in the sky and from far to the East, out over the South China Sea, the RNZAF Bristol Freighter approached. It would soon be followed by USAF Hercules. The end had come.

We had not surrendered any swords nor left our colours behind. The democratic Western governments and peoples at home had self-defeated

---

* The First was the independence war against France and the Third was the one between the two Vietnams that started in 1973 and ended with the final fall of Saigon in 1975.

as Ho Chi Minh had prophesised before his death. Blown this way and that by every breeze of opinion, they were not capable of remaining steadfast of difficult purpose for a prolonged period. Commitment to a principle will always cave in if it disrupts the selfish, convenience and material interest of an electorate too much and for too long.

A democracy is the only completely right form of collective organisation for reasoning beings and I hope that, in or out of uniform, I shall always be its champion. However, as it allows the weak, unworthy and near-sighted and equal influence to the strong, brave and far-sighted, it has flaws that will be exploited by those with simpler, more autocratic and quicker systems and we should be on our guard.

Just under ten years later, I was glad that in the Falklands war we achieved victory within three months. Even during that short period, there were some Britons who were either so terrified of the principle of direct action or so resentful of the paltry (by international standards) cost of the campaign, that they would have abandoned their stalwart pioneering overseas countrymen to an evil South American military dictatorship.

If it had bogged down into a long campaign, the British public would have been subjected to a gathering daily onslaught by fractionally informed or partisan journalists, broadcasters and wittily debunking intellectuals. The slogans would have been a mixture of: 'thou shalt not kill'; the enemy are really reasonable people; compromise with no matter whom and over no matter what; it is all too expensive and inconvenient; the government in power really wants the war to distract attention from problems at home and to get rid of dissidents, etc.

As with the Americans of the Sixties, the national resolve of the British of the Eighties would doubtless have finally collapsed before the battering. Those who needed help would have been ratted on, the country's faithful and competent armed forces would have been dishonoured and years later when the real situation had dawned it would all have been too late. Poor 'John' Marrett had been on the worst end of this syndrome a couple of times already at the hands of the governments and people of France. He, and many of his generation of French soldiers had been emotionally broken by what they saw as feebleness and treachery at their backs.

The New Zealanders gathered about me in readiness to embark. Groups of Americans, South Vietnamese, Cambodians and Montagnard also arrived to bid us farewell.

The Bristol Freighter landed and an astonishing thing happened. As soon as it came to a halt and opened its door, an inordinate number of overweight and perspiring senior RNZAF officers in lightweight flying

266

suits poured out and started photographing each other against the backdrop of the aircraft, the jungle and the assorted troops.

As it was undoubtedly the last RNZAF flight into a combat zone of this particular war, it was a moment of history not to be missed. They could also say that they had been to Vietnam and might qualify for the campaign medal.

"Hey! What are those fellas doing?" a youthful Wing Commander said as he furiously snapped and re-snapped our Montagnard local defence section.

I explained.

"But we're in a huge USAF base – aren't we?" he asked in alarm.

I told him how it had been abandoned some time ago.

"Well what are they protecting us from?" he went on. "You don't mean there's VC and NVA out there do you?"

I said that it was a possibility.

To be fair, they did have the honesty not to attempt any brave poses and all simultaneously crushed back into the tiny circular doorway. The engines started revving.

We shook our colleagues hands and said that somehow we should meet again. The aircraft made loud impatient roars and so my group started to file on and take up the seats that were left.

I dismissed the guard force, gave Charlie a hug and walked over to join our senior New Zealand special forces officer who was waiting for me. Once he had counted us all onto the aircraft, his unhappy duty in this shame was over. He indicated that I was to climb up the two steps that he stood beside. My English schooling in manners made me unthinkingly make an after you gesture. Just as reflexively, he entered the aircraft. I followed him, took first my left foot and then my right foot from Vietnam, pulled the steps up behind me and helped a crewman push the door shut.

I was truly the very last of Her Majesty's combatant Vietnam soldiers.

The New Zealand special forces team members sat in silent wretchedness during the five hours flight back to Singapore. We flew over Nui Dat, where everyone had served on earlier optimistic tours. Only a few looked down from the windows, and they pulled their heads back sharply and angrily.

Some of us had even thought of totally disassociating ourselves from the pull-out by deserting and serving on with local forces. However, a soldier's first lesson is always that obedience to his lawful national command is his primary duty and so we had meekly done what we were told. The impossible idea of trying to smuggle a few orphans onto an aircraft, and formally adopting them later crossed my mind. I might have given at least a tiny part of Vietnam a life in a free society.

I was also not very proud of the way that I had broken the news of our sudden departure to Lan during the preceding weekend.

Like my companions, I felt personally ashamed for what my previously worshipped democratic West was doing and could not say that it was an irrevocable end. I had said, therefore, that we were sure to be back. She obviously sensed that I did not believe it – which was just as well.

Why had I not swept the slender and lovely girl, with the long, lustreous and shiny blue-black hair, up with one arm and, with my kitbag under the other, have carried her home as a war prize? I knew that she wanted to be with me always and my family would have been enchanted with her.

I had said goodbye to her for the last time late on the Sunday afternoon outside her poor, but neat, little wooden house with a concrete floor. As I drove away, I had not been able to look back immediately as I had to negotiate the quagmire of the lane. When I had looked, I had seen such a little girl standing and alone, waving goodbye forever in a shabby street full of puddles. She was Vietnam itself – several times courted by foreigners, charmed, seduced, used and deserted.

The Sunday afternoon had been one of those oasis-like events that happen rarely, but are remembered for a lifetime.

We had left the comparative security of the base and the village and had walked for about a mile through the coastal scrublands to the beach. It had been a rash thing to do in what was theoretically an enemy occupied area. Lan had been in a pale blue pyjama suit and wore a traditional large conical straw sun hat on her head. A pink ribbon, tied in a bow under her chin, held it on. I wore a pair of civilian shorts, a shirt and a pistol in a holster. The pistol would have been almost useless if an NVA patrol, armed with fully automatic AK47 assault rifles, had come upon us. However, we had been too absorbed to be concerned about danger.

We had been granted that piece of a day to be a normal girlfriend and boyfriend – just like proper lovers in a secure and free world. I had swum, splashed and fooled about in the muddy sea. Lan had paddled and had got her pyjama trousers wet. She had giggled helplessly and often had to bury her face in her hands. Later in the afternoon she had insisted that I wear her hat as protection against the sun and she had flopped my shirt over her own head as cover and had looked sweetly comical. She had been like an innocently happy and pretty child.

Lan and I had not cared about the noise we made as we had laughed and called to each other and rarely had I troubled to look along the beach or across the mangroves and the scrub.

Just for a while there was no war, no one was being killed with terrible pain, no lost and dying babies and infants were eating the gravel from around where they lay, the Vietnamese were not about to be abandoned to enslavement and we both were not whores.

# ⌐EPILOGUE⌐

Two cartoons appeared in editions of *Punch* during, and just before, 1975. One depicted a standard, uniformed peace demonstrator (long uncared for hair and beard and jeans) standing before his television set. On the screen are scenes showing the final American withdrawal from Vietnam and the Vietnamese refugees fleeing from the invading communists. The demonstrator is waving his fist and shouting:

"Heartless bastards!"

In the corner of his room are all his old placards saying 'Yanks Out' and 'Murderers Go Home.'

The other, by a different cartoon artist, showed three of the same type of character. One is walking by in a state of extreme distress and distraction. The other two, in the foreground, are studying and discussing him. One of these two is saying sadly:

"The ending of the war in Vietnam took a lot out of him."

The war – or various imagined versions of it – had been put to use by so many for such a long time. A species of Journalist and photographer had evolved that did nothing but live off that war. In return for putting up with the heat, dust, sweat and smell of Vietnam and occasional danger, the rewards for keeping up a constant outflow of material that the 'bleeding hearts' of the world wanted to hear, could be rich. One could also become a celebrity in a way that no one who actually had to fight the war could.

"Dead Soldiers don't bother me – only dead civilians," one English member of the club said cooly when being interviewed on television. Soldiers, presumably, are either a sub-species of no importance or they start wars on their own initiative and deserve all that they get.

The Vietnam War Reporting Industry could also be quite an easy thing, in practical terms too. The United States military headquarters gave full briefings on all activities and issued printed handouts and photographs of even the goriest scenes taken by Army war photographers. All the journalist/photographer had to do was select and arrange the material to support whatever he, or she, wanted to say. Almost all the material that the Americans supplied to the Western media was used against them, to a

270

greater or lesser extent.

Many of those who rode on the war's back produced books and grew rich. It is unlikely that any donations were made to the suffering civilians and soldiers of both sides who provided the occasion and the subjects for academic observation.

The reporters were looked after by the Western armies, given free use of the combatants' eating, sleeping and drinking facilities and had the independence of action and spare time to make far greater use of the cheap and beautiful girls of Vietnam. Journalists and photographers could accompany operations and film or write what they liked. There was no censorship.

An Australian journalist accidentally left his Editor's written instructions behind at Nui Dat. It clearly stated that evidence of allied aggression was all that was wanted. The vast civil aid projects and other efforts to help the Vietnamese to help themselves, almost never got a mention.

After the Falklands war, the journalists complained loudly and at length that the military authorities had not allowed them the opportunity to report as they wished. They said that their professional and ethical standards could have been trusted. Perhaps they could have been. However, there must undoubtedly have been a memory of how the American military had been used, abused and harmed. It is known that altruism in the Fourth Estate must, in the final instance, be subordinate to the careers of journalists and editors and the sale of newspapers or viewer/listener ratings. The advanced note given about the possibility of our attack on the Argentine garrison at Goose Green resulted in its considerable reinforcement and may have caused more British deaths than was necessary. We heard that if Colonel 'H' had not died in battle, he would have brought a civil action against some areas of the media for their killing of his men.

Communist regimes, of course, do not allow freedom of speech by anyone, and particularly not by people who publish and circulate their criticisms to a vast readership.

Once the North's invasion was complete and reporting became very difficult and dangerous, and there were no junketings, the Western press melted quickly away. A veil was drawn and the communists could inflict their misery without world scrutiny.

The My Lai massacre came to light during my first tour. The killing of communist villagers by an American patrol was a criminal act and is in total opposition to moral standards, the international Geneva Convention, to which the United States is a signatory, and all American military teaching. It was a random action made on the personal decisions of one particular over-stressed group of soldiers and they were made to answer for it.

The Communists, however, did the same thing to pro-Saigon government civilians daily, on a far larger scale and as a deliberate policy. They did not, of course, have independent reporters and photographers with them, were not called to task and no discussion of it would have been permitted.

A friend of mine who went to University in New Zealand after completing his extended National Service in Vietnam found a tiny back page article about one of these communist massacres of Southerners. He pinned it on to the Students' Union notice board and wrote "Protest demonstration this afternoon outside the Soviet and North Vietnamese embassies."

When he returned to the notice board a short while later, his notice was covered in obscenities and the figure for the dead non-communist civilians had been heavily scored out. When he returned yet again, the article had been ripped down. Fortunately, however, he had made a lot of photo-copies and kept putting the article up again and again for some weeks.

North Vietnam's official title was the Democratic Republic of Vietnam. Communists, and indeed socialists of every degree, seem particularly prone to using titles, slogans and other forms of word mincing in lieu of facts.

The Oxford dictionary says that Democracy is "government by the people . . . all citizens have equal rights." It says that a Republic is "A State in which the people, or its elected representatives, is formally acknowledged . . . members regard each other as equals." North Vietnam was run by a single party, an unelected ruling gang who did what they liked, kept the people as slaves and servants and answered to no-one. The State was not even *of Vietnam* as its rulers were not wanted by the majority of the Vietnamese. The area of Vietnam has also, throughout its history, been three separate states – as symbolised by the three red bars across the South's yellow flag – so the North could not claim a historical right concerning unification.

North Vietnam was, therefore, the total antithesis of the title that it's rulers had adopted for it.

Power in the South (The Republic of Vietnam) was only gained by persons with wealth and influence – so it could not truly claim to be republican. However, it did not strive to regiment and totally control the thoughts, words and deeds of its population and invade its neighbours. It had, therefore, to be very much the lesser evil.

In direct proportion to the number of words in the title of any left-wing government or movement that have been selected from the following

'The Peoples', 'Popular', 'Democratic', 'Patriotic', 'Liberation', 'Republic', will be the measure of its despotism.

Appropriately enough, this time, it was a Labour government minister who was waiting at RNZAF Whenuapai to use Her Majesty's returning New Zealand Soldiers as the background props for his speech to the TV cameras. The New Zealand Labour party had gained office a few weeks earlier.

"Well, we said we'd get you all out for Christmas . . ." he said smugly, "and we have – just!"

If he had expected a ragged cheer from gaunt and hollow-eyed, battle fatigued veterans pathetically grateful for deliverance, he did not get it. No-one wanted by choice to stay longer than was necessary in the grim and risky world of the Vietnam war. However, anything was better than the knawing bitterness of national, professional and personal shame. Apparently, they all stared resentfully. Mercifully, I was not there.

I had been granted four week's leave in Singapore and had managed to purchase an indulgence passage on an RAF flight to Britain.

I arrived at Brize Norton in a tropical shirt and trousers – the only civilian clothes I had available. It was two o'clock in the morning and snowing. Within minutes the cold pierced my unacclimatized and unwrapped body to the core.

I tried to control my shivers as my little kit bag and person were given the most thorough search that I have ever had.

"We occasionally get a few of you Vietnam lot through here," a Customs officer said – not unkindly.

"Yanks and Aussies – we've been warned that you're usually loaded with captured weapons and drugs."

I had sent a telegram to my parents a few minutes prior to embarking at Changi and – joy of joys – my father and brother were beaming at me through the glass of the outside wall of the reception area.

I was driven to my parents house sound asleep on the rear seat of the station waggon and wrapped in the only warm covering available – which were the dogs blankets from the back. It was Christmas Eve.

I awoke fully that evening and got dressed in a sports jacket and trousers, that my father had lent me, just in time to be ready for a ring on the doorbell.

Bathed in the porch light were a very impressive group of about half a dozen men. They were dressed in blazers and regimental ties and *requested* that my father and I accompany them to *The Star*. Some were youngish and some were very old. They were villagers who, between them, had served in every British war of the twentieth century. Naturally, they required to be briefed on this latest event where soldiers had fought with the emblem of the British Sovereign's Crown on their colours and uniforms.

As I entered the cosy pub that wintery evening, with the heros of my boyhood, I was initially exulted, then overawed and finally rather ashamed to think that my inconsequential performance in the most mismanaged and saddest of wars might cause these noble men to include me in their company.

The peace talks continued to delude most of the Western world – or, more likely, most were happy to be deluded. The few who had encountered Asian communists in general, and the North Vietnamese in particular knew that the exercise had about as much point as trying to come to a deal with a fox to stop it eating your chickens if you intended to leave the hen house open and unguarded.

All the communists wanted was: the bombing of their capital stopped, as their population was getting tired of glorious sacrifice for the ruling gang and their invasion efforts were being interfered with; the mines out of Haiphong harbour so that Eastern block war supplies could keep coming and all foreign Western armies out of the South because their skills and technology kept defeating them in conventional battles.

To achieve these aims they were happy to waffle about cease fires, plebiscites, unarmed international monitoring forces, power sharing and almost anything else that kept the Americans happy – and sliding, with their allies, out of South Vietnam.

Le Duc To, the North's Paris representative, was a professional revolutionary who looked upon peace negotiations as just another aspect of guerilla warfare. As with everything else, one went to win – never to compromise. There were those in his movement who were allocated to the business of planning future communist worlds. Le Duc To, however, had dedicated a lifetime exclusively to sabotaging, defeating and destroying 'what was' by any and every means to clear the way. There was no constructiveness in him. He was single minded to his cause. He had no personal vanity to distract him – and endless patience.

Apparently, he soon saw that his enemy, Dr Kissinger, was a political and academic snob who was desperate to be A Man of History and the 'Man Who Ended The War In Vietnam' and achieved 'Peace with Honour'. He also knew that a portion of American public opinion wanted to pull all their troops out no matter what and – as America was a true democracy – they were not only allowed to make their opinion known, but would actually have importance and influence too.

It was an unequal contest. 200,000 NVA on Southern soil were not removed under the foreign troops clause; there was a lull in the fighting to allow the North to get organised for the final thrust and an international

274

monitoring force appeared for a while and gave the Saigon whores the experience of still more transient and ineffective military men of even more nations. Within a few days of the ending of the Second Indo-China War, the communists – despite having given their word of honour and signed the Paris treaty – had started the Third Indo-China War.

It seems to me that there is a descending order of main winners and losers in the war.

The Winners:

1. The North Vietnamese ruling gang.

2. The USSR, until it collapsed twenty years later, who got a fairly obedient colony and a host of military bases in SE Asia.

3. Weapons designers, manufacturers and suppliers (as always).

4. The reporters, photographers and writers who made their careers and fortunes out of displaying aspects of the war.

5. Distant Western satirical film and play producers, pop stars and social occasion wits who gained personally by skilled debunking and belittling of attempts to keep invaders out of South Vietnam.

6. Distant Western youth who used the war as an excuse to fornicate more ('making love not war') and to dignify mob disorder, vandalism, shop looting, obscene language and violence against public servants ('peace demonstrations').

The Losers:

1. All the people of Vietnam, except those in Serial 1 above. They now live as slaves to the state. The young men still occasionally fight and die in subsequent spin-off conflicts. They have still not been given peace. The former followers of the Saigon government arrived in this situation by invasion and defeat and those who dedicated themselves to the cause of Hanoi got into this state because they allowed themselves to be duped.

2. The soldiers of South Vietnam's allies who were committed to fight a uniquely defensive and, therefore, unwinnable war. They were leashed and muzzled dogs with tergiversate owners who were put against unconstrained, ruthless and resolute foes who had a clear and simple goal.

3. Communist China. Having constantly supported the various struggles of the Vietnamese over the years, they had every reason to expect that they would finally get a colony, locally ruled by their version of communism, out of it. However, the Soviets prevailed instead. The

Sino-communists were set-up by their Russian-following comrades to be eradicated during the Tet Offensive. China has even had to subsequently fight a border war with their erstwhile *protegés* – and they did not do very well.

4. Anyone in Western society who openly said in fashionable circles that it was not unreasonable for non-communists to fight back against infiltration and invasion – and be helped to do so. They had to put up with the bore of constant verbal assault by the endlessly repeated slogans of almost everyone else, who was young or youngish, as all were Liberal Intellectuals. It was an era when knowledge was not a pre-requisite of being an expert on something. Today, those who considered the reasons for the war to be understandable now have the even more exasperating experience of hearing some of the auto-protest generation (now middle-aged members of the Establishment) say unrepentantly in pompous and round about ways, as usual, that they were previously wrong.

The Neutrals:

The imprecisely known millions of civilian and military dead of the war. One can only hope that those who were able to think during their last moments, died believing that their particular side was finally going to make Vietnam a happy place after achieving victory.

There were other, rather peripheral – but still sad-types of casualties from the war. Marriages amongst American and ANZAC troops was one of them. When I was in New Zealand for the nine months between leaving Vietnam and being sent to the Kashmir conflict, New Zealand Army Officers' Messes seemed to abound with young infantry Captain and Lieutenant divorcees.

The Royal New Zealand Infantry Regiment used to deploy to Vietnam from the Singapore garrison. The Servicemen would spend two years in South East Asia. Their first six months would be spent in Singapore and those who were married would have their families with them. The menfolk would then go to fight in Vietnam for a standard year's tour – leaving their wives and children, of course, in their married quarters. After their time in Vietnam, they would have a final six months in Singapore before returning to New Zealand.

The ANZUK garrison in Singapore also contained Australians who commuted to the war. However, there were mainland British who did not.

There was little likelihood of a military threat to Singapore, and so military duties were not arduous. Local servants took care of the routine of life so socialising had to be one of the main occupations of most of the European community. The younger people got bored. As always, "the Devil finds work for idle hands."

There were usually some very historic and prettily uniformed British regiments in the garrison containing amongst their officers some very smooth and dashing roués. The provincial girls were mostly pretty, rather disorientated and very lonely. The inevitable sequence of events was repeated and repeated. Things were the same in the non-commissioned community.

However, Singapore was not the indirect cause of every infidelity. There was a sad case of a Gun sergeant from my Battery whose brother stole his wife, back in New Zealand, while he was on his first tour in the war. His brother was his only remaining blood relative so he lost everyone.

After that, he kept going back and back to Vietnam. There was always good and loyal company there and plenty going on to stop the mind dwelling on bitter things. The Royal New Zealand Artillery headquarters also knew that he would always go without complaint.

However, one day Venus must obviously have decided to briefly make at least some restitution for her previous poor treatment of him. What befell is a noble tale and goes a long way to restoring ones faith in correctly spirited and patriotic womankind in general.

The Sergeant reported to Auckland International Airport to verify the flight that would take him for his fourth year in Vietnam. He was required there urgently and was being sent to Singapore on the first available civil flight – as a routine trooping flight was not scheduled until later in the month. The ground hostess during the checking-in confirmed that his flight was the following dawn and the military would be moving him onwards from Singapore.

He asked the young lady's advice concerning the cheapest local motel and turned to go.

A vision of classical female loveliness who was standing beside the counter said, "Are you really going to Vietnam?"

The Sergeant said that he was.

"But you might die!" she went on in a shocked tone.

The Sergeant confirmed that this was a possibility – albeit he was hoping not.

"Where are your family to see you off?" she demanded. "Surely they will not let you leave – just like that – on your own?"

He said that he had no one; it did not matter and thanked her for her obviously sincere compassion. He then turned to go again, but saw that the beautiful air hostess, who had been by the counter to keep her ground

277

hostess friend company, was deeply moved.

"What are you going to do on your last night?" she demanded.

The Sergeant said that he would be alright. In fact, he usually ate something with chips in the cheapest restaurant and then got drunk in the lowliest bar.

"No. You are not going to go believing that nobody cares!" she stated and, slipping her arm through his, she led him away to her sports car.

He was astounded. He was a strong and valiant man. However, he knew that she was from an expensive and beautifully groomed world where she turned all heads. The sort of world that, with his artless manners and dress sense, he would be laughed from.

She took him to her apartment where she changed into breathtaking evening wear and then to a palatial restaurant where she bought him exotic and utterly delicious foreign things to eat and drink in great quantity. Next she took him home again and lavished every possible womanly care and attention upon him and finally, the following dawn, with a last passionate kiss from her tear streaked face, she propelled his weakened, but deliriously happy, form into the airport departure lounge.

He remained in a vacantly smiling trance for about a week at Nui Dat. We wondered what was the matter with him and started to get quite worried.

One of the Special Forces Sergeants at Vinh Giat went from a happy and secure marriage to a divorce within a few days.

After six months of faithful longing in Vietnam, his mid-tour point and the week of his R and R arrived. He was to spend it in Hawaii with his wife. Unfortunately, a few nights before his flight, he went to a local bar with some friends and his generally pent up feelings led him, in a careless and foolish moment, to be persuaded to give a bar girl company.

However, by the time he met his young wife, the hazy events of a drunken night out were forgotten and they fell happily into total absorption of each other.

Sadly, the brief bar incident left them both with a highly undesirable souvenir. The wife returned to mainland America, soon discovered the problem, contacted a doctor and a lawyer on the same morning – it is a matrimonial offence permitting an instant divorce – and the lawyer sent a telegram notifying our Sergeant of his instant change of marital status.

He had had delays with his return flights and so got back to Vinh Giat some days after his wife got home. He arrived chatting happily about his fabulous leave, and lovely wife, and a post room orderly innocently handed him the envelope containing the shattering telegram.

The total of people directly killed by this war was about two million. The Western allies lost a quarter of a million men, the communists lost nearly one million. The wounded in action outnumbered the killed in action by about six times. Some of the wounds of modern weapons are horrendous. I saw men still alive whose legs, and other things, had been taken off from the level of the groin. Half a million South Vietnamese civilians died as a direct result of the fighting. North Vietnamese civilians killed mostly by air raids, make up the rest of the two million.

Added to this, two million should be the killed of other parts of the Indo-China Wars, such as Cambodia and Laos. This would be hundreds of thousands. Later, after 1975, of course, the Cambodian communists (the Khymer Rouge) methodically killed several million of their own people. These are, of course, additional to the total of dead for the Second Indo-China War.

In addition to the battle casualties, there would be the other type of war dead – the indirect casualties: those killed by war related accidents; those who died of illnesses and diseases caused by the unhealthy climate of war; the tiny, elderly or infirm who died because the war caused them to be neglected and those who killed themselves or died for no better reason than the unhappy wretchedness of it all. The total numbers of this group can never be accurately known. However, from the examples of past wars, it probably exceeds the total of all those directly killed by the war.

Centuries of enduring unending war, enslavement and every kind of suffering seems to have made the Vietnamese stoic in life and in death.

I remember once turning angrily on a laughing young New Zealand Gunner who was recounting a tale to his friends. However, I did not remonstrate with him because I saw that the false laughter held in check the tears and the shame that were in his eyes.

The night before he had bought a young Vietnamese woman and had taken her to a local hotel. When he woke up at dawn, the thin little girl lay dead in his bed. She had died quietly and unobtrusively during the night. She must have been very ill but had carried on working, no doubt, for the grandparents and the tiny brothers and sisters that she supported.

The New Zealand teenager had dressed her, as well as he was able, to try and give her some dignity and had carried her out into the deserted dusty street. He did not know what he was going to do.

A very old rickshaw operator, who was the only other person about, indicated that he should put the poor little prostitute in his cart. The youth gave him a considerable sum of money – although he asked for nothing – and he slowly towed the lifeless and tragic little form to a graveyard or refuse tip, out of town. At no time had the old man's expression changed in the slightest degree. We all knew that face of Old

Vietnam. Many years before he had become as profoundly sad as it is possible to be.

Of the several of Her Majesty's wars in which I have served, I have found that in the years that follow, the day by day sequence of events and much of the chronological detail is forgotten. What seems to remain is the atmosphere of the war, one's part therein, and random but unforgettable, pictures and sensations.

The word, or thought, Vietnam triggers: young, thin, sweaty, wary, determined, filthy, green-clad professionals of many nationalities in the speckled jungle twilight; the pain to the eyes upon bursting out into the piercing pale gold glare of a clearing; the ceaseless biting of insects; soreness, sweatyness, hot and unhealthy feet and crotch, weariness, boredom, frustration, excitement, interesting natural sights and terrible fear; the vicious hiss of a cigarette burning into a blood-bloated leech and the odd sensation of a medic with tweezers, unscrewing a bamboo tick that has bored into your body; an ancient skull with a bullet hole through the forehead and an old fashioned French sun helmet, with a matching bullet hole through the front lying in some remote bushes; noisy, fly-infested and littered villages; toddlers wise and cynical well beyond their years who hold out their grubby little golden hands for anything that you can give; lines of immaculate school girls (or 'cherry girls') in their all-white *au-dai* and conical sun hats; exquisitely beautiful, but humiliated, older girls; smooth, cocksure and smiling South Vietnamese army officers; stray dogs, pigs and chickens everywhere; laughing men and women in the red glow of a bar and the clank and ping of the pin tables above the Sixties pop music; stately oxen; masses of dangerously driven Hondas; red dust; the serene loveliness of a sleeping Vietnamese girl; a crouching frightened young North Vietnamese prisoner of war; weeping, tough men at burial ceremonies; damaged, ripped, torn, smashed, dismembered, rotted and burnt humans and how identical the faces of people of all races look when they are in terrible pain.

It was also a war of distinctive sounds: the 'whop-whop' of the Iroquois helicopter blades; the rushing scream of the Skyhawks and Phantoms. The senses-battering racket of contact; shells passing overhead and their jungle-muffled explosions, the roar of the gunships' Gatlings, the ground jerking concussion of bombs; the distressing noises of the wounded and dying; the distinctive signature tune, chirpy DJs and popular records of AFVN; the uneven musical sound of the tonal Vietnamese language; the night barking of jungle deer and the buzzing, chirping and calls of the jungle's thousands of other life forms.

Some of the scents are also unforgettable: the rich and damp jungle; pungent Vietnamese village cooking; the exhaust stink of chugging fire base generators; the fearful mixture of burnt out fuel and phospherous after a napalming; the distinctive and different dirty human smell of troops who have been long in a jungle, the natural sweetness of a Vietnamese girl's pale gold, velvet textured skin; cordite; pungent wounds; the newly dead and the long dead; the dust that was in your nostrils for most of the time that you were out of the jungle and daytime air that, except when a coastal breeze was encountered, was like warm glue.

The popular songs of the war – that we listened to and sang along with, when possible, are particularly evocative when I hear them on the radio these days:

*Galveston* by Glenn Campbell; *Ruby* by Kenny Rogers; *Goodbye* by Mary Hopkins; *Two Little Boys* by Rolf Harris; *Country Road* by Olivia Newton-John and several others.

Some nights I dream that I am back in the Vietnamese war and, during those few moments before full wakefulness, when dreams still seem real, although I am frightened, I am glad to be back. The small upturned dark 'Imperial' that I grew in that jungle so long ago – which used to get me likened to a First War Turkish Officer – is now grey. However, I am still fairly lean and if I ever thought that those poor people wanted me to serve in some pro-democracy resistance again, I should go.

I went to the war in vanity. I wanted to round off the process that the British had started and make myself a whole soldier. I also felt that the cause was good and that made everything alright. I started out as a sort of jobbing knight errant or mildly principled mercenary. However, I found unexpected love that rewarded me, frustrated me, caused me to be scared and hurt, eluded me and finally broke my heart.

I did not despair totally by our shameful flight from South Vietnam as, like so many, I comforted myself with the hope that a miracle might happen and a communist regime would keep its word or the South forces might prevail. Three years later in 1975 my spirits were crushed when the, internationally well-backed communist forces, finally overran the abandoned pro-Western states of Indo-China.

What then came to pass was even worse than the prophesies of we who had been intimately involved. Vietnam and Laos became prisons and Cambodia became a charnel house.

Western politicians, intelligensia, journalists, chatterers and all the distant voices of liberty and enlightenment turned their backs without conscience, it seems, and gave newer high-profile events the benefit of their talk.

President Nixon and Vice President Agnew had risked political unpopularity to support the cause of the South Vietnamese, and the allied soldiers who fought with them, and had so skilfully baffled the

281

uninformed and imprecise waffle of the liberals with terse and accurate counter-arguments that they had made themselves marked men. In a system where high position at any sort is only possible when combined with a commercial ability, unfortuantate combinations of ambitious are a constant problem. One could possibly pin something on all prominent Americans – fashionable liberals and journalists included. The President and Vice President had spoken too well, had made some of the greatest egos in the land look foolish and so had to be toppled and humiliated.

With their public demise, the liberals, pacifists-at-anyone's-cost, isolationists and moral cowards could feel with satisfaction that the last loose ends of the West's Vietnam involvement had been tied up and total victory was theirs. Only the Vietnamese have had to live with the ensuing reality. Occasionally, when the plight of boat people has been too awful, the Vietnamese have annoyingly returned to the headlines. Fortunately, however, as reporting accurately and in detail on life in Vietnam itself is difficult, and unfashionable, journalists tend to leave it alone.

By the 1990s the British government was repatriating Vietnamese boat-people refugees from Hong Kong even though Asian communism was openly demonstrating its changeless face in China with the arbitrary murder of pro-democracy advocators. The West also eventually got round to supporting the slippery Prince Norodom Sihanouk and his, by then, associates – the Khymer Rouge.

No one wants the brave escapees. Sweden, the country that never stands up to be counted in any war, could be directed by the United Nations to take a large number of Vietnamese refugees. During the war, their national policy was total opposition to the allies' assistance and they gave sanctuary to any and every draft dodger. They could now atone for the consequences of the result that they advocated.

Foreign countries, other than the Free World allies of the Second Indo-China War have contributed to Vietnam's current situation.

The French have much to answer for as it was their vain and unenlightened colonial methods that first made communism seem a discipline that might bring a better life, the 'You Have Nothing To Lose Except Your Chains' movement of the 1930s, 40s and 50s

Japanese organised moronic and murderous sadism was also, of course, of immeasurable assistance to communist resistance groups in Vietnam, as it was in every other place that they occupied.

The British contribution to the Vietnam situation is unforgivable. The British were the only ones to bring peace to Vietnam. After their victory in SE Asia in 1945, they had all the trouble makers in prison camps. The

Vichy French, the Japanese, the nationalist Viet Minh and the communist Viet Minh. They then did the same as they did with much of the British, Laurence of Arabia, liberated and unified Middle East after the First World War; they gave it to the French Empire to look after and set it on the road to the present day. Incredibly, French rubber planters, who worked on long after French authority had been withdrawn, and often locally assisted both sides in the Second Indo-China War for commercial reasons, used to shake their heads in amusement and wisdom when they met us and say that we would never do any good as we did not know the people and the country as the French did.

From the most ancient times, every Asian Empire strove to own the area called 'The Rice Bowl' – the rich and fertile lands that border the beautiful Mecong River.

In *The Times* Saturday Review of November 17, 1990, Richard West in the principal essay entitled 'Who Really Won The War?' gave a detailed account of life in modern Vietnam under the usual nasty and deteriorating communist system. In his conclusion, he wrote of the American [allied] Vietnam soldiers:

"It was right and honourable to try to prevent the spread of communism and, in particular, to defend South Vietnam, where communism is more unpopular than ever."

Finally, alone in a Sussex Cottage on a Saturday afternoon in an armchair in front of the fire, I shed the tears that I had kept in check for twenty years. For so long I had become hardened to always expect that my companions cause, dedication, suffering and death would be disparaged. To see our simple belief at last clarioned, and by the profession that made itself our secondary enemy, rendered me temporarily defenceless.

The Labour government of Great Britain apparently tried to prevent the award of a campaign medal to Her Majesty's Vietnam soldiers. The North Vietnamese were heros to many of its members.

However, as the death toll of local boys grew, the Governors General of Australia and New Zealand threatened to strike a colonial campaign medal. To avert any sort of constitutional crisis, therefore, Her Majesty's Office of Chancery produced a Vietnam Medal.

It has The Sovereign's profile on its face and a Classical warrior figure protecting one world and fending off another on the obverse. The ribbon is the flag of The Republic of Vietnam with stripes of dark blue, scarlet and light blue down its edges – acknowledging, respectively, the navies, armies and air forces.

To date, there have been only four full British campaign medals struck since the Second World War. In order, these are for: the Korea War, the

Vietnam War, the Falklands War and the Gulf. The Vietnam Medal is the most unique as it was the first in our history that could not be awarded to all Her Majesty's soldiers – only to Her Australasian ones.

Within a few months of leaving Vietnam, I was with a United Nations military mission in a mountain conflict in Kashmir for two and a half years. After that, I returned to mainland British forces and served in Northern Ireland and the Falklands war. I became about the most multi-campaigned veteran of my era.

My experience and military standing were, of course, revered, respected and eagerly taken up. I was used in high level instructional and high profile military image areas. I was promoted to ranks where my uniqueness could have the greatest influence and inspire the young and those without experience of the realities of soldiering. Actually, I was a Junior Officer for the rest of my time and my home-based interludes were spent in military backwaters.

It is perhaps a correct situation. The mainstream military must bide their time together and keep their experiences common, administrate themselves and prepare together for the day when they may all go to a vast nation-saving event. If random veterans of obscure, one-off wars are given too much influence they may sidetrack national policies into wrong directions because of convictions inspired by impressive, but irrelevant, personal experience.

I had inadvertently distanced myself from the true "military." It was a profession that I had neither the qualifications nor experience to belong to and so, after the Falklands War, it was time for me to leave.

Even those amongst my peers and seniors who actually asked me about my campaigns said later that I kept "telling war stories." After a while, I anecdoted only of peacetime and pre-Service days.

I enjoyed being a very old junior level training officer for most of my last period, as preparation is realistic in peace as well as war and must go on and one has a physical life style with the keen, young troops in the fresh air all the time.

The Imperial knights of my youth and their ladies, who had either uncomplainingly kept home fires indefinately burning or made civilized communities in hostile lands, all seemed to be gone.

Some modern officers' wives, who were mostly not from military families, said things like: "When *we* got promoted," "Oh, he's one of *our* officers" and "Darling, do you remember that super Sergeant *we* had in Germany?"

One of my last (non-Army) superiors asked me to remove the two rows of coloured silk ribbons from my best tunic in the interests of uniformity and "so as not to cause any ill feeling."

The peace time careerists had become monarchs of all they surveyed. Absurdly, militarily unfulfilled seniors could be bitterly jealous and vindictive. The intensity and subtlety of it was very impressive.

However, the best type of war prize of all awaited me upon my return home from Vietnam, in the New Year of 1973, in the form of Lynn from Hailsham. She was a gorgeous, elegant, yet "hour glass" figured girl with big bright blue eyes, a smile that made your heart take flight, a delightfully pretty little gap between her two upper front teeth and long rich and heavy brown hair. I resolved to make her permanently mine. Surprisingly for a British girl in her mid-twenties, she had had no previous lovers and, just before I returned to the New Zealand Army and the Kashmir conflict, she held me and actually said:

"I have waited so long for you."

She married a civilian factory engineer a few months later – and despite my loving letters. The news reached me in Jammu. However, by then individual humans could no longer hurt me. I had come to rejoice in our unreliability. It is what makes us different from the animals.

These days, I have permission to use the bar of a local Officers' Mess on quiet evenings when there are no official functions. As always, it is a most convivial and elegant private club. One may consort with people with whom one has something in common. The drink is good value.

As my visits are early in the evening, before dinner at home, I am occasionally lucky enough to hear a military band nearby, either at practice or holding a late parade rehearsal. The tunes of glory fill my head and direct my thoughts and I am very happy.

The modern Junior Officers all gather together at the bar and talk in the same brave and careless way that I and my friends once did. I sit alone in a corner and dream the way that "has-beens" do. There is just about the same age difference between the young officers and myself as there was between myself, when newly commissioned, and the World War II men. The time gap between the present and the Second Indo-China War is about the same as between the late 1960s and 1945. As a fortyish and greying Old Soldier – who has retained his figure – I occasionally get some brief, but often quite breathless, attention from the youngest officers of the female services. It is very gratifying.

A couple of times a year, a band will do a 'Beating of the Retreat' on the beautiful mess lawns. The civic dignatories and the senior officers and all their wives are seated on chairs in front of the open French windows. The more junior officers and their wives stand around and behind them. The guests from the municipality are in evening dress and traditional robes, the serving officers wear mess uniform and the ladies are aglitter with evening finery. The people and their surroundings form a lovely, and typically British, scene and the stirring military spectacle of the 'The Retreat' makes a perfect prelude to their formal dinner evening.

The band's uniforms are magnificent, the drill impresses, the pulse and rattle of the Corps of Drums thrills and the noble music stirs.

As I am not a dining member, I make a covered approach from behind some flanking rhodedendron bushes and get into a position from where I can see but not be seen.

As the band plays *Sunset* and the cascade of massed trumpets and bugles sound the *Last Post* I doff my English countrymans' Harris Tweed hat and stand at attention. That sort of thing has always been one of my favourite aspects of it all.

There was a very mixed crowd of young men and women, of quite a variety of Services and military callings, in the bar the other evening.

A jet fighter pilot suddenly strode over to my alcove and, pointing at me with all the fingers of his right hand, said:

"Hey! We were talking about you last night. Someone said you'd been in the Korean war. Is that true?"

"Vietnam," I said.

"Ouch!" he exclaimed softly, snapped his fingers and smote himself lightly on the forehead with the base of his open palm in a modern manner of strong men showing amused self-criticism.

"Sorry!" he said with a beaming friendly smile.

"That was the one!" and, after giving me a cheery wink, he returned to his group.

I looked out of the window at the golden Summer evening glory of a mature English formal garden and pondered the fact that the same sun that shone through our clear air would soon be shining through the thicker atmosphere of Indo-China.

Those lovely former bar girls, and probably their grown up daughters, would be up to their firm, smooth and heavenly bare thighs in the mud of the rice paddy. Life would be grey, frugal and totally controlled; fighting still went on and my poor, poor dear Cambodian friends and their wives and children were all murdered long ago.

I should have told the *arsehole* Kabul to Kandahar or the Ashanti Wars, I thought, to see if it made any difference.

THE END